Joey Green's Magic Brands

1,185 Brand-New Uses for Brand Name Products

By the author of *Clean Your Clothes with Cheez Whiz*®
and *Polish Your Furniture with Panty Hose*

RODALE

Printed in the United States of America
Rodale Inc. makes every effort to use acid-free (∞), recycled paper ♻

Cover Designer: Tara A. Long
Cover Photographer: Mitch Mandel/Rodale Images

Library of Congress Cataloging-in-Publication Data

Green, Joey.
 Joey Green's magic brands : 1,185 brand-new uses for brand name products / Joey Green.
  p. cm.
 " "The material in this book has previously been published as Polish your furniture with panty hose © 1995 by Joey Green, Paint your house with powdered milk © 1996 by Joey Green, and Wash your hair with whipped cream © 1997 by Joey Green"—T.p. verso."
 Includes index.
  ISBN 1–57954–452–5 hardcover
  1. Home ecomonics. 2. Brand name products—United States. I. Title.
 TX158 .G6783 2001
 640—dc21   2001001864

  4 6 8 10 9 7 5 3   hardcover

Visit us on the Web at www.rodalebooks.com, or call us toll-free at (800) 848-4735.

WE **INSPIRE** AND **ENABLE** PEOPLE TO IMPROVE
THEIR LIVES AND THE WORLD AROUND THEM

Contents

And Now, a Word from Our Sponsor

When I wrote *Polish Your Furniture with Panty Hose*, I had no idea that anyone else on the planet would actually share my enthusiasm for the hundreds of offbeat uses for brand-name products kept secret from the American public. I was convinced I was all alone, a misguided consumer with too much time on his hands, a fluke of the universe.

But with the publication of that book, overzealous Americans from all walks of life came out of the woodwork. I was inundated with hundreds of letters. I suddenly realized that I could turn my love affair with brand-name products into a full-time career, spending the rest of my life investigating the myriad uses for items like Wrigley's Spearmint Gum, Scotch Tape, Miller High Life, and Crayola Crayons. I was ecstatic.

I was truly amazed to find myself on the NBC *Today* show and *CNN Headline News*, polishing furniture with SPAM. Next thing I knew, my picture was in the *New York Times* pouring a can of Coca-Cola into a toilet bowl. And then I was on television again, this time teaching Tammy Faye Bakker how to shave with Jif peanut butter. The American public's fascination with the hundreds of quirky uses for brand-name products was bigger than I ever thought possible. I had opened Pandora's box.

In a strange way, I had become a public servant, destined to open the clandestine files on America's favorite brand-name products and share their secrets with the world. After all, the public has a right to know the offbeat uses for products like ChapStick, Dixie Cups, Jell-O, Reddi-wip, and Saran Wrap—although I'm not quite sure you'll find that in the Bill of Rights.

Alberto VO5 Conditioning Hairdressing

Just a Touch Gives... Healthy, Manageable Naturally Shiny Hair In Just Seconds!

Alberto **VO5**®

CONDITIONING HAIRDRESSING
Clean feeling with 5 organic conditioners

NORMAL, DRY HAIR

- **Prevent silver from tarnishing.** Apply a thin coat of Alberto VO5 Conditioning Hairdressing with a soft cloth to clean, polished, dry silver candlesticks, picture frames, silver sets, and other decorative items. Wipe off excess, leaving behind a very thin, virtually invisible, protective coating. VO5's organic protectants actually prevent tarnishing.

- **Remove a ring stuck on a finger.** Rub on a little Alberto VO5 Conditioning Hairdressing, then hold your hand up toward the ceiling to drain the blood from the area and slide off the ring.

- **Make cleaning up after painting or doing a messy auto grease job easy.** Lightly coating your hands with Alberto VO5 Conditioning Hairdressing before painting or fixing the car allows you to clean them off afterward without harsh solvents.

- **Soften your feet.** Before going to bed, coat your feet with Alberto VO5 Conditioning Hairdressing and put on a pair of socks.

- **Soften dry cuticles and moisturize dry elbows and heels.** Rub on a dab of Alberto VO5 Conditioning Hairdressing.

- **Prevent spray paint from sticking in your hair.** Before spray painting, slick a dab of Alberto VO5 Conditioning Hairdressing the size of a quarter over your hair so you can wash away the paint more easily.

- **Prevent static electricity in your hair.** Comb a dab of Alberto VO5 Conditioning Hairdressing through your hair.

- **Protect your scalp during a permanent.** Rub some Alberto VO5 Conditioning Hairdressing into the scalp before giving yourself a perm.

- **Minimize drying out your hair in a chlorinated pool.** Rub a long dab of Alberto VO5 Conditioning Hairdressing through your hair before taking a swim.

- **Prevent hair coloring from dyeing your skin.** Dab a little Alberto VO5 Conditioning Hairdressing on your forehead and around the hairline and ears to help keep the color from staining your skin.

- **Remove makeup.** A dab of Alberto VO5 Conditioning Hairdressing on a tissue or cotton ball gently removes makeup.

- **Glitter your face for a holiday party.** Rub a little Alberto VO5 Conditioning Hairdressing onto your cheeks, then dust lightly with glitter.

- **Moisturize your face.** Rub a little Alberto VO5 Conditioning Hairdressing in the lines around your eyes to help prevent dry lines.

- **Remove an adhesive bandage painlessly.** Rub a little Alberto VO5 Conditioning Hairdressing into the bandage wings, wait a few minutes, then peel off.

- **Soothe chapped lips and skin.** Rub in a small amount of Alberto VO5 Conditioning Hairdressing.

- **Soothe your legs after shaving.** Rub some Alberto VO5 Conditioning Hairdressing into your skin after a bath or shower to make your legs feel velvety smooth.

- **Make zippers glide easily.** Rub a little Alberto VO5 Conditioning Hairdressing into the teeth of the zipper.

- **Condition leather.** If you're all out of mink oil, substitute Alberto VO5 Conditioning Hairdressing.

- **Protect leather shoes and boots from winter salt and ice.** Rub in Alberto VO5 Conditioning Hairdressing.

- **Shine vinyl and patent leather shoes.** Rub in a little Alberto VO5 Conditioning Hairdressing, then buff.

- **Protect your dog's or cat's paw pads.** Rub in a little Alberto VO5 Conditioning Hairdressing before sending your pet outdoors.

- **Prevent shoes from squeaking.** Give squeaky shoes a coat of Alberto VO5 Conditioning Hairdressing.

- **Detangle and shine a dog's coat.** Comb in a small amount of Alberto VO5 Conditioning Hairdressing.

- **Prevent cat hair balls and static electricity on your cat's coat.** Rub in a little Alberto VO5 Conditioning Hairdressing. (Don't worry if your cat licks its fur; Alberto VO5 Conditioning Hairdressing is natural and non-toxic.)

- **Shine a horse's hooves.** Rub in a little Alberto VO5 Conditioning Hairdressing.

- **Prevent a leather saddle from drying out.** Rub in a little Alberto VO5 Conditioning Hairdressing.

- **Detangle a horse's mane and tail.** Brush in a little Alberto VO5 Conditioning Hairdressing.

- **Stop windows from sticking in their tracks.** Lubricate the tracks with a little Alberto VO5 Conditioning Hairdressing.

- **Lubricate pipe joints.** A thin layer of Alberto VO5 Conditioning Hairdressing on pipe connections will make them fit together more easily.

- **Prevent nuts and bolts from rusting together.** Lubricate the nuts and bolts with a dab of Alberto VO5 Conditioning Hairdressing before screwing them together.

- **Prevent tools from rusting.** Give your tools a light coat of Alberto VO5 Conditioning Hairdressing.

- **Stop a faucet from screeching.** Remove the handle and stem, coat both sets of metal threads with Alberto VO5 Conditioning Hairdressing, and replace.

- **Stop refrigerator racks from sticking.** Coat the edges of the racks with a thin layer of Alberto VO5 Conditioning Hairdressing so the racks glide easily.

- **Prevent squeaky door hinges.** Apply a little bit of Alberto VO5 Conditioning Hairdressing.

- **Lubricate furniture drawers.** Rub a little Alberto VO5 Conditioning Hairdressing on the casters of drawers so they slide open and shut easily.

- **Keep shower curtains gliding easily.** Apply a thin coat of Alberto VO5 Conditioning Hairdressing to the curtain rod.

- **Prevent sliding doors on a medicine cabinet from sticking.** Rub a little Alberto VO5 Conditioning Hairdressing onto the glides.

- **Clean wooden knickknacks and other wood objects.** Lightly coat the wood with Alberto VO5 Conditioning Hairdressing, then buff.

- **Avoid splattering paint on windows, hinges, doorknobs, and lock latches.** Coat them with Alberto VO5 Conditioning Hairdressing to prevent paint from adhering to the surfaces. After painting, wipe clean with a cloth.

- **Hide scratches on wood furniture.** Put a dab of Alberto VO5 Conditioning Hairdressing on a clean, soft cloth, then buff the spot.

- **Prevent wood paneling from drying out.** Just rub on Alberto VO5 Conditioning Hairdressing with a clean, soft cloth, then buff well, giving the paneling a soft glow.

- **Remove wax drippings from candlestick holders.** Coat the candlestick holders with Alberto VO5 Conditioning Hairdressing before inserting the candles.

- **Make a stainless steel sink sparkle.** Shine the sink with a dab of Alberto VO5 Conditioning Hairdressing on a soft cloth.

- **Shine chrome faucets, handles, and car bumpers.** Put a little Alberto VO5 Conditioning Hairdressing on a soft, dry cloth and buff lightly.

- **Clean plant leaves.** Apply a small dab of Alberto VO5 Conditioning Hairdressing to the leaves with a soft cloth.

- **Break in a baseball glove.** Rub the center of the glove with Alberto VO5 Conditioning Hairdressing, place a baseball in the glove, fold the mitt around it, and secure with rubber bands. Tuck the glove under a mattress overnight.

- **Lubricate roller skates, skateboard wheels, and bicycle chains.** Use a dab of Alberto VO5 Conditioning Hairdressing.

- **Prevent a sailboat's spinnaker pole fittings from jamming or sticking.** Lubricate with Alberto VO5 Conditioning Hairdressing.

- **Make golf clubs shine.** Clean the shafts with a dab of Alberto VO5 Conditioning Hairdressing on a clean cloth.

✳Invented
1956

✳The Name

Alberto VO5 is named after Alberto, the chemist who invented Alberto VO5 Conditioning Hairdressing. "VO5" stands for the five *vital organic* emollients in the hairdressing. Oddly, no one at Alberto-Culver can recall Alberto's first name.

A Short History

In the 1950s, a chemist named Alberto developed Alberto VO5 Conditioning Hairdressing to rejuvenate the coiffures of Hollywood's movie stars from the damage of harsh studio lights. The five vital organic emollients in Alberto VO5 Conditioning Hairdressing restore resiliency and flexibility to dull, dry hair, smooth frizzies and split ends, help control static flyaway, and protect hair from further damage.

Alberto's partner, Blaine Culver, marketed the company until 1955, when thirty-six-year-old Leonard Lavin and his wife, Bernice, bought the Los Angeles–based beauty supply firm for $400,000 and relocated it to Chicago. That same year, the company ran the first television commercial for VO5, and within three years Alberto VO5 Conditioning Hairdressing was the best-selling hair conditioner in the United States.

Ingredients

Mineral oil, petrolatum, lanolin, PEG-8 dilaurate, paraffin, isopropyl myristate, fragrance, BHA

Strange Fact

- In 1972, Alberto-Culver changed advertising by combining two thirty-second television commercials into the industry's first sixty-second spot.

Distribution

- Alberto VO5 is the number-one hair conditioner in the United States.
- Alberto VO5 Conditioning Hairdressing is available in Normal Formula, Gray Formula, Extra Body, and Unscented Formula.

- Alberto-Culver markets Alberto VO5 shampoos and hair treatments, SugarTwin sweetener, Mrs. Dash seasonings, and Kleen Guard furniture polish.
- Alberto-Culver owns the world's largest chain of beauty supply stores, Sally Beauty Supply. Sally Beauty operates more than 1,400 outlets offering salon products and appliances to professional and retail customers.
- Alberto-Culver sells its personal use products in more than 100 countries.

For More Information

Alberto-Culver USA, Inc., 2525 Armitage Avenue, Melrose Park, IL 60160. Or telephone 1-708-450-3000.

Alberto VO5 Hair Spray

- **Immobilize flying insects.** Spray Alberto VO5 Hair Spray on a flying insect to stiffen its wings, bringing the pest spiraling to the ground.

- **Protect artwork.** When sprayed on a chalk drawing, Alberto VO5 Hair Spray acts as a fixative, preventing artwork from fading.

- **Remove ink stains from clothes, vinyl, or skin.** Spray Alberto VO5 Hair Spray on the stain, blot until the stain comes up, and wash.

- **Kill plant lice on African violets.** Spray Alberto VO5 Hair Spray into a plastic bag (not directly onto the plant), place the bag over the plant, secure shut with a twist tie, and let sit overnight.

- **Thread a needle.** Stiffen the end of the thread with Alberto VO5 Hair Spray so it can be easily poked through the eye of a needle.

- **Laminate recipe cards.** Spray with Alberto VO5 Hair Spray to give the cards a protective gloss.

- **Stiffen ruffled curtains.** Hold the fabric taut and spray with Alberto VO5 Hair Spray.

- **Preserve floral arrangements.** Spray Alberto VO5 Hair Spray on baby's breath, broom grass, and cattails to help preserve them.

- **Make wrapping paper.** Spray Alberto VO5 Hair Spray on the comics section from the Sunday paper to seal in the ink and give the paper a shiny gloss.

- **Remove dry glue from bottles.** Spray Alberto VO5 Hair Spray on the dry glue, wipe off, and wash the bottle in soapy water. The propanes, butanes, and acetones in Alberto VO5 Hair Spray dissolve glue.

- **Remove pet hair from furniture.** Spray a tissue with Alberto VO5 Hair Spray and, while the tissue is sticky, pick up those hairs.

- **Protect decorative copper or brass from tarnish.** After polishing decorative copper or brass, spray with Alberto VO5 Hair Spray to add a protective coating.

⭑Invented
1961

⭑The Name

Alberto VO5 is named after Alberto, the chemist who invented Alberto VO5 Conditioning Hairdressing. "VO5" stands for the five vital organic emollients in the hairdressing. Oddly, no one at Alberto-Culver can recall Alberto's first name.

⭑A Short History

A chemist named Alberto developed Alberto VO5 Conditioning Hairdressing to rejuvenate the coiffures of Hollywood's movie stars from the damage of harsh studio lights. Alberto's business partner, Blaine Culver, marketed the company. In 1955, Leonard Lavin and his wife, Bernice, bought the Los Angeles–based beauty supply firm that manufactured VO5 from Blaine Culver for $400,000 and relocated it to Chicago. That same year the company ran the first television commercial for VO5, and within three years it was the best-selling hair conditioner in the United States.

In 1960, Alberto-Culver built a new plant and headquarters in Melrose, Illinois, and the company went public the following year. Alberto-Culver introduced Alberto VO5 Hair Spray in 1961, Alberto VO5 shampoo in 1962, New Dawn hair color in 1963, and FDS in 1966. Leonard Lavin's son-in-law and daughter, Howard and Carol Bernick, assumed management of Alberto-Culver in 1992. Two years later, Howard Bernick was named CEO, and Carol Bernick became president of the Alberto-Culver USA unit.

Ingredients

SD alcohol 40, dimethyl ether, water, butane, octylacrylamide/acrylates/ butylaminoethyl methacrylate copolymer, vinyl acetate/crotonates/vinyl neodecanoate copolymer/amino-methyl propanol, dimethyl stearamine, fragrance, MEA-borate, MIPA-borate

Strange Facts

- Alberto VO5 Hair Spray was the world's first crystal-clear hair spray.
- In 1972, Alberto-Culver changed advertising by putting two thirty-second television commercials together and creating the industry's first sixty-second spot.

Distribution

- Alberto-Culver markets Alberto VO5 shampoos and hair treatments, SugarTwin sweetener, Mrs. Dash seasonings, and Kleen Guard furniture polish.
- Alberto-Culver owns the world's largest chain of beauty supply stores, Sally Beauty Supply. Sally Beauty operates more than 1,400 outlets offering salon products and appliances to professional and retail customers.
- Alberto-Culver sells its personal use products in more than 100 countries.

For More Information

Alberto-Culver USA, Inc., 2525 Armitage Avenue, Melrose Park, IL 60160. Or telephone 1-708-450-3000.

Alka-Seltzer

- **Clean a toilet.** Drop in two Alka-Seltzer tablets, wait twenty minutes, brush, and flush. The citric acid and effervescent action clean vitreous china.

- **Clean a vase.** To remove a stain from the bottom of a glass vase or cruet, fill with water and drop in two Alka-Seltzer tablets.

- **Polish jewelry.** Drop two Alka-Seltzer tablets into a glass of water and immerse the jewelry for two minutes.

- **Clean a thermos bottle.** Fill the bottle with water, drop in four Alka-Seltzer tablets, and let soak for an hour (or longer, if necessary).

- **Remove burned-on grease from a pot or pan.** Fill the pot or pan with water, drop in six Alka-Seltzer tablets, let soak for one hour, then scrub as usual.

- **Unclog a drain.** Clear the sink drain by dropping three Alka-Seltzer tablets down the drain followed by a cup of Heinz White Vinegar. Wait a few minutes, then run the hot water.

- **Get short-term relief from nicotine withdrawal symptoms.** As long as you're not on a low-sodium diet and don't have peptic ulcers, drink two Alka-Seltzer tablets dissolved in a glass of water at every meal.

- **Soothe insect bites.** Dissolve two Alka-Seltzer tablets in a glass of water, dip a cloth into the solution, and place the cloth on the bite for twenty minutes.

*Invented
1930

*The Name

Alka-Seltzer is a coined word that suggests *alka*linity and the carbonation of *seltzer*.

*A Short History

In 1928, Hub Beardsley, president of Dr. Miles Laboratories, discovered that the editor of the local newspaper in Elkhart, Indiana, prevented his staff from getting influenza during a severe flu epidemic by giving them a novel combination of aspirin and baking soda. Beardsley immediately set his chief chemist, Maurice Treneer, to work devising a tablet containing the two ingredients.

In 1978, Bayer acquired Miles Laboratories. Bayer, founded by Friedrich Bayer in 1863 to develop synthetic dyes, became a pioneer in the modern German chemical industry—developing the first synthetic pesticide in 1892, aspirin in 1899, synthetic rubber in 1915, a treatment for African sleeping sickness in 1921, and the first sulfa drug in 1935—and pioneered the development of polyurethanes. In 1992, Bayer merged its U.S. holdings—Miles Laboratories, Mobay, Agfa, and management holding company Bayer USA—under the name Miles, Inc. In 1994, Bayer acquired the North American over-the-counter drug company Sterling Winthrop, paving the way for the company to change Miles, Inc.'s name to Bayer Corporation.

✳Ingredients

Each Alka-Seltzer tablet contains 325 milligrams of aspirin, 1,916 milligrams of heat-treated sodium bicarbonate, and 1,000 milligrams of citric acid. Alka-Seltzer in four ounces of water contains principally the antacid sodium citrate and the analgesic sodium acetylsalicylate.

✳*Strange Facts*

- An Alka-Seltzer tablet fizzing in a glass of water prompted a hung-over W. C. Fields to joke, "Can't anyone do something about that racket?"
- Early promotions for Alka-Seltzer featured Speedy Alka-Seltzer, a baby-faced puppet with red hair and a tablet-shaped hat, created in 1951. Stop-motion animation brought Speedy to life in 212 television commercials between 1954 and 1964, requiring nineteen plaster heads with various lip positions, two sets of legs and arms, and as many as 1,440 adjustments for a single sixty-second commercial. Voice-over talent Dick Beals provided Speedy's voice. Speedy Alka-Seltzer co-starred with Buster Keaton, Martha Tilton, Sammy Davis Jr., and the Flintstones. Speedy Alka-Seltzer celebrated America's Bicentennial, participated in the 1980 Winter Olympics, attended thousands of holiday dinners, and has helped Santa Claus.
- The original six-inch-high Speedy Alka-Seltzer working model became so famous that it was insured for $100,000 and kept in the vault of a Beverly Hills bank. In 1955, a plastic Speedy doll was issued in a limited edition.
- The buffered aspirin in Alka-Seltzer peaks within thirty minutes, whereas regular aspirin tablets peak in about two hours.
- In the 1970s, Alka-Seltzer became widely known for its innovative television commercials, launching the catchphrases "Mama mia, that's a spicy meatball," "Try it, you'll like it," and "I can't believe I ate the whole thing."
- The "Plop, Plop, Fizz, Fizz, Oh, What a Relief It Is!" vintage theme song for Alka-Seltzer, written by Tom Dawes in 1977, remains one of the most recognized commercial melodies and a favorite of popular culture trivia buffs.

✳Distribution

- Alka-Seltzer is the best-selling antacid/pain reliever in the United States.
- Alka-Seltzer is available in Alka-Seltzer Original, Alka-Seltzer Gold, Alka-Seltzer Lemon Lime, Alka-Seltzer Cherry, Alka-Seltzer Extra Strength Pain Reliever, Alka-Seltzer Caplets, Alka-Seltzer Liqui-Gel Antacid, Alka-Seltzer Anti-Gas, and Alka-Mints in Spearmint, Tropical, and Cherry.
- Bayer operates in 150 countries.

For More Information

Bayer Corporation Consumer Care Division, Morristown, NJ.

Arm & Hammer Baking Soda

- **Clean a microwave oven.** Sprinkle Arm & Hammer Baking Soda on a damp sponge, scrub, and rinse.

- **Remove tarnish from silver.** Mix a thick paste of Arm & Hammer Baking Soda with water, apply to the silver with a damp sponge, rub, rinse, and buff dry.

- **Clean a stainless steel sink.** Sprinkle Arm & Hammer Baking Soda on a damp sponge, scrub the sink, and rinse clean.

- **Boost the strength of liquid laundry detergent.** Add one-half cup Arm & Hammer Baking Soda, with the usual amount of detergent, to your regular wash cycle.

- **Clean a fiberglass bathtub or shower.** Sprinkle Arm & Hammer Baking Soda on a damp sponge, scrub, and rinse clean.

- **Clean bathroom tile.** Sprinkle Arm & Hammer Baking Soda on a damp sponge, scrub, and rinse clean.

- **Maintain your septic tank.** Flush one cup Arm & Hammer Baking Soda down the toilet once a week. Baking soda helps maintain proper pH and alkalinity, controlling sulfide odors.

- **Deodorize cloth diapers.** Mix one-half cup Arm & Hammer Baking Soda in two quarts of water, and soak diapers in the solution.

- **Deodorize a disposable diaper pail.** Sprinkle liberally with Arm & Hammer Baking Soda.

- **Deodorize garbage disposals and sink drains.** Instead of throwing out that old box of Arm & Hammer Baking Soda that's been sitting in the refrigerator or freezer, gradually pour it down the drain and flush with water. Or better yet, pour two tablespoons Arm & Hammer Baking Soda down the garbage disposal every week.

- **Clean a refrigerator.** Sprinkle Arm & Hammer Baking Soda on a damp sponge, scrub, and rinse clean.

- **Deodorize a dishwasher.** Sprinkle one-half cup Arm & Hammer Baking Soda on the bottom of the dishwasher between loads.

- **Boost the strength of dishwashing liquid.** Add two full tablespoons Arm & Hammer Baking Soda to the usual amount of detergent you use.

- **Remove burned-on food from cookware.** Dampen area, sprinkle with Arm & Hammer Baking Soda, let soak overnight, then scrub with a sponge, rinse, and dry.

- **Clean and deodorize a cutting board.** Sprinkle Arm & Hammer Baking Soda on a damp sponge, rub the cutting board, and rinse clean.

- **Deodorize food containers.** Mix one-quarter cup Arm & Hammer Baking Soda with one quart water, swish food containers in the solution, let soak overnight, then rinse clean.

- **Clean coffee pots and teapots.** Wash in a solution of one-quarter cup Arm & Hammer Baking Soda and one quart warm water, then rinse clean.

- **Deodorize kitchen garbage.** Sprinkle a handful of Arm & Hammer Baking Soda in the garbage pail each time you add garbage.

- **Deodorize carpet.** Sprinkle Arm & Hammer Baking Soda lightly over the dry carpet, let sit for fifteen minutes, then vacuum up.

- **Deodorize a cat litter box.** Cover the bottom of the litter box with one-quarter inch Arm & Hammer Baking Soda, then add the litter.

- **Maintain the proper alkalinity in a swimming pool.** Add one and a half pounds of baking soda for every ten thousand gallons of water in the pool to raise total alkalinity by 10 ppm (parts per million), keeping the total alkalinity of the pool within the range of 80 to 150 ppm. Maintaining a proper level of total alkalinity minimizes changes in pH when acidic or basic pool chemicals or contaminants enter the water, reducing chloramine formation and the corrosivity of water, consequently reducing eye irritation and unpleasant odors while improving bactericidal effectiveness.

- **Soothe poison ivy rash or insect bites.** Make a paste of Arm & Hammer Baking Soda and water, and apply to the affected area.

- **Soothe sunburn, windburn, and prickly heat.** Dissolve one-half cup Arm & Hammer Baking Soda in a tepid bath. Soak in the bath for fifteen minutes.

- **Take a refreshing bath.** Dissolve one-half cup Arm & Hammer Baking Soda in a tub of warm water for soft, smooth-feeling skin and a relaxing bath.

- **Brush your teeth.** Plain baking soda is a gentle abrasive that cleans like the strongest toothpaste. Apply Arm & Hammer Baking Soda to a damp toothbrush, brush as usual, and rinse. Of course, Arm & Hammer Baking Soda does not contain fluoride.

- **Wash your mouth.** Add one teaspoon Arm & Hammer Baking Soda to one-half glass warm water, and swish through teeth for a refreshing mouthwash.

- **Neutralize vomit odor.** Sprinkle Arm & Hammer Baking Soda generously to cover the stained area, let sit for an hour, then vacuum up.

- **Soothe tired feet.** Add three tablespoons Arm & Hammer Baking Soda to a basin of warm water and soak feet in the solution.

- **Use as a deodorant.** Dust Arm & Hammer Baking Soda under arms.

- **Clean dirt, grime, and scuff marks from doors, stoves, laminated table-tops, linoleum floors, and tile.** Sprinkle Arm & Hammer Baking Soda on a damp sponge, wipe clean, and dry.

- **Remove coffee or tea stains from china.** Dip a damp cloth in baking soda, gently rub the china, and rinse clean.

- **Minimize the smell of dirty laundry.** Sprinkle some Arm & Hammer Baking Soda into your hamper or laundry bag.

- **Deodorize a closet.** Place an open box of Arm & Hammer Baking Soda on a shelf.

- **Deodorize garment storage bags.** Sprinkle Arm & Hammer Baking Soda into the bottom of the bags.

- **Deodorize shoes or sneakers.** In the evening, sprinkle Arm & Hammer Baking Soda inside shoes to eliminate odors. Shake out in the morning.

- **Remove crayon marks from walls or wallpaper.** Sprinkle Arm & Hammer Baking Soda on a damp sponge, scrub gently to avoid mussing the paint or wallpaper, then wipe clean.

- **Clean dirt and grime from hands.** Sprinkle Arm & Hammer Baking Soda onto wet hands with liquid soap, rub vigorously, rinse, and dry.

- **Remove conditioner and styling gel buildup from hair.** Wash hair once a week with a tablespoon of Arm & Hammer Baking Soda mixed with your regular shampoo; rinse thoroughly, then condition and style as usual.

- **Refresh stuffed animals.** Sprinkle Arm & Hammer Baking Soda on the stuffed animals, let sit for fifteen minutes, then brush off.

- **Clean high chairs, car seats, strollers, and plastic mattress protectors.** Sprinkle Arm & Hammer Baking Soda on a damp sponge, wipe clean, and dry.

- **Clean baby bottles, nipples, and bottle brushes.** Soak in a solution of warm water and Arm & Hammer Baking Soda, then sterilize before use.

- **Make baby clothes smell even fresher.** Add one-half cup Arm & Hammer Baking Soda to baby's laundry.

- **Boost bleach.** Use one-half cup Arm & Hammer Baking Soda with your normal liquid bleach to boost the bleaching action and freshen the wash.

- **Whiten socks and dirty clothes.** Add one-half cup Arm & Hammer Baking Soda to regular laundry detergent.

- **Clean up pet accidents.** Apply Canada Dry Club Soda to the stain, rub it in, wait a few minutes, sponge it up, let dry thoroughly, then sprinkle on Arm & Hammer Baking Soda, allow to sit for fifteen minutes, then vacuum up.

- **Clean chrome bumpers and hubcaps.** Sprinkle Arm & Hammer Baking Soda on a damp sponge, rub surface, and wipe clean with a dry cloth.

- **Remove dead insects from a car or truck windshield.** Sprinkle Arm & Hammer Baking Soda on a damp sponge, clean glass, and wipe clean with a dry cloth.

- **Deodorize carpeting in a car.** Sprinkle Arm & Hammer Baking Soda on the carpet, let sit for fifteen minutes, then vacuum up.

- **Degrease and clean barbecue grills.** Make a paste by mixing equal parts Arm & Hammer Baking Soda and water, apply with a wire brush, wipe clean, and dry with a cloth.

Invented

1846

The Name

Sodium bicarbonate, more commonly known as bicarbonate of soda, was originally used as an ingredient in cake batter to make cakes rise; hence the combination of the words *baking* and *soda*. The Arm & Hammer symbol was first used in the early 1860s by James A. Church, who ran a spice-and-mustard business called Vulcan Spice Mills. When Church joined his father, Dr. Austin Church, in the baking soda business in 1867, he brought with him the trademark depicting the muscular arm of Vulcan, god of fire, with steel hammer in hand about to descend on an anvil.

A Short History

In 1846, John Dwight started making baking soda in the kitchen of his Massachusetts home. In 1847, he formed John Dwight and Company with his brother-in-law, Dr. Austin Church, introducing Cow Brand as the trademark for Dwight's Saleratus (aerated salt, as baking soda was then called). Church formed Church & Company to produce the baking soda, identifying his brand as Arm & Hammer. In 1896, the descendants of the founders of these two companies consolidated their interests under the name Church & Dwight Co., Inc.

Ingredients

100 percent sodium bicarbonate

Strange Facts

- The Arm & Hammer logo ranks among the nation's most recognized product symbols.
- Baking soda has an almost unlimited shelf life.

- A box of baking soda can be found in nine out of ten refrigerators. According to the *Los Angeles Times*, "More refrigerators are likely to have baking soda than working lightbulbs."
- Baking soda was used to clean the Statue of Liberty for the 1976 Bicentennial celebration.
- Baking soda is the main ingredient in Alka-Seltzer.
- Baking soda was promoted as a key ingredient in 25 percent of all toothpastes sold in 1994.
- When mixed in cake batter and heated, baking soda releases a carbon dioxide gas that causes the cake to rise.
- Baking soda chemically neutralizes odors by turning into a sodium salt and giving off water and carbon dioxide.
- Baking soda cleanses by neutralizing fatty acids found in most dirt and grease.
- Arm & Hammer Baking Soda has been used to reduce air pollution in factory smokestacks. Arm & Hammer Baking Soda, when pulverized to an appropriate particle size, is, like other sodium sorbents, one of the most effective collectors of sulfur dioxide. Injecting Arm & Hammer–brand sorbent-grade sodium bicarbonate directly into the flue gas ducts of coal-fired boiler systems desulfurizes flue gas. The baking soda reacts with sulfur dioxide to form sodium sulfate, and the cleaned flue gas exits through the stack.
- Arm & Hammer Baking Soda has been used to increase the effectiveness of sewage treatment plants. Baking soda helps maintain proper pH and alkalinity in biological digesters, fostering trouble-free operation of both anaerobic and aerobic treatment plants. Used in maintenance doses, baking soda boosts sludge compaction, alkalinity, and methane gas production while reducing biological oxygen demand and controlling sulfide odors. Plus, it's environmentally safe.
- Baking soda can restore lakes damaged by acid rain. In 1985, Cornell professor James Bisongi Jr. restored Wolf Pond, a virtually dead fifty-acre lake in the Adirondacks, by adding nearly twenty tons of baking soda to the water to dramatically reduce the acidity.
- The U.S. Environmental Protection Agency and the navy's Civil Engineering Lab have jointly developed an inexpensive method of using baking soda to decontaminate soil laced with halogenated organic chemicals. The halogenated contaminates are decomposed by excavating, crushing, and screening the soil; mixing in baking soda at 10 percent of

its weight; and then heating the soil to 630°F for one hour. The treated soil can then be returned to its original location.

- Arm & Hammer Baking Soda has been used to increase the butterfat content of cow and goat milk. High-grain diets typically increase acid formation in ruminant animals, interfering with the bacteria that aid digestion. Adding baking soda to cow and goat feed increases the pH in the animals' rumina, lowering the acidity, making for a more favorable environment for the microbacteria that aid digestion, elevating the rate of feed intake, and increasing milk production and the butterfat content of the milk.

✳Distribution

- Arm & Hammer Baking Soda, the only nationally distributed brand-name baking soda, can be found in virtually every household in the United States.
- Arm & Hammer Baking Soda is available in 8-ounce, 16-ounce, 32-ounce, 64-ounce, and 10-pound boxes. It is also available in 20-ounce "Fridge-Freezer Packs" with "Spill-Proof Vents" that will prevent the baking soda from spilling if the container is knocked over in the refrigerator or freezer.

For More Information

Arm & Hammer, Division of Church & Dwight Co., Inc., 469 North Harrison Street, Princeton, NJ 08543. Or telephone 1-800-524-1328 (in New Jersey, telephone 1-800-624-2889).

Aunt Jemima Original Syrup

- **Prolong the life of a Christmas tree.** Cut an extra inch off the bottom of the tree, stand the tree in a bucket of cold water to which one cup of Aunt Jemima Original Syrup has been added, and let the tree soak for two or three days before decorating.

- **Condition hair and prevent split ends and frizzies.** Massage Aunt Jemima Original Syrup into dry hair, cover hair with a shower cap for thirty minutes, then shampoo and rinse thoroughly.

- **Make maple frosting.** Combine one stick of margarine, one-third cup of Aunt Jemima Original Syrup, and three to four cups powdered sugar. Beat until desired thickness.

- **Make a Maple Yogurt Smoothie.** In a blender, combine one cup ice cubes, one cup plain yogurt, one-half cup low-fat milk, one-third cup Aunt Jemima Original Syrup, and one peeled banana. Cover and blend on high speed until smooth and thick.

- **Substitute syrup for sugar when cooking.** Use three-quarters cup of Aunt Jemima Original Syrup for each cup of sugar.

- **Revive an ailing house plant.** Add two tablespoons Aunt Jemima Original Syrup at the base of the plant once a month.

- **Relieve a sore throat.** Take two teaspoons Aunt Jemima Original Syrup to coat and soothe the throat.

- **Sweeten a cup of coffee or tea.** Substitute a teaspoon of Aunt Jemima Original Syrup for each teaspoon of sugar or honey.

- **Lure insects away from an outdoor party or barbecue.** Coat a few small pieces of cardboard with Aunt Jemima Original Syrup and place around the perimeter of the yard. Stinging insects, like wasps, bees, and yellow jackets, will be attracted to the syrup instead of your guests.

Invented
1964

The Name

While seeking a name and package design for the world's first self-rising pancake mix, creator Chris L. Rutt saw a vaudeville team known as Baker and Farrell whose act included Baker singing the catchy song "Aunt Jemima" dressed as a Southern mammy. Inspired by the wholesome name and image, Rutt appropriated them both to market his new pancake mix.

A Short History

In 1889, Chris L. Rutt, a newspaperman in St. Joseph, Missouri, began working on creating a self-rising pancake mix. Within a year, he and two associates developed the first pancake mix ever made. Unable to raise the money to promote Aunt Jemima pancake mix, Rutt and his associates sold their company to R. T. Davis Mill and Manufacturing Company, which promoted the new product at the World's Columbian Exposition in Chicago in 1893. The company hired Nancy Green, a famous African-American cook born in Montgomery County, Kentucky, to play the part of Aunt Jemima and demonstrate the pancake mix. As Aunt Jemima, Nancy Green made and served over one million pancakes by the time the fair closed, prompting buyers to place over fifty thousand orders for Aunt Jemima pancake mix. For the next thirty years, Green played the part of Aunt Jemima at expositions all over the country. In 1924, the Quaker Oats Company bought the Aunt Jemima Mills.

✳Ingredients

Corn syrup, sugar syrup, high-fructose corn syrup, water, maple syrup, cellulose gum, salt, artificial and natural flavors, caramel color, sodium benzoate and sorbic acid (preservatives), sodium hexametaphosphate

✳Strange Facts

- A caricature of Nancy Green as a black mammy was pictured on early packages of Aunt Jemima pancake mix. In 1917, Aunt Jemima was re-drawn as a smiling, heavyset black housekeeper with a bandanna wrapped around her head. In 1989, the company modernized Aunt Jemima, making her thinner, eliminating her bandanna, and giving her a perm and a pair of pearl earrings.
- In 1923, Nancy Green died in an automobile accident at the age of eighty-nine.
- Before Aunt Jemima pancake mix was invented, pancakes were strictly a breakfast food. The appeal and convenience of Aunt Jemima pancake mix made pancakes a standard for lunch and dinner.
- The Boys Club of Rockford, Illinois, was built and is operated solely from funds raised annually by Rockford Kiwanians and Aunt Jemima.
- Frank Zappa recorded an album titled *Electric Aunt Jemima*.
- In 1994, pop singer Gladys Knight became a spokesperson for Aunt Jemima Lite Syrup.

✳Distribution

- In 1994, Aunt Jemima sold over $105 million worth of syrup, accounting for 18 percent of the syrup category.

For More Information

The Quaker Oats Company, P.O. Box 049003, Chicago, IL 60604-9003. Or telephone 1-800-407-2247.

Avery Laser Labels

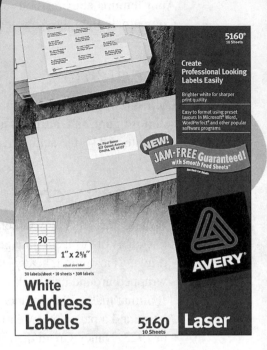

White Address Labels 5160 Laser

- **Label your eyeglass case.** Print your name, address, and phone number on an Avery Laser Label and adhere it inside your eyeglass case.

- **Identify your camera.** Print your name on an Avery Laser Label and adhere it to the back of your camera so you can easily identify it at family get-togethers or parties where many people bring the same type of camera.

- **Label Halloween candy.** Print your name, address, and phone number on Avery Laser Labels and adhere them to the wrappers of the candy you give out for Halloween, so parents will know whom the candy comes from.

- **Label your books and compact discs.** Print your name, address, and phone number on Avery Laser Labels and adhere them to books and CDs.

- **Label your child's school supplies.** Print your child's name on Avery Laser Labels and adhere them to rulers, crayon boxes, lunch boxes, and thermos bottles, then cover with transparent tape.

- **Label frozen foods and leftovers.** Print information about the contents and the date you place the food in the refrigerator or freezer on Avery Laser Labels.

- **Label computer discs.** Use Avery Laser Labels. Avery Dennison also makes diskette labels.

- **Label storage boxes.** Label the contents of any box you put into storage or in the attic or garage with an Avery Laser Label so you can easily identify the contents.

✳Invented
1935

✳The Name

Avery Laser Labels are named after company founder R. Stanton Avery.

✳A Short History

In 1935, Stan Avery founded Kum-Kleen Products, making self-adhesive labels using machinery he had developed from an old washing machine motor and sewing machine. Avery renamed his company Avery Adhesives, which incorporated in 1946 and became the Avery Adhesive Label Corporation, with 80 percent of its sales stemming from industrial labels sold to manufacturers to label their own products.

In 1952, Avery lost its patent rights for self-adhesive labels, compelling Avery to create a new division—the Avery Paper Company—to produce and market self-adhesive base materials.

In 1961, Avery went public, and grew rapidly over the next three decades, establishing new production facilities around the world, and introducing new, technologically superior adhesives. Major acquisitions extended the company's reach in office products and specialty chemicals, expanding Avery's product line and strengthening its market position. The company's primary brand names—Avery, in office products markets, and Fasson, for industrial customers—became recognized worldwide leaders in their industries.

In 1990, Avery International Corporation merged with Dennison Manufacturing Company. The merger created Avery Dennison, a substantially strengthened company with global leadership in office products, adhesives, and label converting technology.

✳Ingredients

Paper, adhesive

✳Strange Facts

- Dennison Manufacturing, which merged with Avery International in 1990, was founded by Andrew Dennison and his son Aaron Dennison in 1844. The company made jewelry boxes, and later manufactured tags, labels, and tissue paper.
- Avery Dennison works closely with leading software companies to incorporate preset layouts for Avery labels directly into the software. These preset layouts enable computer users to print labels almost effortlessly without the hassles of having to adjust margins, set tabs, or create tables.
- In 1977, Avery began supplying adhesives for disposable diapers.
- Avery Dennison makes self-adhesive postage stamps for the United States Postal Service.

✳Distribution

- Avery Dennison produces a wide variety of address labels. Avery labels are available in white, clear, or fluorescent colors, and are specially designed for laser or ink jet printers. Avery labels are also available for copiers, dot matrix printers, and typewriters.
- Avery Dennison also manufactures and markets pressure-sensitive adhesives and materials, office products, tags, retail systems, and specialty chemicals.

- Avery Dennison makes the best-selling office address labels in the United States.
- Avery Dennison operates two hundred manufacturing facilities and sales offices in thirty-six countries.
- In 1996, Avery Dennison sold more than $3.2 billion worth of pressure-sensitive adhesives and materials.

For More Information

Avery Dennison Corporation, Avery Division, Consumer Service Center, P.O. Box 5244, Diamond Bar, CA 91765-4000. Or telephone 1-800-462-8379.

Barbasol

- **Remove spots from rugs or carpets.**
  Squirt Barbasol on stain, scrub, and
  wash with water.

- **Clean upholstery.** Apply Barbasol sparingly to stain and rub gently with a
  damp cloth.

- **Make finger paint.** Let children paint
  with Barbasol on a kitchen table or vinyl tablecloth. For color, sprinkle
  in powdered tempera paint or add a drop of food coloring.

- **Clean grease from hands.** Rubbing Barbasol between your hands will
  dissolve grime without water. Keep a can of it at the workbench.

- **Remove latex paint from hands.** The emollients and moisturizers in Barbasol ease latex paint from skin.

- **Keep your bathroom mirror from fogging up.** Spread Barbasol on and wipe
  off. Can last two to three weeks.

- **Lubricate squeaky hinges.** Spray the joint with Barbasol.

- **Break in a baseball glove.** Rub the center of the glove with Barbasol, place a baseball in the glove, fold the mitt around it, and secure with rubber bands. Tuck the glove under a mattress overnight.

- **Prevent ski goggles from fogging up.** Spray the goggles with Barbasol, then wipe clean.

*Invented
1920

*The Name

Barbasol is a combination of the Roman word *barba* (meaning 'beard,' and the origin of the word *barber*) and the English word *solution*, signifying that the shaving cream is similar to the solution used by barbers. The stripes on the can evoke the familiarity of barbershop pole stripes.

*A Short History

In 1920, Frank B. Shields, a former chemistry instructor at the Massachusetts Institute of Technology who had founded the Napco Corporation in Indianapolis to make vegetable glue, developed the formula for Barbasol, one of the first brushless shaving creams on the market. The white cream provided a quick, smooth shave and eliminated the drudgery of having to lather up shaving soap in a mug with a shaving brush and then rubbing it onto the face. It immediately won the allegiance of thousands. The Barbasol factory and offices were both located in a small second-floor room in downtown Indianapolis. The tubes were filled, clipped, and packaged by hand. At the most, only thirty or forty gross made up an entire day's production schedule. By December 1920, Barbasol had outgrown the Napco Corporation and the Barbasol Company was created.

Barbasol was widely advertised on early radio by musical performers—most memorably Harry 'Singin' Sam' Frankel—and by the catchy jingle 'Barbasol, Barbasol . . . No brush, no lather, no rub-in . . . Wet your razor, then begin.'

In 1962, Pfizer—the pharmaceutical company founded in 1849 in

Brooklyn by Charles Pfizer and his cousin, confectioner Charles Erhart, to manufacture camphor, citric acid, and santonin—acquired the Barbasol line of shaving products, extending and updating the popular old brand.

✷Ingredients

Water, stearic acid, triethanolamine, isobutane, laureth-23, fragrance, propane, sodium lauryl sulfate

✷Strange Facts

- A typical shave will cut about 20,000 to 25,000 facial hairs.
- Company founder Frank Shields developed Barbasol especially for men with tough beards and tender skins because he had both of those shaving problems.
- During the 1920s, Barbasol was endorsed by Knute Rockne, Florenz Ziegfeld, and other celebrities of the day.
- The Depression had practically no effect on the Barbasol Company because shaving cream was not a luxury.
- In the 1936 Indianapolis 500, Barbasol sponsored the Barbasol Special #12, painted to look like a tube of Barbasol Brushless Shaving Cream. The car finished 21st after crashing in the main stretch in the 119th lap of the 200-lap race. Today, Barbasol sponsors a NASCAR team.
- Shaving in the shower wastes an average of ten to thirty-five gallons of water. To conserve water, fill the sink basin with an inch of water and vigorously rinse your razor often in the water—after every second or third stroke.
- A typical razor blade today is good for about ten shaves.
- Among the 90 percent of males who shave, roughly 30 percent use electric razors.
- Shaving daily with a wet razor exfoliates the beard area of the face, loosening and removing the top layer of skin cells, which is believed to help the skin retain its vitality and youthful appearance.
- According to archaeologists, men shaved their faces as far back as the Stone Age—twenty thousand years ago. Prehistoric men shaved with clamshells, shark teeth, sharpened pieces of flint, and knives.
- Ancient Egyptians shaved their faces and heads so the enemy had less to grab during hand-to-hand combat. Archaeologists have discovered gold

and copper razors in Egyptian tombs dating back to the fourth century B.C.

- The longest beard, according to the *Guinness Book of Records*, measured 17.5 feet in length and was presented to the Smithsonian Institute in 1967.
- Aerosol shaving cream cans were introduced in the 1950s.
- Shave gels, which turn to foam after being worked into the beard, were introduced in the late 1970s.
- The first shaving creams specifically targeted to women were introduced in 1986.
- Seventy percent of women rate clean-shaven men as sexy.

✱Distribution

- Barbasol is available in Aerosol Foam (Original, Menthol, Lemon/Lime, Skin Conditioner, Sensitive Skin, and Aloe), Shave Gel (Regular, Lime, Skin Conditioner, and Sensitive Skin), and Brushless Shave Cream.
- Barbasol accounts for 20 percent of all shaving preparations sold in the market.
- Pfizer, which mass-produced penicillin during World War II, discovered Terramycin, and made Salk and Sabin polio vaccines in the 1950s, is today one of the world's leading pharmaceutical companies. It also makes BenGay, Desitin, Bain de Soleil, Cortizone, and Visine.

For More Information

Consumer Health Group, Pfizer Inc., 235 East 42nd Street, New York, NY 10017.

Bounce

- **Repel mosquitoes.** Tie a sheet of scented Bounce through a belt loop when outdoors during mosquito season.

- **Eliminate static electricity from your television screen.** Since Bounce is designed to help eliminate static cling, wipe your television screen with a used sheet of Bounce to help prevent dust from resettling.

- **Dissolve soap scum from shower.** Clean with a used sheet of Bounce.

- **Freshen the air in your home.** Place an individual sheet of scented Bounce in a drawer or hang one in the closet.

- **Prevent thread from tangling.** Run a threaded needle through a sheet of Bounce to eliminate the static cling on the thread before sewing.

- **Eliminate static cling from panty hose.** Rub a damp, used sheet of Bounce over the hose.

- **Prevent musty suitcases.** Place an individual sheet of scented Bounce inside empty luggage before storing.

- **Freshen the air in your car.** Place a sheet of scented Bounce under the front seat.

- **Clean baked-on food from a cooking pan.** Put a sheet in the pan, fill with water, let sit overnight, and sponge clean. The antistatic agents apparently weaken the bond between the food and the pan while the fabric softening agents soften the baked-on food.

- **Eliminate odors in wastebaskets.** Place a sheet of scented Bounce at the bottom of the wastebasket.

- **Collect cat hair.** Rubbing the area with a sheet of Bounce will magnetically attract all the loose hairs.

- **Eliminate static electricity from venetian blinds.** Wipe the blinds with a used sheet of Bounce to prevent dust from resettling.

- **Wipe up sawdust from drilling or sandpapering.** A used sheet of Bounce will collect sawdust like a tack cloth.

- **Eliminate odors in dirty laundry.** Place an individual sheet of scented Bounce at the bottom of a laundry bag or hamper.

- **Deodorize shoes or sneakers.** Place a sheet of scented Bounce in your shoes or sneakers overnight so they'll smell great in the morning.

Invented
1972

The Name

The name Bounce signifies the way the sheet of fabric softener tumbles with the load during a typical drying cycle, distributing its softening ingredients.

A Short History

When different dry fabrics rub together in the dryer, the electrons in one fabric transfer to another, creating static electricity. When one fabric has more electrons than another, the fabrics cling together. To prevent static cling, Procter & Gamble developed Bounce to act as a conductor, releasing molecules of fabric softener that give the fabrics similar surface characteristics, preventing electron transfer.

✳ Ingredients

Fabric softening agents (cationic and/or nonionic surfactants), an antistatic agent (hydrophilic polymer or nonionic surfactant), an agent to provide more uniform ingredient release (bentonite), in a non-woven cloth

✳ Strange Facts

- The actual sheet is nine inches square and made from nonwoven porous rayon cloth.
- Bounce reduces the amount of effort needed during ironing because its softening agents act to smooth fibers, reduce wrinkles, and help the iron glide more easily.

✳ Distribution

- Bounce fabric softener sheets can be found in more than one out of every four homes in the United States. (Fabric softener can be found in 85 percent of all homes in the United States; 78 percent of those homes use Bounce.)
- Bounce is available in Outdoor Fresh Bounce, Gentle Breeze Bounce, and Bounce Free (with no fragrance).

For More Information

Procter & Gamble, Co., 391 East 6th Street, Cincinnati, OH 45202. Or telephone 1-800-5-BOUNCE.

Canada Dry Club Soda

- **Clean diamonds, rubies, sapphires, and emeralds.** Simply soak the gems in Canada Dry Club Soda.

- **Make fluffy pancakes, waffles, and matzah balls.** Substitute Canada Dry Club Soda for the liquid used in the recipes.

- **Make a poor man's lava lamp.** Fill a glass with Canada Dry Club Soda and drop in two raisins. The carbonation will cause the raisins to repeatedly bob to the surface and then sink again.

- **Clean grease stains from double-knit fabrics.** Pour on Canada Dry Club Soda and scrub gently.

- **Make inexpensive soft drinks.** Add Canada Dry Club Soda to fruit juice for a low-cost, healthy beverage.

- **Remove wine spills or other spots from carpet.** Apply Canada Dry Club Soda to the stain, rub it in, wait a few minutes, then sponge it up.

- **Clean and shine porcelain fixtures.** Pour Canada Dry Club Soda over the fixtures.

- **Clean chrome or stainless steel.** Use Canada Dry Club Soda in a spray bottle.

- **Water your plants.** Feed flat Canada Dry Club Soda to your houseplants or outdoor plants. The minerals in club soda are beneficial to green plants.

- **Remove food stains from clothes.** Immediately blot up the spills on any washable fabric, sponge with Canada Dry Club Soda, then wash the item in the washing machine through a regular cycle.

- **Clean countertops.** Pour Canada Dry Club Soda directly on the counter, wipe with a soft cloth, then rinse with warm water and wipe dry.

- **Relieve an upset stomach.** Drink Canada Dry Club Soda to soothe indigestion.

- **Clean grease from a car windshield.** Use a spray bottle filled with Canada Dry Club Soda and wipe with paper towels.

- **Loosen rusty nuts and bolts.** Pour Canada Dry Club Soda over them. The carbonation bubbles away rust.

- **Change blond hair dyed green by chlorine back to its original color.** Simply rinse your hair with Canada Dry Club Soda.

- **Preserve newspaper clippings.** Dissolve one Milk of Magnesia tablet in one quart Canada Dry Club Soda. Let the mixture stand overnight. The next day, stir the mixture well, then soak your clipping in the solution for one hour. Blot the newspaper clipping between two sheets of paper towel and place on a screen to dry.

✳Invented
1930

✳The Name

Toronto pharmacist J. J. McLaughlin named his first ginger ale McLaughlin's Pale Dry Ginger Ale, later changing the name to Canada

Dry Pale Ginger Ale. The word *Canada* denotes the country of the soft drink's origin and the word *dry* suggests nonalcoholic beverages. McLaughlin designed the original Canada Dry trademark—a map of Canada, emblems of the Canadian provinces, and a crouching beaver (the national animal)—inside a shield capped with a crown to symbolize "king-like quality."

A Short History

In 1904, J. J. McLaughlin, a Toronto pharmacist who had started a small plant that manufactured soda water to be sold to drugstores as a mixer for fruit juices and flavored extracts, developed a new "dry" ginger ale while trying to improve upon old-style ginger-ale recipes.

Although corner drugstores were the only outlets for distributing carbonated beverages, McLaughlin pioneered techniques for mass bottling that made it possible to serve Canada Dry at baseball games and public beaches.

In 1923, McLaughlin's heirs sold the company for $1 million to P. D. Saylor and J. M. Mathes, who founded the present-day Canada Dry Corporation. In 1930, Canada Dry introduced Tonic Water, Club Soda, Collins Mix, and fountain syrup. In 1986, Cadbury Schweppes, the world's first soft-drink maker, purchased Canada Dry and Sunkist.

Ingredients

Carbonated water, sodium bicarbonate, sodium citrate, potassium sulfate, disodium phosphate

Strange Fact

- Canada Dry was the first major soft drink company to put soft drinks in cans (1953) and introduce sugar-free drinks (1964).

Distribution

- Canada Dry also makes Seltzer and Sparkling Water, Vichy Water, Ginger Ale, Collins Mixer, Tonic Water, Sour Mixer, Lemon Sour, Jamaica Cola, Island Lime, Hi-Spot, Half and Half, Concord Grape, Wild Cherry, California Strawberry, Cactus Cooler, Black Cherry Wishniak, Birch Beer, Barrelhead Root Beer, Vanilla Cream Soda, Tahitian Treat, Sunripe Orange, Peach Soda, and Piña Pineapple.

- Cadbury Schweppes products are sold in more than 110 countries worldwide.
- In 1991, Cadbury Schweppes sold over $3.4 million worth of beverages.
- London-based Cadbury Schweppes uses 800 independent bottlers in the United States, a bottling network second only to the Coca-Cola Company.

For More Information

Canada Dry U.S.A., A division of Cadbury Beverages Inc., Six High Ridge Park, Stamford, CT 06905-0800. Or telephone 1-203-968-5600.

Carnation Nonfat Dry Milk

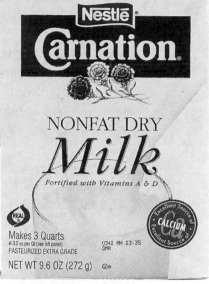

- **Paint your house.** Mix one and a half cups Carnation Nonfat Dry Milk and one-half cup water until it is the consistency of paint. Blend in a water-based color to make the desired hue. Thin the paint by adding more water; thicken the paint by adding more powdered milk. Brush on as you would any other paint. Let the first coat dry for at least twenty-four hours before adding a second coat. Let the second dry for three days. Early American colonists made their milk paint from the milk used to boil berries, resulting in an attractive gray color. This paint is extremely durable. To strip milk paint, apply ammonia, allow it to dry for about four days, then apply bleach. Make sure you are stripping the paint in a well-ventilated area.

- **Remove makeup.** Mix a teaspoon of Carnation Nonfat Dry Milk with warm water, apply with a cotton ball, wipe clean, and rinse.

- **Thaw frozen fish.** Mix one and one-third cups Carnation Nonfat Dry Milk in three and three-quarters cups water. Place the frozen fish in a pan and cover with the milk solution. Milk eliminates the frozen taste, returning the fresh-caught flavor.

- **Soothe poison ivy, insect bites, and sunburn.** Mix ten ounces Carnation Nonfat Dry Milk and twenty-five ounces water in a quart container. Fill up the container by adding ice cubes and two tablespoons salt. Apply to infected area with a cloth for twenty minutes, three or four times daily.

- **Take a milk bath.** Add one-half cup Carnation Nonfat Dry Milk to warm water for a soothing bath.

- **Make a slight crack in a dish or plate disappear.** Mix one and one-third cups Carnation Nonfat Dry Milk with three and three-quarters cups water. Place the dish or plate in a pan, cover with the milk solution, then bring to a boil and simmer for forty-five minutes at low heat. In most cases, the crack will vanish.

- **Clean plant leaves.** Mix one and one-third cups Carnation Nonfat Dry Milk with seven and three-quarters cups water, and using a soft cloth, wipe the leaves.

- **Substitute for whipped cream.** Whip one cup Carnation Nonfat Dry Milk in a cup of ice water for five minutes. Use immediately.

- **Clean silver.** Mix five ounces Carnation Nonfat Dry Milk, twelve ounces water, and one tablespoon Heinz White Vinegar or ReaLemon lemon juice. Let silver stand overnight in the mixture, then rinse clean and dry thoroughly.

Invented
1954

The Name

Legend holds that company founder Elbridge Amos Stuart noticed a box of Carnation cigars in the window of a Seattle shop and decided to use the name for his evaporated milk. The cigars were probably named Carnation to suggest opulence while simultaneously hinting at the word *Corona*.

A Short History

In 1899, Elbridge Amos Stuart founded the Carnation company in Kent, Washington, to manufacture evaporated milk. Purportedly, Stuart had designed a brightly colored label for his cases of evaporated milk before deciding upon a name for his company. Nestlé acquired Carnation in 1985.

Ingredients

Milk, vitamin A, vitamin D_3

Strange Facts

- Bread factories often add nonfat dry milk to their breads to improve the flavor and enhance the nutritional quality.
- Nestlé is the world's largest food company.

Distribution

- Nestlé also makes Carnation Evaporated Milk, Carnation Condensed Milk, Carnation Instant Breakfast drink, and Carnation Breakfast Bars.
- In the United States, Nestlé's well-known brands include Nestlé, Stouffer's, Hills Bros., Libby's, Carnation, Contadina, Nestea, Nescafé, Taster's Choice, Ortega, and Friskies.

For More Information

Nestlé USA Inc., 800 North Brand Boulevard, Glendale, CA 91203. Or telephone 1-818-549-6000.

Cascade

- **Get your whites whiter than white.** Mix one-half cup Cascade and one gallon hot water in a plastic bucket. Soak clothing in this mixture overnight, dump the solution and clothes into the washing machine, and wash as usual. Add one-half cup Heinz White Vinegar to the rinse water.

- **Remove coffee and tea stains from glass cookware.** Soak the glassware in a solution of two tablespoons Cascade to two quarts warm water.

- **Clean a thermos bottle.** Fill the bottle with two tablespoons Cascade and hot water. Let sit for thirty minutes, then swish clean with a bottle brush and rinse thoroughly.

- **Prewash stains on clothes.** Wet the fabric and sprinkle Cascade on the stain. Scrub gently with an old toothbrush, rinse, and run through the regular wash cycle.

- **Clean dirt, grease, and grime from walls, glass, porcelain, wooden furniture, and the outsides of appliances.** Dissolve one-quarter cup Cascade in one gallon of very hot water. Scrub, then wipe clean with a dry cloth. Cascade is spot-resistant and contains water-softening agents, so everything gets shiny clean without rinsing.

- **Whiten white polyester.** Mix one cup Cascade and one gallon warm water in a plastic bucket. Soak the clothes in this mixture overnight, then run them through the washing machine. Cascade removes the gray due to detergent residue buildup from white polyester.

- **Clean a vase.** Place one teaspoon Cascade in a dirty glass vase, fill with water, and let sit overnight. The next morning, simply rinse clean.

- **Clean bathtub rings.** Sprinkle Cascade on a wet sponge and scrub.

- **Clean cooked-on oil from a popcorn popper or baked-on food from a pot or pan.** Mix a heaping tablespoon of Cascade with hot water, put it in the popper (or pot or pan), and let soak overnight.

Invented
1955

The Name

The word *cascade* suggests the way the crystals cascade over the dishes to clean them.

A Short History

In the 1950s, when postwar prosperity made the automatic dishwasher popular, Procter & Gamble developed a detergent specially blended to capitalize on the new home market for these machines. In 1955, blue-green, pine-scented Cascade came in a box wrapped in gold paper, changed to green in 1958. In 1972, Procter & Gamble introduced Lemon Scent Cascade. In 1976, a new color dye was used, and the phosphate content was reduced from 12.9 to 8.3 percent in response to legislation barring high levels of phosphates. In 1983, Cascade was repackaged in a green laminated box. Cascade's phosphate content was lowered to 8.1 percent in 1989. In 1990, Cascade was reformulated without any dyes, and in 1992, the phosphate content was lowered again, to 7.5 percent.

✳Ingredients

Water softeners (complex sodium phosphates and sodium carbonate), cleaning agent (chlorine bleach), water spot prevention agents (nonionic surfactant), dishwasher and china protection agent (sodium silicate), processing aids (sodium sulfate), and perfume

✳Strange Facts

- After World War II, complex phosphates, primarily sodium tripolyphosphate, were a key factor in the development of the first synthetic detergent.
- Phosphates contain the element phosphorus, one of many nutrients essential to water plants and algae. Since phosphorus also contributes to accelerated eutrophication—the excessively rapid growth of aquatic plant life in water bodies—many state governments have banned the sale of detergents with phosphates.
- Since 1976, Procter & Gamble has reduced the amount of phosphate in Cascade by more than 41 percent, adding extra surfactants to boost the cleaning power.
- State legislatures that have banned detergents that contain phosphates have made an exception for automatic dishwasher detergents because, until recently, no automatic dishwasher detergent would work without phosphates.

✳Distribution

- Cascade is the best-selling automatic dishwashing detergent in the United States.
- Cascade is also available in Lemon (King Size and Family Size), Liquid Gel (Baking Soda Fresh Scent and Family Size), and Lemon Liquid Gel (King Size and Family Size).

For More Information

Procter & Gamble, One Procter & Gamble Plaza, Cincinnati, OH 45202. Or telephone 1-800-765-5516.

ChapStick Lip Balm

- **Stop bleeding while shaving.** Dab on some ChapStick if you nick yourself.

- **Prevent car battery corrosion.** Smear ChapStick on clean car battery terminals.

- **Lubricate a zipper.** Rub ChapStick along the teeth of the zipper to make it zip smoothly.

- **Moisturize skin.** Rubbing ChapStick on your face protects the skin from windburn while snow skiing.

- **Remove a ring stuck on a finger.** Coat finger with ChapStick and slide the ring off.

- **Lubricate nails and screws.** Nails and screws rubbed with ChapStick will go into wood more easily.

- **Groom a mustache or eyebrows.** A little ChapStick will keep the ends of a mustache waxed together and keep bushy eyebrow hairs in place.

- **Shine leather shoes.** In a pinch, rub ChapStick over the leather and buff with a dry, clean cloth.

- **Lubricate furniture drawers and windows.** Rub ChapStick on the casters of drawers and windows so they slide open and shut easily.

- **Prevent hair coloring from dyeing your skin.** Rub ChapStick along your hairline before coloring your hair.

✳Invented
Early 1880s

✳The Name

ChapStick is apparently named for the fact that you can heal *chap*ped lips by applying the *stick* of balm.

✳A Short History

In the early 1880s, Dr. C. D. Fleet, a physician and pharmacological tinkerer who lived in Lynchburg, Virginia, invented a lip balm in the form of a wickless candle wrapped in tinfoil and called it ChapStick. The lip balm was sold locally without much success. In 1912, another Lynchburg resident, John Morton, bought the rights to ChapStick for five dollars. In the family kitchen, his wife melted the pink ChapStick mixture on her kitchen stove, poured the liquid through a small funnel into brass tubes held in a rack, and then set the rack on the porch to cool. The Mortons cut the molded ChapStick into sticks and placed them into containers for shipping.

In 1963, the A. H. Robins Company acquired ChapStick lip balm from Morton Manufacturing Corporation and, in 1971, added four flavors. In 1989, American Home Products Corporation, makers of Chef Boyardee foods and a leader in women's health care products, acquired A. H. Robins.

✳Ingredients

ACTIVE INGREDIENTS: 44 percent petrolatums, 1.5 percent padimate 0, 1 percent lanolin, 1 percent isopropyl myristate, 0.5 percent cetyl alcohol;

INACTIVE INGREDIENTS: arachadyl propionate, camphor, carnauba wax, D&C red 6 barium lake, FD&C yellow 5 aluminum lake, fragrance, isopropyl lanolate, methylparaben, mineral oil, 2-octyl dodecanol, oleyl alcohol, polyphenylmethylsiloxane 556, propylparaben, titanium dioxide, wax paraffin, white wax

Strange Facts

- Suzi Chaffey, a member of the United States Olympic Women's Alpine Skiing Team, became a spokesperson for ChapStick in the 1970s, using the nickname Suzi Chapstick.
- In the 1994 movie *Clifford*, Clifford (Martin Short) substitutes lipstick for ChapStick in Martin's (Charles Grodin's) pocket, and Martin applies the lipstick shortly before giving a toast at dinner with his future in-laws.

Distribution

- ChapStick lip balms are available in five flavors: Regular, Orange, Cherry, Strawberry, and Mint. ChapStick lip balm is also available in Medicated, Ultra SPF 30, Petroleum Jelly Plus, and Lip Moisturizer SPF 15 with Vitamin E and Aloe.
- Whitehall-Robins Healthcare's parent company, American Home Products, sold $819 million worth of food products in 1995.
- American Home Products makes the estrogen drug Premarin, the most prescribed drug in America, and the contraceptive implant Norplant. The company also makes Advil, Anacin, Chef Boyardee, Crunch 'n Munch, Denorex, Gulden's, Jiffy Pop, Pam No Stick Cooking Spray, Preparation H, and Robitussin.

For More Information

Whitehall-Robins Healthcare, 1 Campus Drive, Parsippany, NJ 07054. Or telephone 1-201-660-5500.

Clairol Herbal Essences

- **Remove ring-around-the-collar.** Since the dirt rings in collars are oil stains, oily hair shampoo will remove them when rubbed into the fabric.

- **Wash dishes.** If you run out of dish-washing soap, wash your dishes in the kitchen sink with Herbal Essences. It's perfect for camping because it's biodegradable.

- **Make a bubble bath.** Pour one capful of Herbal Essences under a running tap in the bathtub.

- **Clean grease from your hands.** A dab of Herbal Essences cuts through the grime on your hands.

- **Wash your car.** Add two capfuls of Herbal Essences to a bucket of water and soap up your car with the biodegradable suds.

- **Clean hairbrushes and combs.** Add a capful of Herbal Essences to warm water. Shampoo cuts through sebum oil, leaving brushes clean and fresh.

- **Shave.** Apply Herbal Essences to wet skin as a substitute for shaving cream.

Invented
1971

The Name

Clairol is apparently a combination of the French word *clair* (clear) and the suffix *-ol* (oil). Herbal Essence, the name of the original green shampoo, referred to the shampoo's herbal fragrance, not its ingredients. In 1995, Clairol reformulated the shampoo with all-natural ingredients and renamed it Herbal Essences.

A Short History

The scalp releases sebum oil into the hair, which in turn causes dirt to stick to the hair. In the 1890s, German chemists discovered the detergents that would wash sebum oil from hair, although British hairdressers had already coined the word *shampoo* from the Hindi *champoo* (to massage) to refer to cleansing formulas made from water, soap, and soda. In the United States, John Breck, captain of a Massachusetts volunteer fire department, developed several shampoos—including a shampoo for normal hair in 1930 and shampoos for oily and dry hair in 1933. Clairol concocted green Herbal Essence shampoo to target the back-to-nature sentiment embraced by the youth movement of the early 1970s. In 1995, Clairol reformulated, repackaged, and relaunched Herbal Essence as a complete line of biodegradable shampoos blended from organic herbs and botanicals in pure mountain springwater, renaming the product Herbal Essences.

Ingredients

Water, sodium laureth sulfate, sodium lauryl sulfate, cocamidopropyl betaine, aloe extract, chamomile extract, passion flower extract, cocamide MEA dihydroxypropyl PEG-5 linoleaminium chloride, fragrance, citric acid, propylene glycol DMDM hydantoin, iodopropynyl butycarbamate, D&C Orange no. 4, Ext. D&C violet no. 2, FD&C yellow no. 5

✴Strange Facts

- Biodegradable Herbal Essences is made from natural herbs and botanicals and plant-derived ingredients from renewable plant sources. The herbs and botanicals are grown under certified organic conditions without petrochemicals or pesticides.
- Herbal Essences is not tested on animals, nor does it contain any animal by-products.
- The see-through bottles, featuring botanical graphics and a flip-top cap, are made from recyclable polyethylene and contain 2.5 percent postconsumer polyethylene plastic.
- Herbal Essences financially supports environmental and natural causes devoted to preserving the earth's rain forests, parks, and endangered plant species.

✴Distribution

- Herbal Essences is available in four clear formulas: Moisture-Balancing Shampoo (chamomile, aloe vera, and passion flower), Replenisher Shampoo (rose hips, vitamin E, and jojoba), Extra Body Shampoo (marigold flowers, angelica, and thyme), and Clarifying Shampoo (rosemary, jasmine, and orange flower).

For More Information

Clairol Inc., Stamford, CT 06902. Or telephone 1-800-223-5800.

Clorox Bleach

- **Extend the life of freshly cut flowers.** Add one-quarter teaspoon (twenty drops) Clorox bleach to each quart of water used in your vase.

- **Deodorize coolers and thermos bottles.** Wash with diluted Clorox bleach, then rinse.

- **Remove mold and mildew from outdoor siding, tile, brick, stucco, and patios.** Clean with a mixture of three-quarters cup Clorox bleach per gallon of water.

- **Remove coffee or tea stains from china cups.** Soak clean china cups for five to ten minutes in a solution of one tablespoon Clorox bleach per gallon of water.

- **Disinfect garbage cans.** Wash the garbage cans with a solution made from three-quarters cup Clorox bleach to one gallon water. Let stand for five minutes, then rinse clean.

- **Bail out a boat.** Cap an empty, clean Clorox bleach bottle, cut diagonally across the bottom, and scoop out the water.

- **Make a scooper.** Cap an empty, clean Clorox bleach bottle, cut diagonally across the bottom, and use it to scoop up flour, sugar, rice, dog food, sand, fertilizer, or snow.

- **Make a pooper scooper.** Cut an empty, clean Clorox bleach jug in half. Use the half with the handle to scoop.

- **Clean butcher blocks to prevent bacteria from breeding.** Wash the cutting board with hot, sudsy water and rinse clean. Then apply a solution of three tablespoons Clorox bleach per gallon of water. Keep wet for two minutes, then rinse clean.

- **Make a hot cap.** Cut off the bottom of an empty, clean Clorox bleach jug and place the jug over the seedlings. Take the cap off during the day, and replace the cap at night. To anchor these hot caps, simply cut off the top of the handle, insert a sharp stick, and drive the stick into the ground.

- **Remove stains from baby clothes.** Mix one-quarter cup Clorox bleach to one gallon of water in a plastic bucket. Add colorfast clothes and soak for five minutes. Rinse well, then run the clothes through the regular cycle in the washing machine.

- **Sift soil.** Cut the bottom off an empty, clean Clorox bleach bottle at an angle to make a scooper. Insert a six-inch-diameter piece of one-quarter-inch hardware cloth to rest above the handle hole. Scoop up dirt, sift through the narrow opening, and stones will be caught by the hardware cloth.

- **Make a fishing or boating buoy.** Cap an empty, clean Clorox bleach jug tightly, tie a rope to the handle, and tie a weight to the other end of the rope. These buoys can also be strung together to mark swimming and boating areas.

- **Make a carrier for small children's toys and crayons.** Cut a hole in the side of an empty, clean Clorox bleach jug opposite the handle.

- **Clean mops.** Rinse mops in a bucket of sudsy water and three-quarters cup Clorox bleach per gallon of water.

- **Clean caulking around bathtubs.** Scrub with a solution of three-quarters cup Clorox bleach to a gallon of water.

- **Make a clothespin holder.** Cut a hole in the side of an empty, clean Clorox bleach jug opposite the handle, and punch small holes in the bottom for drainage. Hang your new clothespin holder on the clothesline.

- **Whiten a porcelain sink.** Fill the sink with a solution of three-quarters cup Clorox bleach per gallon of water. Let sit for five minutes.

- **Make a paint bucket.** Cut a hole in the side of an empty, clean Clorox bleach jug opposite the handle.

- **Make an anchor.** Fill an empty, clean Clorox bleach bottle with gravel.

- **Clean a toilet bowl.** Pour in one cup Clorox bleach. Let it stand for ten minutes. Brush and flush.

- **Clean a rubber sink mat.** Fill the sink with water, add one-quarter cup Clorox bleach, and soak the sink mat for five to ten minutes.

- **Improvise a funnel.** Cut an empty, clean Clorox bottle in half, remove the cap, and keep it in the trunk of your car as an emergency funnel for motor oil, antifreeze, and water.

- **Make a bird feeder.** Cut a hole in the side of an empty, clean Clorox bleach jug opposite the handle, and fill with birdseed.

- **Freshen and disinfect old sponges.** Soak sponges for five to ten minutes in a mixture of three-quarters cup Clorox bleach per gallon of water, then rinse well.

- **Make a hip bucket for harvesting fruits or berries.** Cut a large hole in the side of an empty, clean Clorox bleach bottle opposite the handle, then string your belt through the handle.

- **Clean mildew from shower curtains, shower caddies, bath mats, and plastic soap dishes.** Place all the bathroom accessories in the bathtub, fill with two gallons water, and add one and a half cups Clorox bleach. Soak for five to ten minutes, then rinse and drain. The Clorox bleach will have cleaned the bathtub also, so sponge it down too.

- **Deodorize the garbage disposal in your sink.** Pour one cup Clorox bleach down your drain, then run the hot water for two minutes.

- **Make dumbbells.** Fill two empty, clean Clorox bleach bottles with sand.

- **Make a megaphone.** Remove the cap and cut off the bottom of an empty, clean Clorox bleach bottle.

- **Clean mildew from grout.** Mix three-quarters cup Clorox bleach with one gallon of water, and use an old toothbrush to scrub off the mildew.

- **Store rock salt for melting snow.** Ice melting products are much easier to dispense from Clorox bleach bottles.

- **Make glasses sparkle and silverware shine.** Add a capful of Clorox bleach to the dishwasher.

Invented
1916

The Name

Clorox seems to be a combination of the words c*hlor*ine and *sodium hydroxide*, the two main ingredients used to make sodium hypochlorite bleach.

A Short History

French chemist Claude Louis Berthollet (1748–1822) introduced sodium hypochlorite as an industrial bleach. In 1913, five Oakland investors founded The Electro-Alkaline Company to make industrial-strength bleach using water from salt ponds around San Francisco Bay. The following year the company registered the brand name Clorox and its diamond-shaped trademark. In 1916, the company formulated a less concentrated household bleach, and in 1928, went public. In 1957, Procter & Gamble bought Clorox, resulting in antitrust litigation by the FTC for the next decade. Procter & Gamble was ordered to divest itself of Clorox, and in 1969, Clorox again became an independent company.

Ingredient

5.25 percent solution sodium hypochlorite

Strange Facts

- According to The Clorox Company, Clorox bleach is an environmentally sound choice because it breaks down naturally after use to little more than salt and water.
- The shape of the Clorox bottle is a registered trademark of The Clorox Company.
- Never mix bleach with other household chemicals, such as toilet bowl cleaners, rust removers, acids, or products containing ammonia. To do so will release hazardous gases.
- Never use Clorox on silk or wool; sodium hypochlorite destroys these fibers.
- *Fortune* magazine named Clorox a top ten United States environmental leader in 1993.

Distribution

- Clorox is also available in Fresh Scent, Lemon Fresh, and Floral Fresh.
- Clorox sells its products in ninety-four countries and produces them in more than thirty plants in the United States, Puerto Rico, Canada, Mexico, Argentina, and South Korea.
- Clorox also manufactures Brita water filtering systems, Clorox Clean-Up cleaner, Clorox 2 all-fabric bleach, Combat insect control systems, Formula 409 all-purpose cleaner, Fresh Step cat litter, Hidden Valley Ranch salad dressing, K.C. Masterpiece barbecue sauce, Kingsford charcoal briquets, Kitchen Bouquet browning and seasoning sauce, Liquid-Plumr drain opener, Pine-Sol cleaner, Soft Scrub mild abrasive liquid cleanser, Stain Out soil and stain remover, and Tilex mildew remover.
- In 1995, The Clorox Company's sales topped $1.9 billion.

For More Information

The Clorox Company, 1221 Broadway, Oakland, CA 94612-1888. Or telephone 1-510-271-7000.

Coca-Cola

- **Clean a toilet bowl.** Pour a can of Coca-Cola into the toilet bowl. Let the Real Thing sit for one hour, then brush and flush clean. The citric acid in Coke removes stains from vitreous china, according to household-hints columnist Heloise.

- **Remove rust spots from chrome car bumpers.** Rubbing the bumper with a crumpled-up piece of Reynolds Wrap aluminum foil dipped in Coca-Cola will help remove rust spots, according to household-hints columnist Mary Ellen.

- **Clean corrosion from car battery terminals.** Pour a can of carbonated Coca-Cola over the terminals to bubble away the corrosion, according to Heloise.

- **Cook with Coca-Cola.** The Coca-Cola Consumer Information Center offers a free packet of recipes, including a Mustard Herb Dressing (an Italian-style salad dressing made with one-half cup Coca-Cola), a Twin Cheese Dip (requiring three-quarters cup Coca-Cola and doubling as a sandwich filling), and Sweet-Sour Cabbage (using one-half cup Coca-Cola and two tablespoons bacon drippings).

- **Loosen a rusted bolt.** Mary Ellen suggests applying a cloth soaked in a carbonated soda to the rusted bolt for several minutes.

- **Bake a moist ham.** Empty a can of Coca-Cola into the baking pan, wrap the ham in aluminum foil, and bake. Thirty minutes before the ham is finished, remove the foil, allowing the drippings to mix with the Coke for a sumptuous brown gravy.

- **Remove grease from clothes.** Empty a can of Coke into a load of greasy work clothes, add detergent, and run through a regular wash cycle. The Coca-Cola will help loosen grease stains, according to Mary Ellen.

Invented
May 8, 1886

The Name

Bookkeeper Frank M. Robinson, one of Coca-Cola inventor Dr. John Styth Pemberton's four partners, suggested naming the elixir after two of the main ingredients: the coca leaf and the kola nut. He suggested spelling *kola* with a *c* for the sake of alliteration. Robinson wrote the name in his bookkeeper's Spencerian script, much the way it appears today.

A Short History

Dr. John Styth Pemberton, inventor of Globe of Flower Cough Syrup, Indian Queen Hair Dye, Triplex Liver Pills, and Extract of Styllinger, was eager to duplicate Vin Mariani, a popular wine elixir made with coca. In his backyard at 107 Marietta Street in Atlanta, Georgia, Pemberton developed a thick syrup drink from sugar water, a kola nut extract, and coca.

Pemberton brought his new syrup elixir to Jacob's Drug Store, where druggist Willis Venable added carbonated water. The rights to the name and formula were bought and sold several times before Asa G. Candler acquired them in 1888. Candler kept the formula a well-guarded secret, and on January 31, 1893, trademarked the name. The distinctively shaped Coke bottle was designed by Alexander Samuelson at Root Glass in Terre Haute, Indiana.

Since 1893, the recipe for Coca-Cola has been changed only once. In 1985, when Pepsi-Cola outsold Coca-Cola in the United States for the first time in history, the Coca-Cola Company sweetened the product and renamed it New Coke. Within three months, consumers forced the company to bring back the old formula. It became known as Coca-Cola Classic, and New Coke, considered the marketing fiasco of the decade, soon disappeared from the marketplace.

✳Ingredients

Carbonated water, high fructose corn syrup and/or sucrose, caffeine, phosphoric acid, caramel color, glycerin, lemon oil, orange oil, lime oil, cassia oil, nutmeg oil, vanilla extract, coca, and kola

✳Strange Facts

- Coca-Cola stock went public in 1919 at $40 per share. In 1994, one of those shares was worth $118,192.76, including dividends.
- Rumor contends that a piece of meat left in a glass of Coca-Cola overnight will be completely dissolved by the following morning. It won't. A piece of meat soaked in Coca-Cola overnight will, however, be marinated and tender.
- During the 1960s, the Coca-Cola jingle was sung by Roy Orbison, the Supremes, the Moody Blues, Ray Charles (who sang the Diet Pepsi jingle in the 1990s), the Fifth Dimension, Aretha Franklin, and Gladys Knight and the Pips.
- The World of Coca-Cola, a three-story pavilion in Atlanta, features exhibits (including a 1,000-piece memorabilia collection and John Pemberton's original handwritten formula book), soda fountains of the past and future, bottling exhibits, samples of Coca-Cola products from around the world, and films of Coca-Cola commercials.
- If all the Coca-Cola ever produced was in regular-size bottles and laid end to end, it would reach to the moon and back 1,045 times. That is one trip per day for two years, ten months, and eleven days.
- "Good to the Last Drop," a slogan used by Maxwell House coffee, was first used by Coca-Cola in 1908.

- Shaking up a bottle of Coca-Cola for use as a douche immediately after sexual intercourse has been considered an effective method of contraception among the uneducated. It does not work.
- *The Coca-Cola Catalog*, a mail order catalog filled with Coca-Cola memorabilia from boxer shorts to "O" gauge boxcars emblazoned with the Coca-Cola logo, is available for free by calling 1-800-872-6531.

⚹Distribution

- On the average day in 1993, consumers drank 705 million servings of Coke and other Coca-Cola soft drinks worldwide.
- 2,386.7 million gallons of Coca-Cola Classic were sold in 1992.
- Coca-Cola outsells Pepsi worldwide by a more than two-to-one margin.
- Coca-Cola is available in Coca-Cola Classic, Caffeine Free Coca-Cola Classic, Diet Coke, Caffeine Free Diet Coke, Cherry Coke, Diet Cherry Coke, and Coke II (previously known as New Coke).

For More Information

Consumer Information Center, Coca-Cola USA, One Coca-Cola Plaza, Atlanta, GA 30313. Or telephone 1-800-GET COKE.

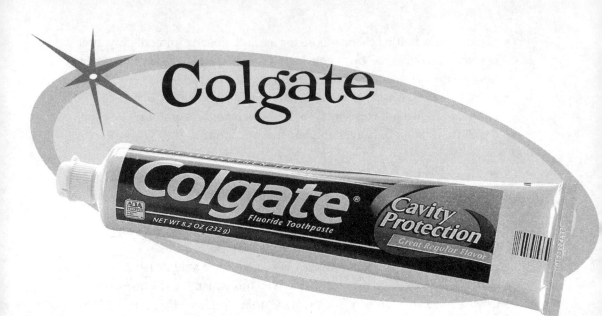

- **Polish silverware, silver, or gold.** Colgate will shine up silver and gold. Rinse thoroughly.

- **Clean piano keys.** Squeeze Colgate on a damp cloth. Rub the keys well, wipe dry, and buff with a soft, dry cloth.

- **Remove ink spots from cloth.** Squeeze Colgate on spot, scrub, and rinse thoroughly.

- **Dry up acne pimples.** Dab Colgate on pimples.

- **Remove crayon from walls.** Brush the marks with Colgate on an old toothbrush.

- **Remove scratches on glassware.** Polish with a dollop of Colgate.

- **Deodorize smelly hands.** Squeeze an inch of Colgate into your palm and wash hands under running water.

- **Remove Kool-Aid mustaches from kids' faces.** Rub on Colgate and rinse thoroughly.

- **Deodorize "sour" baby bottles.** Scrub with Colgate and a bottle brush.

- **Remove scuffs on shoes.** Apply Colgate with a tissue, rub, and wipe off.

- **Remove tar from skin.** Squeeze on Colgate and rub.

- **Fill small holes in walls.** Use a small dab of Colgate as emergency spackling to fill in small holes in plaster walls. Let dry before painting.

Invented
1896

The Name

The Colgate Company named the white toothpaste after the company's founder, William Colgate.

A Short History

In 1806, William Colgate founded his starch, soap, and candle business on Dutch Street in New York City. In 1896, the Colgate Company, run by Colgate's son, Samuel Colgate, introduced Colgate Dental Cream, the first toothpaste packaged in a collapsible tube. In 1968, Colgate toothpaste was reformulated with MFP fluoride (monofluorophosphate), deemed the best possible protection against tooth decay.

Ingredients

Sodium monofluorophosphate (0.15 percent w/v fluoride ion), dicalcium phosphate dihydrate, water, glycerin and/or sorbitol, sodium lauryl sulfate, cellulose gum, flavor, tetrasodium pyrophosphate, sodium saccharin

Strange Facts

- Poison toothpaste is used by the CIA as a weapon for assassinations, according to Larry Devlin, a CIA agent who was instructed to kill ousted

Belgian Congo prime minister Patrice Lumumba. "I received instructions to see that Lumumba was removed from the world," Devlin told *Time* magazine in 1993. "I received poison toothpaste, among other devices, but never used them."

- When wilderness camping, anything that smells like food can attract bears, including toothpaste. Food, soap, and toothpaste should be stored in a waterproof sack hung over a twenty-foot-high rope strung between two trees.
- According to *The First Really Important Survey of American Habits* by Mel Poretz and Barry Sinrod, 72 percent of Americans squeeze the toothpaste tube from the top.

✳Distribution

- Colgate is the best-selling toothpaste worldwide.
- Colgate is available in Great Regular Flavor, Tartar Control Paste, Clear Blue Winterfresh Gel, Tartar Control Gel, Baking Soda, Tartar Control Baking Soda, and Platinum.

For More Information

Colgate-Palmolive Company, 300 Park Avenue, New York, NY 10022. Or telephone 1-800-221-4607.

Conair Pro Style 1600

- **Dry salad greens.** Set a Conair Pro Style 1600 on cool, and dry wet leaves of lettuce.

- **Dry steam off a fogged-up bathroom mirror.** Simply use a Conair Pro Style 1600 to blow hot air at the mirror.

- **Dry wet boots or sneakers.** Insert the nozzle of a Conair Pro Style 1600 into the boot and use on a low setting for five minutes.

- **Thaw frozen windows.** Use a Conair Pro Style 1600 to thaw windows that are frozen shut.

- **Clean crayon marks from wallpaper.** Set a Conair Pro Style 1600 on hot until the wax heats up, then wipe clean with a paper towel.

- **Do your dusting.** Use a Conair Pro Style 1600 to blow cool air to clean dust off high shelves or out from under appliances, pleated lampshades, carved furniture, crevices, and knickknacks.

- **Defrost frozen pipes.** Set a Conair Pro Style 1600 on hot and aim at the pipes.

- **Free a snapshot stuck in a magnetic photo album.** Blow warm air from a Conair Pro Style 1600 underneath the plastic page.

- **Remove Con-Tact paper.** Set a Conair Pro Style 1600 on warm, work on one section at a time, and gently pull the edges.

- **Remove candle wax from a table or countertop.** Blow warm air an inch above the drips, then wipe away the wax with a paper towel.

- **Set cake icing.** Set a Conair Pro Style 1600 on warm and dry cake icing.

- **Remove a bumper sticker.** Blow it with a Conair Pro Style 1600 set on hot for a few minutes, until the adhesive softens, then peel the bumper sticker off.

- **Dry the inside of rubber gloves.** Insert the nozzle of a Conair Pro Style 1600 into the glove and blow warm air.

- **Dry panty hose.** Hang the wet panty hose on the shower rod and blow them dry.

- **Defrost a jammed automatic ice maker.** Hold a Conair Pro Style 1600 eight inches from the frozen mass of ice cubes until they melt apart.

- **Remove an adhesive bandage.** Blowing hot air with a Conair Pro Style 1600 at the bandage will soften the adhesive so you can ease off the bandage.

- **Thaw the frozen lock on a car door.** Before you call the locksmith, use a Conair Pro Style 1600 to thaw the frozen lock.

- **Remove the wrinkles from plastic tablecloths or shower curtains.** Blow with a Conair Pro Style 1600 set on hot until the plastic softens.

- **Determine which windows are leaking heat.** Hold a lit candle just inside a window, while someone else goes outside with a Conair Pro Style 1600 and blows air along the frame. If the flame flickers, the window needs caulking.

- **Dry joint compound.** Use a Conair Pro Style 1600 to speed up the drying process.

- **Warm cold bed sheets.** Use a Conair Pro Style 1600 to make ice-cold sheets toasty warm.

✶Invented
1971

✶The Name

Conair is a conjunction of the words *continental* and *hair*.

✶A Short History

In 1959, with only $100, Leandro P. Rizzuto and his parents, Julian and Josephine, started Continental Hair Products in New York City to market hair rollers for beauty salons. The company developed the hot comb in 1968 and introduced the first hand-held pistol-grip blow dryer to the United States in 1971. The following year, Continental Hair Products went public at $8.75 per share and, in 1973, acquired Jheri Redding Products, makers of shampoos and conditioners. In May 1976, the company changed its name to Conair Corporation. In 1985, company founder Lee Rizzuto bought the company in the largest leveraged buyout to date by an individual at $300 a share.

✶Ingredients

Thermoplastic, mica, nickle chrome heater wire, thermal fuse, thermostat, switches, DC motor, rectifier, plastic impeller, screws, heating element

✶Strange Facts

- The development of the blow dryer enabled hair salons to accomplish in minutes what used to take hours, thus handling more clients in less time, and thereby increasing revenues.

- Other products introduced to beauty salons by Conair include curling irons, brushes, shears, shampoos, conditioners, beauty soap bars, hair rollers, tipping caps, perms, and perm rods.

✳Distribution

- Conair has been the leading designer and manufacturer of professional hair-styling appliances since its founding in 1959.
- Conair also owns Jheri Redding Products, Cuisinart, and Fabergé and manufactures Southwestern Bell Freedom Phones.

For More Information

Conair Corporation, 150 Milford Road, East Windsor, NJ 08520. Or telephone 1-800-3-CONAIR.

Coppertone

- **Remove tar spots from car finishes without damaging the finish.** Apply Coppertone to a cloth and rub until the tar glides off.

- **Prevent skin damage.** Using sunscreen whenever you go out in the sun can prevent wrinkling, discoloration, pronounced blood vessels, and cancerous lesions that may be caused by prolonged exposure to the sun.

- **Prevent chapped lips.** Coppertone keeps lips moist and healthy.

- **Moisturize your hands.** The emollients in Coppertone rejuvenate dry skin.

- **Repel insects.** Slather on Coppertone to keep insects away.

- **Take a soothing bath.** Add two tablespoons Coppertone to a warm bath as a bath oil.

- **Soften fingernails.** Warm Coppertone and use as a hot oil treatment to soften nails.

- **Enjoy a massage.** Coppertone makes an excellent substitute for massage oil.

- **Relieve itching from insect bites.** Applying Coppertone over the affected areas alleviates itching.

- **Remove scuff marks from patent leather shoes.** Apply Coppertone to a soft cloth and rub it into the patent leather.

- **Clean grease and oil from skin.** Rub Coppertone into the skin and wash clean with water.

- **Polish wood surfaces.** Squeeze Coppertone onto a soft cloth to clean and polish natural wood.

- **Remove candle wax.** Rub on a dollop of Coppertone to remove candle wax from furniture, carpeting, and clothing.

- **Clean paint from hands.** Coppertone removes paint and stains from hands more gently than turpentine.

- **Pry apart two bowls or glasses.** Dribble a few drops of Coppertone down the sides, then slip the bowls or glasses apart.

- **Clean grease and dirt.** Squeeze Coppertone onto a soft cloth to remove grease stains from Formica surfaces and oven-range hoods.

- **Remove dried glue and gum left by price tags and labels peeled from glass, metals, and most plastics.** Apply Coppertone and wipe clean.

- **Clean ink from hands and vinyl surfaces.** Apply Coppertone and wipe clean.

- **Lubricate pipe joints.** Coppertone works as an oil lubricant for fitting pipe joints together.

⭑*Invented*
1944

The Name

Coppertone signifies the *copper*-colored skin *tone* sun worshippers strive to obtain.

A Short History

Dr. Benjamin Green, a physician from Miami, Florida, helped the United States military develop sunscreen to protect soldiers stationed in the South Pacific during World War II from getting severe sunburns. After the war, he noticed that tourists in Miami used all kinds of homemade concoctions to bronze in the sun. He began experimenting with different formulas, using his own bald head as a testing ground, until he came up with the recipe for Coppertone suntan cream with the essence of jasmine in 1944. A picture of an Indian chief was on the first bottles, with the slogan "Don't be a Paleface." Little Miss Coppertone replaced him in 1953.

Ingredients

ACTIVE INGREDIENTS: Ethylhexyl p-methoxcinnamate, oxybenzone; INACTIVE INGREDIENTS: Water, sorbitan sesquioleate, sorbitol, glyceryl stearate SE, stearic acid, isopropyl myristrate, triethanolamine, benzy alcohol, octadecene/MA copolymer, fragrance, dimethicone, carbomer, methylparaben, aloe extract, tocopheryl acetate (Vitamin E acetate), jojoba oil, propylparaben, disodium EDTA

Strange Facts

- To figure out how many hours of protection you can expect from a sun screen, take the number of minutes it takes your skin to start burning without sunscreen, multiply by the sun protection factor (SPF) printed on the bottle of Coppertone, and divide the result by sixty. For instance, if you usually burn in thirty minutes, an SPF 8 lotion should protect you for approximately four hours.
- The higher the SPF of a sunscreen, the higher the price.

- The higher in the sky the sun is, the higher the SPF number you need. Also, the closer to the equator you are, the stronger the sunscreen you need.
- Freckles can sometimes be minimized by using sunscreen lotions containing para-aminobenzoic acid (PABA). Freckles are caused by an accumulation of the skin pigment melanin, which responds unevenly to sunlight. Coppertone does not contain PABA.
- Never use a sunscreen that is more than a year old. Abide by the expiration dates.
- As a child, actress Jodie Foster appeared in Coppertone commercials.

Distribution

- Coppertone is the best-selling sunscreen in the United States.

For More Information

Schering-Plough HealthCare Products, Inc., Memphis, TN 38151. Or telephone 1-800-842-4090.

Cover Girl NailSlicks Classic Red

- **Adjust the water in the bath or shower effortlessly.** Turn the bathtub or shower faucets to the temperature you prefer, then mark the faucet(s) and the wall with a dot of Cover Girl NailSlicks Classic Red so the dots can be aligned immediately every time you bathe or shower.

- **Label golf, tennis, and squash balls.** Paint a small mark with Cover Girl NailSlicks Classic Red so you can easily identify your own sports equipment.

- **Make the raised gradation marks on plastic baby bottles clearly visible.** Paint the gradation marks with Cover Girl NailSlicks Classic Red.

- **Label children's toys.** Simply paint your child's name on the bottom of his or her favorite toys with Cover Girl NailSlicks Classic Red so they won't get lost.

- **Repaint faded gradation marks on measuring cups.** Carefully repaint the gradation marks with Cover Girl NailSlicks Classic Red.

- **Label poisons and medicines.** Paint an *X* with Cover Girl NailSlicks Classic Red on containers of poison and medicine bottles, and teach your children to never touch any bottle or box labeled with a red *X*.

- **Label hot water faucets for younger children.** Paint the tops of the hot water faucets with Cover Girl NailSlicks Classic Red for your children's protection.

- **Locate the arrows or markings on childproof caps easily.** Paint the arrows or other markings on childproof medicine bottles with Cover Girl Nail-Slicks Classic Red so you can line them up easier.

- **Thread a needle with ease.** Dip the end of the thread into Cover Girl NailSlicks Classic Red, let dry, and thread.

- **Seal an envelope.** Use Cover Girl NailSlicks Classic Red to seal a letter as you would use sealing wax.

- **Teach your child to push the red button on the phone in an emergency.** Paint a red dot with Cover Girl NailSlicks Classic Red in the middle of the *0* on your telephone so young children can always call for help.

- **Readjust your thermostat quickly.** Paint a dot of Cover Girl NailSlicks Classic Red to mark the temperature at which you usually set your thermostat.

- **Remind yourself to turn off your calculator or camera flash attachment.** Paint the off button with Cover Girl NailSlicks Classic Red.

Invented
1977

The Name

Cover Girl has always been about models—and linking famous magazine "cover girls" with its products.

A Short History

In 1914, pharmacist Dr. George Bunting combined medication and vanishing cream in the prescription room of his Baltimore drugstore to create "Dr. Bunting's Sunburn Remedy." A customer told Bunting, "Your cream knocked my eczema," inspiring Bunting to change the name of his sunburn remedy to Noxzema. For three years, Bunting mixed, heated, and poured Noxzema from a large coffee pot into blue jars—ultimately founding the Noxzema Chemical Company in 1917. With the backing of Bunting's fellow druggists, Noxzema achieved national distribution in 1938.

In 1961, Noxzema launched the Cover Girl line of cosmetics with an advertising campaign using famous and fashionable cover girls raving over the new makeup. In 1966, the company changed its name to the Noxell Corporation. In 1989, Procter & Gamble Cosmetics and Fragrances bought Noxell.

Ingredients

Ethyl acetate, butyl acetate, nitrocellulose, propyl acetate, tosylamide/epoxy resin, dibutyl phthalate, isopropyl alcohol, stearalkonium bentonite, stearalkonium hectorite, camphor, benzophenone-1; MAY CONTAIN: Titanium dioxide, guanine, red 6 barium lake, iron oxides, red #7 calcium lake, yellow #5 aluminum lake, red #34 calcium lake, ferric ammonium ferrocyanide, mica, bismuth, oxychloride

Strange Facts

- In 3000 B.C., Chinese artists combined gum arabic, egg white, gelatin, and beeswax to create varnishes, enamels, and lacquers—which Chinese aristocrats started applying to their fingernails as a status symbol.
- The cosmetics industry in the United States includes face makeup (representing 35 percent of sales in 1992), eye cosmetics (30 percent), lip products (23 percent), and nail products (12 percent).

Distribution

• In the United States, Cover Girl is the number-one cosmetics company, followed by number-two Revlon and number-three Maybelline.

For More Information

Procter & Gamble Cosmetics and Fragrances, 11050 York Road, Hunt Valley, MD 21030. Or telephone 1-888-COVER-GIRL, a toll-free number featuring live operators who offer consumers "mini-makeovers" and product information.

Crayola Chalk

- **Prevent an ant invasion.** Draw a line of Crayola Chalk around windows and doors outside your home, and around water pipes inside your home. Ants will not cross a chalk line.

- **Clean ring-around-the-collar.** Mark the stain heavily with white Crayola Chalk. The chalk will absorb the sebum oil that holds in the dirt.

- **Prevent silverware from tarnishing.** Place a piece of Crayola Chalk in your silver chest to absorb moisture.

- **Cover spots on white suede.** Rub with Crayola Chalk.

- **Prevent tools from rusting.** Place a few pieces of Crayola Chalk in your toolbox to absorb moisture.

- **Prevent dampness in a closet.** Tie together a handful of Crayola Chalk and hang the bundle from the clothes rod to absorb moisture.

- **Prevent a screwdriver from slipping.** Rub Crayola Chalk on the tip.

- **Polish marble and metal.** Pulverize a few sticks of Crayola Chalk with a mortar and pestle until it is a fine powder. Dip a soft cloth in the powder, wipe the marble or metal, then rinse with clear water, and dry thoroughly.

- **Fill a hole in a plaster wall.** Insert a piece of Crayola Chalk into the hole, cut it off even with the wall, then plaster.

- **Repel slugs.** Slugs will not cross a chalk line.

- **Remove grease.** Rub Crayola Chalk on a grease spot on clothing or table linens, let it absorb the oil, then brush off. Launder as usual.

- **Draw on sidewalks.** Create games, maps, and adventures.

- **Prevent costume jewelry from tarnishing.** Place a piece of Crayola Chalk in your jewelry box.

Invented
1902

The Name

Alice Binney, wife of company co-owner Edwin Binney, coined the word Crayola by joining *craie*, from the French word meaning chalk, with *ola*, from *oleaginous*, meaning oily.

A Short History

In 1864, Joseph W. Binney began the Peekskill Chemical Works in Peekskill, New York, producing hardwood charcoal and a black pigment called lampblack. In 1880, he opened a New York office and invited his son, Edwin Binney, and his nephew, C. Harold Smith, to join the company. The cousins renamed the company Binney & Smith and expanded the product line to include shoe polish, printing ink, and black crayons.

In 1900, the company bought a water-powered stone mill along Bushkill Creek near Easton, Pennsylvania, to use slate and other materials from nearby quarries to make slate pencils for schools. The success of the pencils led Binney & Smith to develop chalk for teachers.

Binney & Smith chalk was dustless, made by a process called extrusion, which is still used to this day. Calcium carbonate and water-washed clay are pulverized into powder, mixed together, and then blended with a liquid binder. Balls of dough are then rolled into a cylinder, which is then pressed like toothpaste from a tube. As the long rope of wet chalk emerges, an automatic slicer cuts it into small pieces. The small pieces of chalk are then dried in kilns. For colored chalk, dry powdered pigments are added at the start of the process. Binney & Smith chalk won a Gold Medal for excellence at the 1902 St. Louis Exposition.

Ingredients

Calcium carbonate, water-washed clay, pigments

Strange Facts

- Chalk—or calcium carbonate—is always 40 percent calcium, 12 percent carbon, and 48 percent oxygen, by weight.
- Famous chalk deposits include the white cliffs of Dover, England, and the fossil beds in western Kansas.
- Many chalk deposits were formed during the Cretaceous Period, 136 to 70 million years ago, named from the Latin word for chalk, *creta*.
- Musician Joni Mitchell released an album entitled *Chalk Mark in a Rainstorm* in 1988.
- Chalk is used to make rubber goods, paint, putty, polishing powders, and Portland cement.

Distribution

- Crayola Chalk is available in white, colors, and sidewalk chalk.

For More Information

Crayola Consumer Affairs, P.O. Box 431, Easton, PA 18044-0431. Or telephone 1-800-CRAYOLA.

Crayola Crayons

- **Dye candles.** Melt Crayola Crayons with paraffin to make colored candles.

- **Rewind a bobbin.** Mark the thread with a contrasting color Crayola Crayon a few yards after starting to wind it onto the bobbin. The crayon mark will alert you when the thread is coming to the end.

- **Hide scratches on furniture and Formica.** Rub the nick with a matching Crayola Crayon.

- **Mend a leaking vase.** Hold a match under the pointed end of a Crayola Crayon that matches the color of the vase and let the melted wax drip into the crack. After the wax cools, scrape away the excess.

- **Hide small bleach spots on clothing.** Color the spot with a Crayola Crayon that matches the color of the fabric, then cover with wax paper and iron on a low setting.

- **Renew the worn dial on a washer or other appliance.** Rub the knob with red or black Crayola Crayon until the indentations of the letters and numbers are filled with colored wax. Then wipe off the excess crayon.

- **Seal envelopes.** Melt Crayola Crayons as sealing wax for envelopes.

- **Differentiate hard-boiled eggs from raw eggs in the refrigerator.** Mark the hard-boiled eggs with a Crayola Crayon.

- **Repair a scratch on an automobile.** Find a matching color Crayola Crayon and work it into the scratch.

Invented
1903

The Name

Alice Binney, wife of company co-owner Edwin Binney, coined the word Crayola by joining *craie*, from the French word meaning chalk, with *ola*, from *oleaginous*, meaning oily.

A Short History

The Peekskill Chemical Works, founded in 1864 by Joseph W. Binney to manufacture charcoal and black pigment, was renamed Binney & Smith when Binney's son, Edwin, and his nephew, C. Harold Smith, took over the family business. In 1903, the company made the first box of Crayola Crayons, costing a nickel and containing eight colors: red, orange, yellow, green, blue, violet, brown, and black. The now classic box of sixty-four crayons, complete with built-in sharpener, was introduced in 1958. Hallmark Cards, Inc., the world's largest greeting card manufacturer, acquired Binney & Smith in 1984. In 1993, Binney & Smith celebrated Crayola brand's ninetieth birthday by introducing the biggest crayon box ever, with ninety-six colors.

⋆Ingredients

Paraffin wax, stearic acid, colored pigment

⋆Strange Facts

- In 1949, Binney & Smith introduced another forty colors: Apricot, Bittersweet, Blue Green, Blue Violet, Brick Red, Burnt Sienna, Carnation Pink, Cornflower, Flesh (renamed Peach in 1962, partly as a result of the civil rights movement), Gold, Gray, Green Blue, Green Yellow, Lemon Yellow, Magenta, Mahogany, Maize, Maroon, Melon, Olive Green, Orange Red, Orange Yellow, Orchid, Periwinkle, Pine Green, Prussian Blue (renamed Midnight Blue in 1958 in response to teachers' requests), Red Orange, Red Violet, Salmon, Sea Green, Silver, Spring Green, Tan, Thistle, Turquoise Blue, Violet Blue, Violet Red, White, Yellow Green, and Yellow Orange.
- In 1958, Binney & Smith added sixteen colors, bringing the total number of colors to sixty-four: Aquamarine, Blue Gray, Burnt Orange, Cadet Blue, Copper, Forest Green, Goldenrod, Indian Red, Lavender, Mulberry, Navy Blue, Plum, Raw Sienna, Raw Umber, Sepia, and Sky Blue.
- In 1972, Binney & Smith introduced eight fluorescent colors: Atomic Tangerine, Blizzard Blue, Hot Magenta, Laser Lemon, Outrageous Orange, Screamin' Green, Shocking Pink, and Wild Watermelon.
- In 1990, the company introduced eight more fluorescent colors: Electric Lime, Magic Mint, Purple Pizzazz, Radical Red, Razzle Dazzle Rose, Sunglow, Unmellow Yellow, and Neon Carrot.
- In 1990, Binney & Smith retired eight traditional colored crayons from its 64-crayon box (Green Blue, Orange Red, Orange Yellow, Violet Blue, Maize, Lemon Yellow, Blue Gray, and Raw Umber) and replaced them with such New Age hues as Cerulean, Vivid Tangerine, Jungle Green, Fuchsia, Dandelion, Teal Blue, Royal Purple, and Wild Strawberry. Retired colors were enshrined in the Crayola Hall of Fame. Protests from groups such as RUMPS (Raw Umber and Maize Preservation Society) and CRAYON (Committee to Reestablish All Your Old Norms) convinced Binney & Smith to release the one million boxes of the Crayola Eight in October 1991.
- In 1993, Binney & Smith introduced sixteen more colors, all named by consumers: Asparagus, Cerise, Denim, Granny Smith Apple, Macaroni and Cheese, Mauvelous, Pacific Blue, Purple Mountain's Majesty,

Razzmatazz, Robin's Egg Blue, Shamrock, Tickle Me Pink, Timber Wolf, Tropical Rain Forest, Tumbleweed, and Wisteria.

- Washington Irving used the pseudonym Geoffrey Crayon when he published *The Sketch-Book*, a collection of short stories and essays, including "The Legend of Sleepy Hollow" and "Rip Van Winkle."
- On average, children between the ages of two and seven color for twenty-eight minutes every day.
- The average child in the United States will wear down 730 crayons by his or her tenth birthday.
- The scent of Crayola Crayons is among the twenty most recognizable to American adults.
- The Crayola brand name is recognized by 99 percent of all Americans.
- Red barns and black tires got their colors thanks in part to two of Binney & Smith's earliest products: red pigment and carbon black. Red and black are also the most popular crayon colors, primarily because children tend to use them for outlining.
- Binney & Smith is dedicated to environmental responsibility. Crayons that do not meet quality standards are remelted and used to make new crayons. Ninety percent of Crayola products' packaging is made from recycled cardboard. The company also makes sure that the wood in its colored pencils does not originate from tropical rain forests.

Distribution

- Binney & Smith produces two billion Crayola Crayons a year, which, if placed end to end, would circle the earth four and a half times.
- Crayola Crayons are also available in Changeables, Glow in the Dark, Glitter, GemTones, Magic Scent, Cosmic Colors, Washable So Big, and Washable Large.
- Crayola Crayon boxes are printed in eleven languages: Danish, Dutch, English, Finnish, French, German, Italian, Norwegian, Portuguese, Spanish, and Swedish.
- Binney & Smith also manufactures Magic Markers, colored pencils, chalk, and Silly Putty.

For More Information

Crayola Consumer Affairs, P.O. Box 431, Easton, PA 18044-0431. Or telephone 1-800-CRAYOLA.

Cream of Tartar

- **Clean ring-around-the-collar.** Wet the collar with warm or hot water, rub in Cream of Tartar, then launder as usual.

- **Repel ants.** Sprinkle Cream of Tartar around entrances to ant nests and into cracks and crevices.

- **Clean a bathtub.** Make a paste from Cream of Tartar and hydrogen peroxide, scrub with a brush, and rinse thoroughly.

- **Cook with a buttermilk substitute.** Mix one cup milk with one and three-quarters tablespoons Cream of Tartar for use as a buttermilk substitute in recipes.

- **Clean the blackened inside of an aluminum pot.** Boil a solution of two teaspoons Cream of Tartar and one quart water in the pot for several minutes.

- **Remove rust stains from washable fabrics.** Make a paste of Cream of Tartar and hot water, rub into the stain, let sit for ten minutes, then launder as usual.

- **Clean porcelain.** Sprinkle Cream of Tartar on a damp cloth and rub the porcelain surface.

- **Make tartrate baking powder.** Blend together one-half teaspoon Cream of Tartar, one-quarter teaspoon Arm & Hammer Baking Soda, and one-quarter teaspoon Kingsford's Corn Starch.

Invented

1903

The Name

Cream signifies the refining process used to procure the *tartar* that adheres to the inside of wine barrels.

A Short History

In 1889, McCormick & Company was started in Baltimore in one room and a cellar by twenty-five-year-old Willoughby M. McCormick and his staff of two girls and a boy. The company's first products were root beer, flavoring extracts, and fruit syrups and juices—all sold door-to-door. The company entered the spice field in 1896 when McCormick bought F. G. Emmett Spice Company of Philadelphia and had all the spice machinery shipped to Baltimore. In 1947, the McCormick Company acquired A. Schilling & Company of San Francisco, a coffee, spice, and extract house, gaining coast-to-coast distribution with the slogan "United to serve the nation's good taste."

Ingredient

Potassium bitartrate

Strange Facts

- Cream of Tartar is derived from argol, the crude tartar sediment deposited on the sides of casks during wine-making.

- Cream of Tartar is also called potassium bitartrate and has the chemical formula $KHC_4H_4O_6$.
- Cream of Tartar is also used to manufacture baking soda, to tin plate metals, and as a laxative in medicines.
- Cream of Tartar has an indefinite shelf life if kept tightly closed and stored away from heat.
- McCormick/Schilling obtains its supply of Cream of Tartar from Italy, where short people crawl through the very small holes in open wine casks to scrape out the residue left after the wine has been fermented and drained out.

Distribution

- McCormick products are distributed under the Schilling label in the western United States.
- McCormick & Company, Inc., is the largest spice company in the world, with annual sales of $1.7 billion.

For More Information

McCormick & Company, Inc., P.O. Box 208, Hunt Valley, MD 21030-0208.

Crisco All-Vegetable Shortening

- **Prevent diaper rash.** Use Crisco All-Vegetable Shortening as a balm on a baby's behind.

- **Prevent snow from sticking to a shovel.** Lubricate the shovel with Crisco All-Vegetable Shortening before you start shoveling.

- **Clean grease and dirt from hands.** Rub in Crisco All-Vegetable Shortening before using soap.

- **Make white clown makeup.** Mix two tablespoons Kingsford's Corn Starch with one tablespoon Crisco All-Vegetable Shortening. For colored makeup, add a few drops of food coloring.

- **Remove lipstick from clothes.** Rub in a dab of Crisco All-Vegetable Shortening, then rinse the stained area with Canada Dry Club Soda.

- **Season new cast-iron cookware.** Apply a thin coating of solid, unsalted Crisco All-Vegetable Shortening, and bake in an oven at 200°F for two hours. Repeat this procedure after the first few times of use.

- **Revitalize wooden salad bowls.** Rub with Crisco All-Vegetable Shortening inside and out, let sit overnight, then remove excess with paper towels.

- **Clean ink from hands and vinyl surfaces.** Apply Crisco All-Vegetable Shortening and wipe clean.

- **Preserve a wooden cutting board.** Rub with Crisco All-Vegetable Shortening, let sit overnight, then remove excess with paper towels.

- **Polish rubber galoshes.** Rub on Crisco All-Vegetable Shortening.

- **Remove homemade candles from molds easily.** Apply a thin coat of Crisco All-Vegetable Shortening to the inside of the candle mold before pouring in the hot wax.

- **Remove tar from clothing.** Scrape off as much tar as possible, place a lump of Crisco All-Vegetable Shortening over the spot, wait three hours, then wash.

Invented
1911

The Name

The two suggested names for the vegetable shortening—Krispo (the word *crisp* combined with the then-popular suffix *-o*) and Cryst (an onomatopoeia for the hissing and crackling sound foods make while being fried)—were combined to form the unique hybrid Crisco.

A Short History

In 1837, candlemaker William Procter and soapmaker James Gamble merged their small Cincinnati businesses, creating Procter & Gamble. By 1859, P&G had become one of the largest companies in Cincinnati, with sales of $1 million. In 1879, the company introduced Ivory, a floating soap. Procter & Gamble introduced Crisco, the first mass-marketed, 100 percent vegetable shortening, in 1911.

The first cans of Crisco came with an eight-page circular cookbook cut to fit the lid. Starting in 1913, Procter & Gamble sent six home economists across the country to give week-long demonstrations (advertised as "cooking schools") to show homemakers how to get better results by using Crisco in their cooking. After the demonstrations, the home economists would hand out souvenir baskets of various food samples, one-and-a-half-pound cans of Crisco, and special Crisco cookbooks to the eager audiences.

Ingredients

Partially hydrogenated soybean and cottonseed oils, mono- and diglycerides

Strange Facts

- The first Crisco cookbook, printed in 1911 and titled "Tested Crisco Recipes," has been followed through the years by more than sixty Crisco cookbooks.
- Cooking experts from the *Ladies' Home Journal* and other women's magazines worked out Crisco's early cookbooks and tested the recipes in their magazines' kitchens. In 1923, Procter & Gamble set up its own kitchen in Cincinnati to create and test recipes.
- Procter & Gamble's first three radio network programs in 1923 consisted entirely of cake and cookie recipes for Crisco.
- Crisco All-Vegetable Shortening will easily glide out of a bowl or measuring cup that was previously used to beat or measure eggs.
- Procter & Gamble advertising innovations included sponsorship of daytime dramas, the first being *The Puddle Family*, a 1932 radio show.
- Although Crisco appears solid, it actually contains over 80 percent liquid oil. The oil is suspended in a lattice of fat solids much like honey is held in a honeycomb.

✴Distribution

- Procter & Gamble also makes Tide, Spic and Span, Duncan Hines, Charmin, Folgers, Crest, Head & Shoulders, Pampers, Nyquil, Noxzema, Jif, Max Factor, Pringles, Hawaiian Punch, Bounce, Cascade, Cheer, Comet, Downy, Joy, Mr. Clean, Chloraseptic, Clearasil, Cover Girl, Ivory, Luvs, Metamucil, Oil of Olay, Pepto-Bismol, Scope, Secret, Vicks, Vidal Sassoon, and Zest.

For More Information

Procter & Gamble, Box 5558, Cincinnati, OH 45201. Or telephone 1-800-543-7276.

Dannon Yogurt

- **Soothe sunburn pain.** Spread yogurt on the sunburn, let sit for twenty minutes, then rinse clean with luke-warm water.

- **Reduce the occurrence of yeast infections.** The March 1992 issue of the *Annals of Internal Medicine* reports that daily consumption of yogurt containing *Lactobacillus acidophilus* cultures results in a threefold decrease in the incidence of candidal vaginitis (yeast infections).

- **Enhance your immune system.** According to the *International Journal of Immunotherapy*, yogurt with active cultures enhances the body's immune system by increasing the production of gamma interferons, which play a key role in fighting certain allergies and viral infections. Other studies indicate that yogurt can help prevent gastrointestinal infections. (Lactic acid helps inhibit the growth of food-borne pathogens, and yogurt cultures produce bacteriocins that restore natural intestinal cultures.)

- **Prevent diarrhea while taking antibiotics.** Eat Dannon Yogurt with active cultures while taking antibiotics. Antibiotics may kill healthful bacteria in addition to disease-bearing ones, but the *Lactobacillus acidophilus* in yogurt produces bacteriocins.

- **Tighten pores and cleanse skin.** Spread Dannon Yogurt over your face, wait twenty minutes, then wash with lukewarm water.

- **Cure yeast infections.** Use a turkey baster to insert yogurt into the vagina. According to *The New Our Bodies, Ourselves*, some women claim that yogurt in the vagina is a remedy for *candida albicans*.

- **Soothe canker sores.** Eat two servings of Dannon Yogurt a day until the sores clear.

- **Make yogurt cheese.** Yogurt cheese has the same consistency as cream cheese but is much lower in fat. It can he used as a spread for bagels, toast, and crackers or as a low-calorie, low-fat, low-cholesterol substitute for cream cheese in traditional cheesecake recipes. To make yogurt cheese, empty a pint of yogurt into a large, fine-meshed strainer or colander lined with a double thickness of cheesecloth, a coffee filter, or a yogurt strainer. Place a bowl under the strainer to catch the liquid (whey) that drains from the yogurt. Cover the yogurt and refrigerate for eight to 24 hours (texture will vary depending on how long it drains). Save the calcium-rich whey to use in soups and gravies. Makes about one cup yogurt cheese.

Invented
1919

The Name

Dannon is an Americanized version of Danone, the Spanish yogurt manufacturing company founded by Dr. Isaac Carasso and named for his son Daniel. Danone means "Little Daniel."

A Short History

Yogurt is believed to have originated during biblical times. A staple in the Middle East, yogurt was introduced to Europe in the sixteenth century. In

Spain in 1919, Dr. Isaac Carasso perfected the first industrial manufacturing process for yogurt (using bacterial cultures developed at the Pasteur Institute in Paris) and named his company for his son Daniel. In 1942, Daniel Carasso brought the company to the United States, where he Americanized the name to Dannon.

✳Ingredients

Cultured grade A milk and pectin, active yogurt cultures, and *Lactobacillus acidophilus* cultures

✳Strange Facts

- Yogurt is simply cultured milk. When live active cultures are added to milk, they convert the lactose into lactic acid. To label a product "yogurt," the United States Food and Drug Administration requires the use of two live active cultures, *Lactobacillus bulgaricus* and *Streptococcus thermophilus*. Dannon also adds the bacteria *Lactobacillus acidophilus* to the majority of their yogurts. Scientific research has shown that live active cultures boost the body's immune system and help the body digest proteins and lactose.
- All Dannon yogurts contain at least ten million active cultures per gram.
- Dannon plain yogurt was first sold in returnable half-pint glass jars.
- Yogurt helps the estimated 50 million Americans who are milk intolerant—incapable of digesting lactose, the principal sugar found in milk. Because of its high levels of live active cultures, Dannon Yogurt can be eaten by lactose-intolerant people, providing them with all the nutritional benefits of milk.
- Yogurt provides nearly one and a half times more calcium than milk. A single serving of Dannon Yogurt provides 25 to 40 percent of daily calcium requirements.
- In 1992, researchers from the University of Southern California School of Medicine in Los Angeles reported that people who ate yogurt, even as little as three to four times a month, showed lower relative risk of developing colon cancer.

✳Distribution

- Dannon is the best-selling yogurt in the United States, with more than two million cups of yogurt sold every day.
- Dannon Yogurt, with live active cultures, is available in Low Fat Fruit, Low Fat Fruit on the Bottom, Fruit on the Bottom Mini-Packs, Blended Fat Free, Blended Fat Free Mini-Packs, Tropifruta, D'Animals, Sprinkl'ins, Sprinkl'ins Crazy Crunch, Light Fruited, Light Flavored, Light Fruited Mini-Packs, and Light 'n' Crunchy.

For More Information

The Dannon Information Center, P.O. Box 44235, Jacksonville, FL 32231-4235. Or telephone 1-800-321-2174.

Dixie Cups

- **Protect tomatoes from cutworms and insects.** Remove the bottoms of Dixie Cups and push the cups into the soil to encircle young plants.

- **Improvise a funnel.** Punch a hole in the bottom of a Dixie Cup near the edge.

- **Make a weather vane.** Remove the bottom from a Dixie Cup and hang the cup horizontally from a string. The opening will tend to face into the wind.

- **Make a poor man's telephone.** Punch a small hole in the bottom of two Dixie Cups. Then thread the ends of a long piece of string through the holes and tie each end to a button. You and a friend each take a cup and walk apart until the string is straight and taut. Speak into the open end of your cup. Your sound waves travel along the string and can be heard by your friend through the open end of the other cup.

- **Germinate seeds.** Turn a Dixie Cup upside down and use a pencil to poke a hole in the center of the bottom. Then fill half of the cup with soil. Place seed inside and cover with more soil. Follow directions on seed package for proper care. Write plant name on cup with marker.

- **Turn soap slivers into liquid soap.** Place slivers of soap in a Dixie Cup with a little water, then wait a few days.

- **Make a Strawberry Short Cup.** Place a spoonful of whipped topping in the bottom of six nine-ounce Dixie Cups. Alternate filling the cups with strawberries and cubed cake to one inch below the rim. Press down with a spoon to fill any air pockets. Complete with whipped topping and a single whole strawberry. Serves six.

- **Relieve an earache caused by the change in pressure in an airplane.** Dampen a paper towel with hot water, ball it up, and place in the bottom of a Dixie Cup. Then hold the Dixie Cup over your ear. The steam from the hot water will soften the wax in your ear, alleviating the pain.

- **Make an anemometer to determine wind speeds.** Using a hole puncher, punch one hole in four Dixie Cups, about a half inch below the rim. Then take a fifth Dixie Cup and punch four equally spaced holes about a quarter inch below the rim and a fifth hole in the center of the bottom of the cup. Push a straight plastic drinking straw through the hole in one of four cups. When it hits the inside of the cup across from the hole, fold the end of the straw, and staple it to the side of the cup. Slide the free end of the straw through two opposite holes in the fifth cup with the four holes. Then push the free end of the straw through the hole in a second one-hole Dixie Cup. Fold the end of the straw and staple it to the inside of the cup across from the hole, making certain the cup faces in the opposite direction from the first cup. Repeat this procedure using the remaining two cups and a second straight plastic straw, aligning the four cups so that their open ends face in the same direction around the center cup. Push the eraser end of a sharpened pencil through the bottom hole in the center cup, then push a pin through the two straws where they intersect and into the end of the pencil eraser as far as it will go.

    To find the wind speed, multiply the number of revolutions per minute by the circumference of the circle (in feet) made by the revolving paper cups. The result is the speed of the wind in feet per minute.

Invented

1908

The Name

Inventor Hugh Moore's paper cup factory was located next door to the Dixie Doll Company in the same downtown loft building. The word *Dixie* printed on the company's door reminded Moore of the story he had heard as a boy about "dixies," the ten-dollar banknotes printed with the French word *dix* in big letters across the face of the bill. They had been issued in the early 1800s by a New Orleans bank renowned for its strong currency. The "dixies," Moore decided, had the qualities he wanted people to associate with his paper cups, and with permission from his neighbor, he used the name.

A Short History

In 1908, Hugh Moore started the American Water Supply Company of New England to market a vending machine that for one penny would dispense a cool drink of water in an individual, clean, disposable paper cup. Moore soon realized that his sanitary cups had greater sales potential than his water, particularly when Dr. Samuel Crumbine, a health official in Dodge City, Kansas, began crusading for a law to ban the public tin dipper. Lacking the capital to manufacture enough paper cups to abolish the tin dipper, Moore and his associate Lawrence Luellen traveled to New York City with a few handmade samples and eventually hooked up with an investment banker who invested $200,000 in the venture, incorporated as the Public Cup Vendor Company in 1909.

That same year, Kansas passed the first state law abolishing the public dipper and Professor Alvin Davison of Lafayette College published a study reporting that germs of communicable diseases could be found on public dipping tins. As state after state outlawed public tins, Moore and his associates created a paper cup dispenser to be distributed for free to businesses and schools who would buy the paper cups. By 1910 the company had changed its name to the Individual Drinking Cup Company, only to change it again in 1912 to Health Kups and yet again in 1919 to Dixie

Cups. In 1923, Dixie Cups produced a two-and-a-half-ounce Dixie Cup for ice cream, giving the ice cream industry a way to sell individual servings of ice cream and compete with bottled soft drinks and candy bars. The American Can Company purchased Dixie Cups and merged the company with Northern Paper. In 1982, the James River Corporation acquired Dixie Cups/Northern Paper for $455 million.

Ingredients

Paper, wax

Strange Facts

- Etymologists believe that the sobriquet for the southern United States, Dixie Land, originated on the Mississippi River before the Civil War with riverboat men for whom a "dixie" was a New Orleans banknote printed with the word *dix*, French for "ten."
- The Dixie Cups, a popular singing trio comprised of sisters Nadine, Marta, and Lucile LeCupsa, sang the 1964 hit song "Chapel of Love."
- While playing telephone operator Ernestine on *Saturday Night Live*, Lily Tomlin said, "Next time you complain about your phone service, why don't you try using two Dixie Cups with a string?"

Distribution

- Dixie holds the number-one spot in commercial food service, ahead of Sweetheart Cups.
- Dixie also manufactures paper plates.
- Dixie Cups are available in a wide range of designs.

For More Information

James River Corporation, Consumer Products—Dixie, Norwalk, CT 06856-6000. Or telephone 1-800-243-5384.

Efferdent

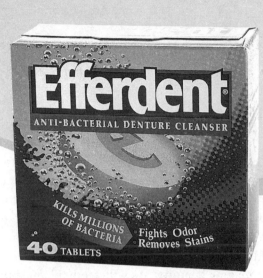

- **Clean a toilet bowl.** Drop several Efferdent tablets into the toilet bowl, scrub, and flush.

- **Polish diamonds.** Drop one Efferdent tablet in a glass of water and immerse diamonds for two minutes.

- **Clean a Thermos bottle.** Fill the bottle with water, drop in three Efferdent tablets, and let soak for an hour or longer if necessary.

- **Unclog a sink.** Drop several Efferdent tablets into the sink and let sit overnight.

- **Clean a vase.** To remove a stain from the bottom of a glass vase or cruet, fill with water and drop in one Efferdent tablet.

- **Clean hubcaps.** Drop one Efferdent tablet into a glass of water, use a cloth to apply the fizzing solution to the hubcaps, and wash clean with water.

★Invented

1966

★The Name

Efferdent is a combination of the words *effervesce* and *dentures*.

★A Short History

The Etruscans made the earliest-known dentures, crafted from stone, wood, and animal teeth. For centuries, skilled artisans constructed dentures, often using gold, silver, and ivory. In 1851, following the discovery of a process to harden the juices of certain tropical plants into vulcanized rubber, porcelain teeth were embedded in gutta-percha or rubber bases. Since World War II, acrylic plastics have replaced the use of rubber and porcelain in making dentures. As with teeth, plaque buildup collects on dentures, producing bacterial odors and leading to denture stains. Throughout history, denture wearers brushed their dentures—until 1967, when Warner-Lambert introduced Efferdent, the world's first denture effervescent cleansing tablet.

★Ingredients

Potassium monopersulfate compound, sodium perborate, sodium bicarbonate, citric acid, sodium carbonate, ethylenediamine tetraacetic acid, tetrasodium salt dihydrate, lathanol, sodium tripolyphosphate, sodium benzoate, magnesium stearate, polytetrafluoroethylene powder, sodium sulfate anhydrous, mint fragrance, FD&C green no. 3, FD&C blue no. 2

★Strange Facts

- More than three billion denture cleanser tablets were sold in the United States in 1993.
- Efferdent kills 99.9 percent of the odor-causing bacteria on dentures.

- Paul Revere, the American patriot best remembered for his midnight ride from Boston to Lexington to herald the news of the British invasion, was also a craftsman who fashioned dentures from ivory and gold.
- George Washington, the first president of the United States, owned at least one pair of dentures made from wood. He never used Efferdent.

Distribution

- Five to seven million Efferdent tablets are produced daily.
- Denture cleansers include effervescent tablets, pastes, gels, and foams. Tablets account for 81 percent of all denture cleanser sales. In 1994, Efferdent accounted for more than 38 percent of all denture cleanser tablet sales, followed by Polident with 28 percent.

For More Information

Warner-Lambert Company, 201 Tabor Road, Morris Plains, NJ 07950. Or telephone 1-800-223-0182.

Elmer's Glue-All

- **Remove a splinter.** Coat the splinter with a drop of Elmer's Glue-All, wait for it to dry, then peel off the dried glue. The splinter should be stuck to it.

- **Seal plants.** Gardeners use Elmer's Glue-All to seal ends of pruned stems and branches against insects and excessive moisture loss.

- **Prevent broken shoelaces from fraying.** Dip the ends into Elmer's Glue-All.

- **Fix small holes in walls.** Small nail holes can be filled by squirting in a drop of Elmer's Glue-All before painting.

- **Make moldable dough that dries without baking.** Mix equal parts Elmer's Glue-All, flour, and cornstarch. Mix and knead well until blended. If too dry, add more glue. If too moist, add more flour and cornstarch. Food coloring may be added if desired. Dough can be molded into any desired shape to create animals, figurines, ornaments, and jewelry. Dough keeps for weeks in a Ziploc Storage Bag.

- **Tighten a screw hole**. When a screw hole is too worn out to hold a screw, soak a cotton ball in Elmer's Glue-All, stuff it into the hole, and let dry for 24 hours. Use a screwdriver to put a new screw into the spot.

- **Make a starch fabric stiffener.** Mix water and Elmer's Glue-All in a bowl to desired consistency. Fabric dipped in the mixture can be shaped and dried in decorative forms and shapes.

- **Teach kids how to write their names.** Use crayon to write the child's name on a piece of paper, then trace over the letters using Elmer's Glue-All. When the glue dries, children can use their fingers to trace along the tactile letters of their names, making it easier to understand the shapes of the letters.

Invented
1947

The Name

In 1936, Borden launched a series of advertisements featuring cartoon cows, including Elsie, the spokescow for Borden dairy products. In 1940, compelled by Elsie's popularity, Borden dressed up "You'll Do Lobelia," a seven-year-old 950-pound Jersey cow from Brookfield, MA, as Elsie for an exhibit at the World's Fair. She stood in a barn boudoir decorated with whimsical props, including churns used as tables, lamps made from milk bottles, a wheelbarrow for a chaise lounge, and oil paintings of Elsie's ancestors—among them Great-Aunt Bess in her bridal gown and Uncle Bosworth, the noted Spanish-American War admiral. This attracted the attention of RKO Pictures, which hired Elsie to star with Jack Oakie and Kay Francis in the movie *Little Men*. Borden needed to find a replacement for Elsie at the World's Fair exhibit. Elsie's husband, Elmer, was chosen, and the boudoir was converted overnight into a bachelor apartment, complete with every conceivable prop to suggest a series of nightly poker parties. In 1951, Borden chose Elmer to be the marketing symbol for all of Borden's glues and adhesives.

A Short History

In 1929, the Borden Co. purchased the Casein Co. of America, the leading manufacturer of glues made from casein, a milk by-product. Borden introduced its first nonfood consumer product, Casco Glue, in 1932. After World War II, Borden expanded into synthetic resin glues that did not use casein. The product known today as Elmer's Glue-All was first introduced in 1947 under the brand name Cascorez, packaged in two-ounce glass jars with wooden applicators. Sales did not take off until 1951, when Elsie's husband, Elmer, was chosen as the marketing symbol. In 1952, Borden repackaged Glue-All into the familiar plastic squeeze bottle with the orange applicator top.

Ingredients

Polyvinyl acetate dispersed in water

Strange Facts

- The Elmer's line now includes nearly 150 types and sizes of adhesives, caulks, and specialty items.
- Elsie the Cow and her husband, Elmer, have two calves, Beulah and Beauregard.

Distribution

- Elmer's Glue-All is the best-selling glue in America.
- Borden's Elmer's Glue operation in Bainbridge, NY, produces approximately 35 million four-ounce bottles of Elmer's Glue-All, School Glue, and GluColors annually.

For More Information

Borden, Inc., Columbus, OH 43215. Or telephone 1-800-426-7336.

Endust

- **Keep ski goggles from fogging up.** Spray the inside of the lens with Endust, then wipe clean.

- **Polish leather shoes.** Spray Endust on shoes and shine with a cloth.

- **Oil a squeaky door.** Lubricate the hinges with Endust.

- **Prevent stains on kitchen drainboards.** Coat rubber drainboard trays with a light application of Endust.

- **Sweep up dust and dirt with ease.** Spray the bristles of your broom or mop with Endust before sweeping.

- **Prevent water spots and soap scum on shower walls and doors.** Coat the tile walls with Endust and wipe clean.

- **Make cleaning grease splatters on the wall behind the stove easier.** Spray the clean, painted wall behind your stove with a generous coat of Endust and buff well. Future grease spatters can be wiped away with a dry sheet of Bounty.

- **Revitalize dull candles.** Spray Endust on a cloth and wipe the candles thoroughly.

- **Clean brass.** Use very fine steel wool sprayed with Endust.

✳Invented
1956

✳The Name

The word *endust* is a clever combination of the words *end* and *dust*, signifying what this wonderful furniture spray does, when used with a dust cloth.

✳A Short History

The Drackett Company of Cincinnati, makers of such products as Windex, introduced Endust in 1956. In 1993, Kiwi Brands acquired both Endust and Behold.

✳Ingredients

Oils, cleaning agents, fragrance

✳Strange Fact

- Endust contains no wax or silicone.

✳Distribution

- Endust is available in Regular, Lemon, and Country Harvest.
- Kiwi Brands also makes Kiwi shoe care products, Ty-D-Bol toilet cleaner, and Behold furniture polish.

- Kiwi Brand's parent company, Sara Lee, makes Bali intimate apparel, Champion activewear, Coach leather goods, Hanes hosiery and apparel, L'eggs panty hose, Playtex intimate apparel, and Ball Park frankfurters.

For More Information

Kiwi Brands, Douglassville, PA 19518-1239. Or telephone 1-800-392-7733.

Food Coloring

- **Tint wallpaper paste.** Add a few drops food coloring to wallpaper paste so you can see how well you are covering the wallpaper.

- **Make your own gift-wrapping paper.** Add five drops food coloring to one cup water, making one cup for each one of the four colors. Stack several sheets of white tissue paper on top of each other, fold them in half, in half again, and in half again. Dip each one of the four corners into a different color solution without soaking the paper. Let the tissue dry on newspaper, unfold, then iron flat.

- **Make colorful macaroni jewelry for kids.** Add a few drops food coloring to a bowl of water. Dip dry macaroni noodles in the water, drain, and dry. Then make necklaces by stringing the colored macaroni noodles together.

- **Paint snow.** Put a teaspoon of food coloring in a spray bottle filled with water and let kids spray designs on snow.

- **Make fried chicken golden brown.** Add a few drops of yellow food coloring to vegetable oil before frying. The chicken will absorb the food coloring and become a golden brown.

- **Color the water in a fish tank.** Adding a few drops of food coloring will make a colorful environment without harming the fish.

- **Differentiate hard-boiled eggs from raw eggs in the refrigerator.** Before hard-boiling eggs, add food coloring to the water to tint them.

- **Recolor small bleach spots on clothing.** Mix food coloring with water to make the proper shade and apply to the spot.

- **Make fingerpaint.** Mix two cups soap flakes, two cups liquid laundry starch, and five drops food coloring in a large bowl. Blend with a wire whisk until the mixture has the consistency of whipped cream. Or mix one-quarter cup Kingsford's Corn Starch with two cups cold water, boil until thick, pour into small containers, and color with food coloring.

- **Tint flowers.** Mix food coloring in warm water and place the flower stems in the solution overnight. The stems will absorb the colors by morning, revealing intriguing designs in different colors.

- **Make clown makeup.** Mix two tablespoons Kingsford's Corn Starch, one tablespoon solid shortening, and several drops food coloring.

- **Make colorful glues.** Fill an empty SueBee honey bear with Elmer's Glue-All and tint with a few drops of food coloring.

Invented
1890

The Name

Food coloring obviously refers to an edible dye used to color food.

A Short History

Spices and condiments were probably used as colors as long ago as 1000 B.C. In all likelihood, colorants taken from natural minerals, plants, and animals were developed along with spices. In the eighteenth and nineteenth centuries, unscrupulous food manufacturers used colorings to disguise spoiled foods. In 1856, Sir William Henry Perkins discovered the first synthetic dye, derived from coal tar.

In the United States, the Federal Pure Food and Drug Act of 1906 attempted to regulate food dyes. The Federal Food, Drug and Cosmetic (FD&C) Act of 1938 made certification mandatory for any synthetic food color. Synthetic food colors, previously known by their common names, were numbered to avoid confusion with inedible dyes. Three categories were created for designated color names: FD&C, D&C, and External D&C. The 1960 Color Additives Amendment gave the Food and Drug Administration (FDA) the authority to set safe limits for the amount of colors permitted in foods, drugs, and cosmetics. The FDA also required all food coloring to undergo premarketing safety clearances.

There are three types of food coloring: natural dyes (anthocyanins, betanins, carotenoids, and chlorophylls), nature identical dyes (synthetic counterparts of colors and pigments derived from natural sources), and synthetic dyes—FD&C dyes (water soluble compounds) and FD&C lakes (aluminum hydrate extensions). As of 1986, FDA regulations permit only nine FD&C dyes and seven FD&C lakes in our food supply.

✷Ingredients

Water, propylene glycol, FD&C yellow No. 5, FD&C red No. 40, FD&C blue No. 1, FD&C red No. 3, 0.1 percent propylparaben (preservative), and sulfiting agents (contained in blue and green colors only)

✷Strange Facts

- The ancient Aztecs used cochineal, a red dye prepared from the dried bodies of female *Dactylopius coccus*, an insect that lives on cactus plants in Central and South America. Cochineal is still used today in food coloring, medicinal products, cosmetics, inks, and artists' pigments.
- In the United States, the first federal regulation concerning food colors was an 1886 act of Congress allowing butter to be colored.
- Studies show that people judge the quality of food by its color. In fact, the color of a food actually affects a person's perception of its taste,

Color Blending Chart	FOR ICINGS & BAKED GOODS	FOR COLORED EGGS
	Gently squeeze sides of bottle, adding color drop by drop to obtain desired shade.	To one-half cup boiling water add one teaspoon vinegar and twenty drops desired color. For other colors, refer to chart. Dip hard-boiled eggs until desired shade is obtained. After color dries, it will not rub off.
COLORS	**NUMBER OF DROPS REQUIRED**	
Orange	1 red, 2 yellow	6 red, 14 yellow
Chartreuse	12 yellow, 1 green	24 yellow, 2 green
Peach	1 red, 3 yellow	—
Turquoise	5 blue, 1 green	15 blue, 5 green
Purple	1 red, 1 blue	10 red, 4 blue
Rose	5 red, 1 blue	15 red, 5 blue

smell, and feel. Researchers have concluded that color even affects a person's ability to identify flavor.

✶Distribution

- McCormick products are distributed under the Schilling label in the western United States.
- An extensive survey conducted by the National Academy of Sciences in 1977 estimated that the average American consumes 327.6 milligrams of FD&C color additives every day. That's sixteen times the Recommended Daily Allowance for iron. According to the survey, every day each American consumes an average of 100 milligrams of FD&C Red Dye No. 40, 43 milligrams of FD&C Yellow Dye No. 5, and 37 milligrams FD&C Yellow Dye No. 6.

For More Information
McCormick & Company, Inc., P.O. Box 208, Hunt Valley, MD 21030-0208.

Forster Toothpicks

- **Apply glue.** Dip one end of a Forster Toothpick into the glue to apply small drops.

- **Improvise a bookmark.** Keep your place with a Forster Toothpick.

- **Plug small nail or thumbtack holes in wood.** Dip the end of a Forster Toothpick in glue, insert into the hole, slice flush with a single-edge razor blade, sand smooth, and refinish the wood.

- **Decorate a cake with ease.** Use a Forster Toothpick to draw your design on the cake, then squeeze the frosting over your lines.

- **Paint small crevices or repair scratches in furniture.** Dip a Forster Toothpick in paint to retouch fine scratches or reach small nooks and crannies.

- **Root a potato or avocado.** Securely insert four Forster Toothpicks equidistantly around the equator of the potato or avocado. (You can use a nail to punch starter holes in the avocado.) Fill a glass with water, set the potato or avocado in the glass so the toothpicks allow only the bottom half of the potato or avocado to sit in the water. Place the glass on a window ledge to get sunlight. When roots and shoots appear, pot the plant in soil.

- **Repair broken eyeglasses temporarily.** If you lose a screw from your eyeglasses, substitute a Forster Toothpick until you can get the glasses fixed properly.

- **Mark the starting point of a roll of masking tape or packaging tape.** Stick a Forster Toothpick under the loose end of the tape so you can find the end easily the next time you use the tape.

- **Clean tight crevices.** Dip a Forster Toothpick in alcohol to clean tight spaces.

- **Make a garlic clove easy to handle.** Stick a Forster Toothpick into a clove of garlic before tossing it into a marinade, so you can remove it easily.

- **Give a broken plant stem first aid.** Make a splint with a Forster Toothpick and Scotch Tape.

- **Identify rare, medium, and well-done steaks on your barbecue grill.** Use colored Forster Toothpicks to mark steaks on the barbecue.

- **Cook sausages with ease.** Use two Forster Toothpicks to skewer two or three sausages together to make them easier to turn and brown evenly.

- **Tighten a loose screw.** Insert a Forster Toothpick into the screw hole, break it off at the surface, and rescrew the screw.

- **Push fabrics through the pressure foot of a sewing machine.** Use a Forster Toothpick to free fabric that gets stuck under the pressure foot.

- **Determine whether a cake is baked.** Insert a Forster Toothpick in the center of the cake and remove. If it comes out clean, the cake is ready.

- **Clean a dog brush.** Run a Forster Toothpick through the rows of bristles.

- **Repair a pinhole in a garden hose temporarily.** Insert a Forster Toothpick into the hole, snap it off flush with the hose's outer skin, then wrap Scotch Mailing Tape around the spot. The wooden toothpick will absorb water, swelling to seal the hole.

Invented
1887

The Name

Forster is named after company founder Charles Forster. The toothpick was named for the purpose of the small piece of wood—to remove food particles from between the teeth.

A Short History

In 1887, Charles Forster began the first wooden toothpick factory in the United States.

Ingredients

White birch

Strange Fact

- In November 1993, Leland's, a premier auctioneer of sports memorabilia, auctioned off Tom Seaver's chewed-up toothpick for $440.

Distribution

- Forster Toothpicks are the best-selling toothpicks in the United States.

For More Information

Forster Manufacturing Company, Inc., P.O. Box 657, Wilton, ME 04294. Or telephone 1-207-645-2574.

Frisbee

- **Hold a paper plate.** Fit a paper plate inside an upside-down Frisbee during a picnic.

- **Improvise a bowl.** In an emergency, an upside-down Frisbee can be used as a bowl or plate.

- **Make a birdbath.** Punch three equidistant holes along the circumference of the Frisbee, insert wire, and hang the Frisbee upside-down from a tree or post. Fill with water, or let the rain do it naturally.

- **Improvise a pet dish.** When camping or hiking, an upside-down Frisbee works well as a food or water dish for your dog.

- **Improvise a cookie tray.** Turn the Frisbee upside-down and fill with cookies.

- **Play Frisbee golf.** Designate a tee-off spot and choose a tree, pole, or other landmark as the "hole." Toss a Frisbee toward the "hole," pick it up wherever it lands, and continue tossing until you hit the "hole." Keep score. The player with the fewest tosses to hit all the holes wins.

★Invented
1957

★The Name

Frisbee was inspired by the *Frisbie* Pie Company of Bridgeport, Connecticut, founded by William Russell Frisbie.

★A Short History

In the 1870s, William Russell Frisbie opened a bakery called the Frisbie Pie Company in Bridgeport, Connecticut. His lightweight pie tins were embossed with the family name. In the mid-1940s, students at Yale University tossed the empty pie tins as a game. In the 1950s, Walter Frederick Morrison, a Los Angeles building inspector determined to capitalize on Hollywood's obsession with UFOs, designed a lightweight plastic disc based on the Frisbie bakery's pie tins, but changed the name to Flyin' Saucer to avoid legal hassles. Morrison sold the rights to the Wham-O Manufacturing Co. of San Gabriel, California, and on January 13, 1957, Americans were introduced to the Frisbee. The Frisbie Pie Company went out of business in 1958. In 1994, Mattel acquired Wham-O.

★Ingredients

Polyurethane

★Strange Fact

- In May 1989, to commemorate the alleged fiftieth anniversary of the Frisbee, Middlebury College in Vermont unveiled a bronze statue of a dog jumping to catch a Frisbee. According to Middlebury legend, five undergraduates driving through Nebraska in 1939 suffered a flat tire. As two boys changed the tire, a third found a discarded pie tin from the Frisbie Pie Company near a cornfield and threw the circular disc into the air. Middlebury President Olin Robison told *Time* magazine, "Our version of the story is that it happened all over America, but it started here."

✦Distribution

- In the United States, more Frisbee discs are sold each year than baseballs, basketballs, and footballs combined.

For More Information

- Mattel, Inc., 333 Continental Boulevard, El Segundo, CA 90245. Or telephone 1-800-580-9786.
- Ultimate Players Association, P.O. Box 2331, Silver City, NM 88062.

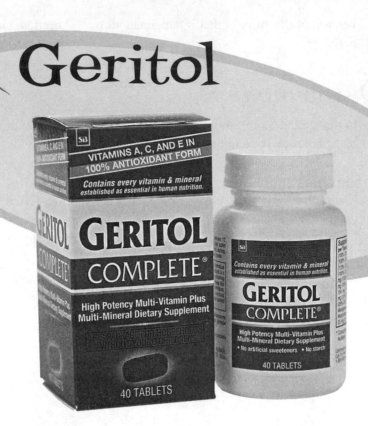

Geritol

- **Revive an ailing houseplant.** Give the plant two tablespoons Geritol twice a week for three months. New leaves should begin to grow within the first month.

- **Polish shoes.** In a pinch, you can shine your brown leather shoes with a few drops of Geritol on a soft cloth.

- **Remove stains, rings, and minor scratches from wood furniture.** Apply Geritol to the wood with a cotton ball, wipe away excess, and polish as usual.

Invented
1950

The Name

Geritol is apparently a combination of the words *geriatric* and *tolerance*.

A Short History

Geritol liquid tonic was introduced in 1950 by Pharmaceuticals Inc. as a remedy for those who felt tired because of iron-poor blood. With Ralph Bellamy and Ted Mack touting Geritol's unique ability to prevent iron-poor blood, Geritol quickly became the number one high-potency iron tonic in America. Pharmaceuticals Inc. sold Geritol to the J. B. Williams Company, which reformulated Geritol in 1967 to include high-potency iron plus seven vitamins, targeting women with iron-poor blood.

Geritol remained the best-selling iron and vitamin supplement until 1979, when health-conscious consumers began seeking more complete vitamin formulas. In 1982, Beecham acquired J. B. Williams and the following year introduced New, Improved Geritol with high-potency iron plus nine vitamins and minerals. Beecham reformulated Geritol again in 1984 as Geritol Complete with iron plus 29 vitamins and minerals, repositioning Geritol as a multivitamin and multimineral supplement—adding beta carotene in 1988. The following year Beecham merged with SmithKline Beckman to form SmithKline Beecham, and in 1993, the company completely repositioned Geritol as a high-potency multivitamin/multimineral supplement, reducing the amount of iron in Geritol to one-third the original formula.

Ingredients

ACTIVE: iron (ferric ammonium citrate), thiamine, riboflavin, niacinamide, panthenol, pyridoxine, cyanocobalamin, methionine, choline bitartrate; INACTIVE: twelve percent alcohol, benzoic acid, caramel color, citric acid, invert sugar, sucrose, water, flavors

Strange Facts

• While one dose of the original formula for Geritol contained twice the iron in a pound of calf's liver, today one dose of Geritol

Complete contains approximately two-thirds the iron in a pound of calf's liver.

- In 1956, Geritol sponsored *Twenty-One*, the game show featured in the 1994 Hollywood Pictures movie *Quiz Show*, directed by Robert Redford and recounting the game show scandal in which producers fed answers to contestants.
- In 1971, Geritol launched the television commercial that created the catchphrase "My Wife, I Think I'll Keep Her," which, in 1994, provided the inspiration for the Mary-Chapin Carpenter song "He Thinks He'll Keep Her."
- Wimbledon tennis champion Evonne Goolagong supplemented her on-court activities with Geritol tablets.
- In 1989, after challenging heavyweight champion Mike Tyson to a fight for the title, former heavyweight champion George Foreman told *Time* magazine, "If I win, every man over forty can grab his Geritol and have a toast."
- Geritol, at less than one calorie per tablet, contains no sodium, sugar, lactose, artificial sweeteners, or preservatives.
- Three out of four people surveyed in 1994 said Bob Barker is the TV game show host most likely to take Geritol.

Distribution

- SmithKline Beecham sells more than 300 products in 130 countries.
- Geritol accounts for less than two percent of SmithKline Beecham's sales.
- SmithKline Beecham sells two of the world's top ten medicines (the anti-ulcer drug Tagamet and the antibiotic Augmentin) and a slew of well-known consumer products including Contac, Tums, Sucrets, Aqua-Fresh, and Brylcreem.

For More Information

Beecham Products, Division of Beecham, Inc., Pittsburgh, PA 15230. Or telephone 1-800-245-1040. In PA, telephone 1-800-242-1718.

GLAD Flexible Straws

- **Unclog a freshly opened ketchup bottle.** Insert a GLAD Flexible Straw all the way into the bottle to add air and start the ketchup flowing.

- **Blow bubbles.** Cut the end of a GLAD Flexible Straw diagonally, dip into bubble soap, and blow.

- **Prevent strings on pull toys from getting tangled.** Run the string through one or more GLAD Flexible Straws and knot it at the end.

- **Extend the spout of an oil can.** Put a GLAD Flexible Straw over the end of the spout of an oil can to reach tight spots.

- **Prevent tangles in fine chain jewelry.** Run the chain through a length of GLAD Flexible Straw and fasten the catch.

- **String plastic straw necklaces.** Let the kids cut up GLAD Flexible Straws instead of macaroni, and run a string of yarn through the straws to make necklaces.

- **Elongate flower stems that are too short for a vase.** Insert the flower stems into GLAD Flexible Straws cut to whatever length you need.

- **Make croquet wickets visible on the lawn.** Run the wickets through GLAD Flexible Straws before sticking them into the ground.

- **Improvise an eyedropper.** Insert a GLAD Flexible Straw into the liquid, cover the open end of the straw with your finger, and lift. The liquid will stay in the straw until you release your finger.

- **Mark a stitch when knitting.** Cut a one-eighth-inch length from a GLAD Flexible Straw and use as a ring to mark a stitch on needles up to size ten.

Invented
Early 1960s

The Name

GLAD apparently signifies the joy consumers will experience when using these convenient flexible straws.

A Short History

In 1917, the National Carbon Company, maker of carbon for streetlights and owner of the Eveready trademark, merged with Union Carbide, manufacturer of calcium carbide—along with Linde Air Products (oxygen), Prest-O-Lite (calcium carbide), and Electro Metallurgical (metals)—to form Union Carbide & Carbon Corporation. In 1920, the company established its own chemicals division, which developed ethylene glycol (antifreeze), eventually marketed as Prestone. In 1957, the company changed its name to Union Carbide Corporation, and in the early 1960s it introduced GLAD plastic household products. In 1985, Union Carbide sold its line of GLAD garbage bags to First Brands Corporation. In 1986, following a catastrophic gas leak in Bhopal, India, and a hostile takeover attempt, Union Carbide put its two consumer products divisions up for sale to raise sorely needed cash. Alfred Dudley, now chairman of First Brands, led other Union Carbide executives in acquiring the company in a leveraged buyout. In 1988, First Brands went public.

✳Ingredient

Plastic

✳Strange Facts

- The Man from GLAD, seen in television commercials during the 1970s, was a take-off on *The Man from U.N.C.L.E.*
- In 1984, a tank at Union Carbide's pesticide plant in Bhopal, India, leaked five tons of poisonous methyl isocyanate gas, killing more than three thousand people and permanently injuring fifty thousand people. It was the world's worst industrial accident in recorded history, resulting in a $470 million settlement in India's Supreme Court in 1989.
- In 1989, the Federal Trade Commission made the First Brands Corporation end its claims that GLAD bags were biodegradable; the bags decomposed in sunlight but not underground in municipal landfills.

✳Distribution

- In 1995, First Brands Corporation sold over $646 million worth of plastic wrap, plastic bags, and related products.
- First Brands Corporation markets the GLAD and GLAD-Lock brands of plastic wrap, sandwich bags, and trash bags; Ever Clean, Jonny Cat, and Scoop Away cat litters; and Simonize and STP car-care products.
- First Brands's principal U.S. manufacturing plants are in Arkansas, California, Georgia, Illinois, Kansas, Mississippi, New Jersey, Ohio, Vermont, and Virginia. The company also has manufacturing plants in Canada, China, Hong Kong, the Philippines, and South Africa.

For More Information

First Brands Corporation, P.O. Box 1999, Danbury, CT 06813-1999. Or telephone 1-800-726-1001.

GLAD Trash Bags

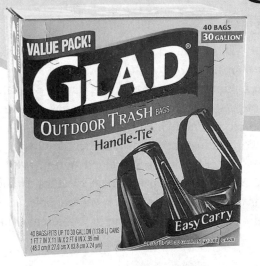

- **Sled down a snow-covered hill.** Tie a GLAD Trash Bag around your bottom like a diaper, and slide down the hill.

- **Improvise a raincoat.** Cut slits in a GLAD Trash Bag for head and arms.

- **Cover your barbecue.** Protect your outdoor grill by covering it with a GLAD Trash Bag.

- **Make a solar-powered camping shower.** Fill a GLAD Trash Bag with water, tie it to a solid tree branch, and let the sun heat the water. After you lather up with soap, poke a small hole in the bag to rinse off.

- **Protect chandeliers and hanging lamps when painting a ceiling.** Pull a GLAD Trash Bag up over the lighting fixture and tie it up as high on the chain as possible.

- **Travel with a plastic laundry bag.** Pack a GLAD Trash Bag in your suitcase.

- **Prevent ice from accumulating on a car windshield.** Cut open a GLAD Trash Bag, place it over the entire windshield, and close the car doors over the edges of the bag to hold it in place. When you're ready to go, brush off any snow and peel off the plastic bag.

- **Make a Hawaiian grass skirt.** Cut off the bottom of a GLAD Trash Bag and cut long strips one inch wide to within three inches of the pull cord.

- **Make waterproof stuffing for outdoor cushions, bathtub toys, and stuffed animals.** Cut a GLAD Trash Bag into strips and use it as the stuffing.

- **Make dust covers for clothes.** Cut a small hole in the center of the bottom of a GLAD Trash Bag and slip the bag over the top of a suit or a dress on a hanger.

- **Make a ground cloth for camping trips.** Place your sleeping bag on top of several GLAD Trash Bags to keep out moisture.

- **Hold bath toys.** Punch holes in a GLAD Trash Bag and hang it on the shower nozzle to hold bath toys.

- **Improvise a plastic sheet.** Cut a GLAD Trash Bag down the sides and place it under the sheets.

- **Make streamers.** Cut a GLAD Trash Bag into strips, starting from the open end and stopping two inches before you reach the bottom.

- **Waterproof a backpack.** Cover the backpack with a GLAD Trash Bag and cut small slits in the bag for the straps of the backpack.

- **Collect aluminum cans for recycling.** Hang a GLAD Trash Bag on the inside of a kitchen cabinet or pantry door.

- **Make a shop apron.** Cut open the bottom of a GLAD Trash Bag, put it over your head, and slip your arms through the handles.

- **Improvise a windbreaker.** Cut holes in a GLAD Trash Bag for your head and arms and wear it under your coat.

- **Store your winter clothes.** Fill a GLAD Trash Bag with your sweaters, add a few mothballs, and seal with a twist tie.

- **Make a scarecrow.** Cut a GLAD Trash Bag into long strips, staple to the lip of a Dixie Cup, and then nail the cup to a tree or a pole in your garden. The plastic strips blowing in the wind will scare birds away.

Invented
Early 1960s

The Name

GLAD apparently signifies the pleasure and joy consumers will experience when their trash is clad in these pleasingly convenient garbage bags.

A Short History

In 1917, National Carbon Company, makers of carbons for streetlights and owner of the Eveready trademark, merged with Union Carbide, manufacturers of calcium carbide—along with Linde Air Products (oxygen), Prest-O-Lite (calcium carbide), and Electro Metallurgical (metals)—to form Union Carbide & Carbon Corporation. In 1920, the company established its own chemicals division, which developed ethylene glycol (antifreeze), eventually marketed as Prestone. In 1957 the company changed its name to Union Carbide Corporation and in the early 1960s introduced GLAD plastic household products. In 1985, Union Carbide sold its line of GLAD garbage bags to First Brands Corporation.

Ingredient
Polyethylene

Strange Facts

- The Man from GLAD, seen in television commercials during the 1970s, was a take-off on *The Man from U.N.C.L.E.*

- In 1984, a tank at Union Carbide's pesticide plant in Bhopal, India, leaked five tons of poisonous methyl isocyanate gas, killing more than 3,000 people and permanently injuring 50,000 people. It was the world's worst industrial accident in recorded history, resulting in a $470 million settlement in India's Supreme Court in 1989.

✳Distribution

- GLAD Handle-Tie Garbage Bags are available in Tall Kitchen Garbage Bags, Regular Trash Size, Large Trash Size, Clear Large Trash Size, and Clear Kitchen Size.

For More Information

First Brands Corporation, P.O. Box 1999, Danbury, CT 06813-1999. Or telephone 1-203-731-2300.

Gold Medal Flour

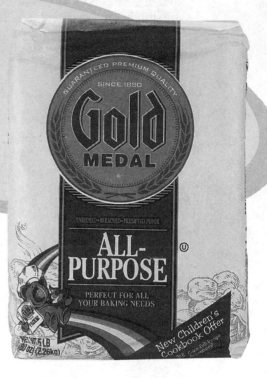

- **Make Play Dough.** Add fifty drops food coloring to two cups water. Then add two cups Gold Medal flour, one cup salt, one teaspoon Cream of Tartar, and two tablespoons Wesson Corn Oil. Mix well. Cook and stir over medium heat for three minutes (or until the mixture holds together). Turn onto a board or a cookie sheet and knead to the proper consistency. Store in an airtight container.

- **Make glue.** Mix Gold Medal flour and water to a pancake-batter consistency for use on paper, lightweight fabric, and cardboard.

- **Make papier-mâché.** In a medium-size bowl mix one cup Gold Medal flour with two-thirds cup water to a thick-glue consistency. To thicken, add more flour. Cut newspaper strips approximately one to two inches in width. Dip each strip into the paste, gently pull it between your fingers to remove excess paste, and apply it to any empty bottle, carton, canister, or disposable container. Repeat until the surface is completely covered. Let dry, then decorate with poster paint. After the paint dries, coat with shellac.

- **Clean white kid gloves.** Rub Gold Medal flour into the leather, then brush clean.

- **Clean brass and copper.** Mix equal parts Gold Medal flour and Morton Salt and add one teaspoon Heinz White Vinegar to make a paste. Spread a thick layer on the brass and let dry. Wash off paste and rinse clean.

- **Clean a deck of playing cards.** Place the deck of cards in a paper bag, add four tablespoons Gold Medal flour, and shake briskly. Remove the cards from the bag and wipe clean.

- **Repel ants.** Fill cracks and make a line with Gold Medal flour where ants enter. Ants will not cross through flour.

Invented
1880

The Name

Gold Medal flour is cleverly named after the gold medal this flour won at an 1880 exhibition.

A Short History

In 1866, Cadwallader Washburn founded the Washburn Crosby Company. After winning a gold medal for flour at an 1880 exhibition, the company introduced the Gold Medal flour trademark. In 1921, the advertising department of Washburn Crosby created a fictional spokeswoman, Betty Crocker (named in honor of a retired company director, William G. Crocker), so that correspondence to housewives could go out with a woman's signature. In 1924, the company introduced Wheaties ready-to-eat cereal. Four years later, James F. Bell, president of Washburn Crosby, consolidated the company with other mills around the country (including Red Star, Rocky Mountain Elevator, Kalispell Flour, and Sperry Flour Company) to form General Mills, the world's largest miller.

✴Ingredients

Wheat flour, malted barley flour, niacin (a B vitamin), iron, thiamin mononitrate (vitamin B_1), and riboflavin (vitamin B_2)

✴Strange Facts

- General Mills introduced Bisquick in the 1930s and Cheerios in 1941, which, along with flour, generated enough sales to allow the company to pay dividends throughout the 1930s and 1940s.
- During the European Renaissance, when the medieval ideal of feminine beauty required a woman's skin to be as white as a lily and her cheeks as red as a rose, peasants, unable to afford expensive cosmetics, made do with wheat flour and beet juice.
- Since 1972, most of the flour found in home kitchens has been used for baking cookies.
- Betty Crocker's first formal portrait was drafted by artist Neysa McMein in 1936. Betty is now in her eighth incarnation.
- In the 1940s, Eleanor Roosevelt was voted the most well-known woman in America, followed by Betty Crocker.

✴Distribution

- General Mills is the second largest cereal manufacturer in the United States.
- Gold Medal flour is available in All-Purpose flour, Whole Wheat flour, Better for Bread bread flour, Better for Bread Wheat Blend flour, Better for Biscuits self-rising flour, Wondra quick-mixing flour, and Softasilk cake flour.
- Besides Gold Medal flour, General Mills also makes Betty Crocker dessert mixes, Cheerios, Cocoa Puffs, Golden Grahams, Kix, Lucky Charms, Raisin Nut Bran, Total, Trix, Wheaties, Bisquick, Bugles, Fruit Roll-Ups, Hamburger Helper, Nature Valley Granola Bars, Pop Secret Microwave Popcorn, Potato Buds Instant Mashed Potatoes, and Yoplait Yogurt.

For More Information

General Mills, Inc., P.O. Box 1113, Minneapolis, MN 55440. Or telephone 1-800-328-6787.

Hartz Parakeet Seed

- **Substitute for rice at weddings.** Instead of throwing rice, which is difficult to clean up, give your guests packets of Hartz Parakeet Seed instead. When the wedding is over, the birds and squirrels will clean up the birdseed.

- **Make a bird feeder.** Punch a hole in the top of an empty cardboard tube (from a used roll of toilet paper or paper towels). Roll the cardboard tube in honey, then roll the honey-coated tube in the Hartz Parakeet Seed. Hang the birdseed-coated tube outdoors.

- **Make artwork.** Paint a design in Elmer's Glue-All on construction paper, then cover the glue with Hartz Parakeet Seed and let dry.

Invented
1926

The Name

Company founder Max Stern named the Hartz Mountain Corporation after the Harz Mountains of Germany, his native country.

A Short History

In 1926, German immigrant Max Stern arrived in New York Harbor with his prized singing canaries and the idea of marketing live pets and pet-care products. The company soon branched out beyond birds to dogs, cats, fish, hamsters, and gerbils. Still family-owned, the Hartz Mountain Corporation is headed today by Edward Stern, grandson of Max Stern.

Ingredients

Millet seed, oat groats, canary grass seed, iodized salt

Strange Facts

- The Harz Mountains were immortalized in Johann Goethe's poetic drama *Faust*.
- Hartz formulated the first antibiotic birdseed, followed by the first vitamin-impregnated birdseed.
- Arthur Godfrey started in radio as a banjo player sponsored by a birdseed company on a station in Baltimore.
- As a boy, Steven Spielberg kept parakeets in his bedroom, flying free. Recalled his mother, Leah, in *Time* magazine: "There would be birds flying around and birdseed all over the floor. I'd just reach in to get the dirty clothes."
- You can tell the sex of an adult budgie parakeet by the color of the skin just above the beak. On males the color is bluish, while on females the color is brownish.
- On an episode of *Gilligan's Island*, the Skipper announces, "Everything grows from seeds."

    "Not everything," objects Gilligan.

    "Yes, everything," insists the Skipper. "Orange trees grow from orange seeds, apple trees grow from apple seeds, and watermelons grow from watermelon seeds."

    "Yeah, but birds don't grow from birdseed," replies Gilligan.

✳Distribution

- Hartz Parakeet Seed is the best-selling parakeet seed in the United States.
- Hartz markets more than one thousand pet-care products distributed to more than forty thousand retail outlets worldwide.
- In addition to bird foods and accessories, Hartz also makes the hugely successful Hartz 2in1 flea and tick collar.

For More Information

Hartz Mountain Corporation, Secaucus, NJ 07094. Or telephone 1-201-271-4800.

Heinz Vinegar

- **Milk cows organically.** Clean milking equipment with unperfumed dish detergent followed with a Heinz Vinegar rinse. Pipes, hoses, and bulk tank will come out squeaky clean without any odor, lowering the bacteria count.

- **Kill bacteria in meats.** Marinating meat in Heinz Vinegar kills bacteria and tenderizes the meat. Use one-quarter cup vinegar for a two- to three-pound roast, marinate overnight, then cook without draining or rinsing the meat. Add herbs to the vinegar when marinating as desired.

- **Dissolve warts.** Mix one part Heinz Apple Cider Vinegar to one part glycerin into a lotion and apply daily to warts until they dissolve.

- **Remove stubborn stains from furniture upholstery and clothes.** Apply Heinz White Vinegar directly to the stain, then wash as directed by the manufacturer's instructions.

- **Grow beautiful azaleas.** Occasionally water plants with a mixture of two tablespoons Heinz Vinegar to one quart water. Azaleas grow best in acidic soil.

- **Relieve arthritis.** Before each meal, drink a glass of water containing two teaspoons Heinz Apple Cider Vinegar. Give this folk remedy at least three weeks to start working.

- **Kill unwanted grass.** Pour Heinz White Vinegar in crevices and between bricks.

- **Remove corns.** Make a poultice of one crumbled piece of bread soaked in one-quarter cup Heinz Vinegar. Let poultice sit for one-half hour, then apply to corn and tape in place overnight. If corn does not peel off by morning, reapply the poultice for several consecutive nights.

- **Clean the hoses and unclog soap scum from a washing machine.** Once a month pour one cup Heinz White Vinegar into the washing machine and run through a normal cycle, without clothes.

- **Cure an upset stomach.** Drink two teaspoons Heinz Apple Cider Vinegar in one cup water to soothe an upset stomach.

- **Kill germs on bathroom fixtures.** Use one part Heinz Vinegar to one part water in a spray bottle. Spray the bathroom fixtures and floor, then wipe clean.

- **Clean soap scum, mildew, and grime from bathtub, tile, and shower curtains.** Simply wipe the surface with Heinz Vinegar and rinse with water.

- **Deodorize the air.** Heinz Vinegar is a natural air freshener when sprayed in a room.

- **Relieve itching.** Use a cotton ball to dab mosquito and other bug bites with Heinz Vinegar straight from the bottle.

- **Clean lime deposits and calcium sludge from an automatic drip coffeemaker.** Once a month fill the reservoir with Heinz White Vinegar and run through the brew cycle. Rinse thoroughly with two cycles of cold water.

- **Relieve a sore throat.** Put two teaspoons Heinz Vinegar in your humidifier.

- **Soothe sunburn pain.** Apply undiluted Heinz Vinegar to the burn.

- **Clean food-stained pots and pans.** Fill the pots and pans with Heinz White Vinegar and let stand for 30 minutes, then rinse in hot, soapy water.

- **Clean rust from tools, bolts, and spigots.** Soak the rusted tool, bolt, or spigot in undiluted Heinz White Vinegar overnight.

- **Turn a chicken bone into rubber.** Soak a chicken bone in a glass of Heinz Vinegar for three days. It will bend like rubber.

- **Prevent bright-colored clothes from fading.** Before putting the article in the washing machine, soak it in Heinz White Vinegar for ten minutes.

- **Keep a garbage disposal clean and smelling fresh.** Mix one cup Heinz Vinegar in enough water to fill an ice cube tray, freeze the mixture, grind the cubes through the disposal, and flush with cold water.

- **Clean a toilet bowl.** Pour in one cup Heinz White Vinegar, let stand for five minutes, and flush.

- **Prevent yeast infections.** Douche with one tablespoon Heinz White Vinegar to one quart warm water to adjust the pH balance in the vagina.

- **Clean dentures.** Soak dentures overnight in Heinz White Vinegar, then brush off tartar with a toothbrush.

- **Remove perspiration stains from clothes.** Apply one part Heinz White Vinegar to four parts water, then rinse.

- **Deodorize a room filled with cigarette smoke or paint fumes.** Place a small bowl of Heinz White Vinegar in the room.

- **Cure the hiccups.** Mix one teaspoon Heinz Apple Cider Vinegar in one cup warm water and drink.

- **Eliminate odors from used jars.** Rinse peanut butter and mayonnaise jars with Heinz White Vinegar.

- **Condition dry hair.** Shampoo, then rinse hair with a mixture of one cup Heinz Apple Cider Vinegar and two cups water. Vinegar adds highlights to brunette hair, restores the acid mantle, and removes soap film and sebum oil.

- **Clean mineral deposits from a steam iron.** Fill the water tank with Heinz White Vinegar. Turn the iron to the steam setting and steam-iron a soft utility rag to clean the steam ports. Repeat the process with water, then thoroughly rinse out the inside of your iron.

- **Remove light scorch marks from fabrics.** Rub lightly with Heinz White Vinegar, then wipe with a clean cloth.

- **Repel ants.** Use a spray bottle or mister filled with a solution of equal parts Heinz Vinegar and water around doorjambs, windowsills, water pipes, and foundation cracks.

- **Keep drains open.** Pour one-half box old baking soda down the drain, followed by one cup Heinz White Vinegar. When the bubbling stops, run the hot water.

- **Prolong and brighten propane lanterns.** Soak new wicks for several hours in Heinz White Vinegar and let dry before inserting. Propane lanterns will burn longer and brighter on the same amount of fuel.

- **Remove decals or bumper stickers.** Soak a cloth in Heinz Vinegar and cover the decal or bumper sticker for several minutes until the vinegar soaks in. The decals and bumper stickers should peel off easily.

- **Deodorize a wool sweater.** Wash sweater, then rinse in equal parts Heinz Vinegar and water.

- **Prevent lint from clinging to clothes.** Add one cup Heinz Vinegar to the wash load.

- **Prevent ice from forming on a car windshield overnight.** Coat the window with a solution of three parts Heinz White or Apple Cider Vinegar to one part water.

- **Prolong the life of flowers in a vase.** Add two tablespoons Heinz White Vinegar plus three tablespoons sugar per quart of warm water. Stems should be in three to four inches of water.

- **Prevent cracked hard-boiled eggs.** Add two tablespoons Heinz White Vinegar per quart of water before boiling to prevent the eggs from cracking. The eggshells will also peel off faster and easier.

- **Clean windows.** Use undiluted Heinz Vinegar in a spray bottle. Dry with a soft cloth.

- **Eliminate cooking odors in the kitchen.** Boil one tablespoon Heinz White Vinegar with one cup water.

- **Remove wallpaper.** Mix equal parts Heinz Vinegar and hot water. Use a paint roller to wet the paper thoroughly with the mixture. Repeat. Paper should peel off in sheets.

- **Eliminate animal urine stains from carpet.** Blot up urine, flush several times with lukewarm water, then apply a mixture of equal parts Heinz White Vinegar and cool water. Blot up, rinse, and let dry.

- **Relieve a cold.** Mix one-quarter cup Heinz Apple Cider Vinegar with one-quarter cup honey. Take one tablespoon six to eight times daily.

- **Deodorize a stale lunch box.** Soak a paper napkin in Heinz Vinegar and leave it inside the closed lunch box overnight.

- **Prevent soapy film on glassware.** Place a cup of Heinz White Vinegar on the bottom rack of your dishwasher, run for five minutes, then run though the full cycle. A cup of white vinegar run through the entire cycle once a month will also reduce soap scum on the inner workings.

- **Unclog a showerhead.** Unscrew the showerhead, remove the rubber washer, place the head in a pot filled with equal parts Heinz Vinegar and water, bring to a boil, then simmer for five minutes.

- **Relieve a cough.** Mix one-half cup Heinz Apple Cider Vinegar, one-half cup water, one teaspoon cayenne pepper, and four teaspoons honey. Take one tablespoon when cough acts up. Take another tablespoon at bedtime.

- **Retard patching plaster from drying.** Add one tablespoon Heinz White Vinegar to the water when mixing plaster to slow the drying time.

Invented
1880

The Name

Vinegar is derived from two French words, *vin* (wine) and *aigre* (sour).

A Short History

Since wine originated at least 10,000 years ago, the first vinegar most likely resulted from spoiled wine. In 5000 B.C., the Babylonians fermented vinegar from date palms, enhancing the flavor by adding tarragon, ruta, absinth, lavender, mint, celery, portulaca, and saffron. Heinz Vinegars were first bottled in 1880, using no additives or preservatives. Vinegar's key ingredient is alcohol. Unlike many budget-brand vinegars that derive their alcohol content from petroleum, Heinz vinegars use only sun-ripened corn or apples and water.

Ingredients

DISTILLED WHITE VINEGAR: select sun-ripened grain, diluted with water to a uniform pickling and table strength of five percent (50 grains) acidity; APPLE CIDER VINEGAR: the juice of apples, diluted with water to a uniform pickling and table strength of five percent (50 grains) acidity

Strange Facts

- Vinegar can be made from virtually any sugary substance that can be fermented to ethyl alcohol, including molasses, sorghum syrup, fruits, berries, melons, coconut, honey, maple syrup, potatoes, beets, malt, grains, and whey. The oldest way to make vinegar is to leave wine made from fruit juice in an open container, allowing microorganisms in the air to convert the ethyl alcohol to acetic acid.

- In 1992, H. J. Heinz hired its first spokesperson for vinegar, Heloise Cruse Evans, the syndicated columnist who writes "Hints from Heloise." "I probably use a gallon a week," Heloise told the *Wall Street Journal*.
- Vinegar lasts indefinitely in the pantry without refrigeration.
- White vinegar is used to pickle vegetables and fruits. Vinegar neutralizes all the water in vegetables and fruits while leaving enough behind to preserve them. Heinz publishes a 32-page booklet with recipes for canning and pickling vegetables and fruits. For a free copy, write to *Heinz Successful Pickling Guide*, P.O. Box 57, Pittsburgh, PA 15230.
- Hannibal, the Carthaginian general, used vinegar to help clear boulders blocking the path of his elephants across the alps. Titus Livius reported in *The History of Rome* that Hannibal's soldiers heated the rocks and applied vinegar to split them.
- According to the *New Testament*, Roman soldiers offered a sponge filled with vinegar to Jesus on the cross. While the act is usually considered cruel, vinegar actually shuts off the taste buds, temporarily quenching thirst, suggesting that the Roman soldiers may have been acting out of kindness.
- Vinegar has served medicinal purposes since biblical times, when it was used as a wet dressing on wounds. Hippocrates, the father of medicine, used vinegar on his patients in 400 B.C. The Assyrians used vinegar to topically treat rniddle-ear infections, and during World War I vinegar was used to treat wounds.

✳Distribution

- The *Progressive Grocer* reported that supermarket sales of vinegar average $112 million a year.

For More Information

- H. J. Heinz Co., P.O. Box 57, Pittsburgh, PA 15230. Or telephone 1-412-456-5700.
- Vinegar Institute, Suite 500G, 5775 Peachtree-Dunwoody Road, Atlanta, GA 30342. Or telephone 1-404-252-3663.

Huggies Baby Wipes

- **Blot up spilled coffee from a rug or carpet.** Huggies baby wipes absorb coffee without leaving a stain.

- **Use as toilet paper after an episiotomy.** Huggies baby wipes are gentle enough for a baby and perfect after an operation on the more sensitive areas of your body.

- **Soothe hemorrhoids.** Use Huggies baby wipes as toilet paper to avoid aggravating sensitive hemorrhoids.

- **Clean hands after pumping gas or changing engine oil.** Keep a box of Huggies baby wipes in the trunk of the car.

- **Store game pieces.** Store loose dice, cards, playing pieces, and small toys in an empty Huggies baby wipes box.

- **Store crayons.** Keep crayons in an empty Huggies baby wipes box.

- **Store screws, nuts, and bolts.** Use empty Huggies baby wipes boxes in the workshop to hold loose screws, bolts, nuts, nails, drill bits, and spare parts.

- **Store crafts.** Organize ribbons, beads, glues, and string in empty Huggies baby wipes boxes.

- **Clean scrapes and bruises.** Huggies baby wipes are great for cleaning minor abrasions.

- **Clean shoes.** Simply wipe the shoes with a Huggies baby wipe.

✳Invented
1990

✳The Name

Huggies describes the way these disposable diapers ideally *hug* an infant's bottom without leaking. Baby Wipes obviously refers to the cloth used to *wipe* a *baby*'s bottom.

✳A Short History

In 1872, John Kimberly, Charles Clark, Havilah Babcock, and Frank Shattuck founded Kimberly, Clark & Company in Neenah, Wisconsin, to manufacture newsprint from rags. In 1889, the company built a pulp-and-paper plant on the Fox River and, in 1914, developed Cellucotton, a cotton substitute used by the U.S. army as surgical cotton during World War I. Army nurses used Cellucotton pads as disposable sanitary napkins, and in 1920 the company introduced Kotex, the first disposable feminine hygiene product, followed by Kleenex, the first throw-away handkerchief, in 1924. Kotex and Kleenex became household words, and in 1928, Kimberly-Clark went public on the New York Stock Exchange. In 1971, Kimberly-Clark entered the disposable diaper market, starting with Kimbies and followed by Huggies in 1978 and Huggies Pull-Ups training pants in 1989.

In 1990, the company introduced Huggies baby wipes with 80 wipes per box. In 1995, the company changed the embossing pattern on Baby

Wipes and gave the wipes a scalloped edge to make it easier to grab an individual Baby Wipe from the box. Later that year, Huggies added a resealable refill pack with 160 wipes.

✳Ingredients

IN PICTURED PRODUCT: Purified water, propylene glycol, PEG-75 lanolin, disodium, cocoamphdiacetate, polysorbate 20, cetyl hydroxyethylcellulose, DMDM hydantoin, methylparaben, malic acid, fragrance

✳Strange Facts

- The town of Kimberly, Wisconsin, founded as a result of the Kimberly-Clark plant, was named in John Kimberly's honor.
- During Operation Bring Hope in Somalia, U.S. troops bartered for Huggies because the disposable diapers, when moistened, provide a refreshing rubdown, almost as good as a bath.

✳Distribution

- Huggies baby wipes are available in Regular (scented and unscented), Natural Care (scented and unscented), and Sensitive Skin.
- Huggies baby wipes, Kleenex tissue, and Huggies disposable diapers are the best-selling brands of those products in the United States.
- Kimberly-Clark sells its products in 150 countries.
- Aside from Huggies baby wipes, Kimberly-Clark markets Kleenex tissues, Huggies diapers, Pull-Ups training pants, Kotex and Lightdays feminine products, Depend and Poise incontinence products, Cottonelle bathroom tissue, and Viva paper towels.

For More Information

Kimberly-Clark Corporation, P.O. Box 2020, Neenah, WI 54957-2020. Or telephone 1-800-558-9177.

Ivory Soap

- **Repulse deer.** Hang bars of Ivory soap around crops.

- **Lubricate a handsaw blade.** Rub Ivory soap across the sides and teeth of the saw to help the blade glide through wood.

- **Make bubble bath.** Hold a bar of Ivory soap under running water to fill the tub with bubbles.

- **Fix small holes in walls.** Rub a bar of Ivory soap over the hole until it looks filled, then paint.

- **Lubricate zippers.** Rub the teeth of the zipper with a bar of Ivory soap to make the zipper glide easier.

- **Prevent campfire soot from sticking to the bottom of pots and pans.** Lightly rub the bottoms of pots and pans with a bar of Ivory soap before using them over an open fire.

- **Lubricate nails and screws.** Nails and screws rubbed with Ivory soap will go into wood easier.

- **Stop insect bites from itching.** Dab the bite with a wet bar of Ivory soap and let dry to desensitize the skin.

- **Make a pincushion.** Using a wrapped bar of Ivory soap as a pincushion makes needles glide through fabric.

- **Keep clothes and linens smelling fresh.** Place an unwrapped bar of Ivory soap in drawers, linen closets, and storage trunks.

- **Lubricate furniture drawers and windows.** Rub Ivory soap on the casters of drawers and windows so they slide open and shut easily.

Invented
1878

The Name

Harley Procter, considering a long list of new names for his white soap, was inspired one Sunday morning in church when the pastor read Psalm 45: "All thy garments smell of myrrh, and aloes, and cassia, out of the ivory palaces, whereby they have made thee glad." A few years later, a chemist's analysis of Ivory soap indicated that 56/1000 of the ingredients did not fall into the category of pure soap. Procter subtracted from 1000, and wrote the slogan "99$\frac{44}{100}$% Pure," which first appeared in Ivory's advertising in 1882. "It Floats" was added to Ivory's slogan in 1891.

A Short History

When Harley Procter decided to develop a creamy white soap to compete with imported castile soaps, he asked his cousin, chemist James Gamble, to formulate the product. One day after the soap went into production, a factory worker (who remains anonymous) forgot to switch off the master mixing machine when he went to lunch, and too much air was whipped into a batch of soap. Consumers, delighted by the floating soap, demanded more, and from then on, Procter & Gamble gave all white soap an extra-long whipping.

*Ingredients

Vegetable oils, animal fats, fragrance, and less than 0.5 percent magnesium sulfate and sodium silicate

*Strange Fact

- Ivory soap is the best-selling soap in America because the air-laden bars dissolve twice as fast as other brands, compelling consumers to buy twice as much.

*Distribution

- Approximately 30 billion cakes of Ivory soap had been manufactured by 1990.

For More Information

Procter & Gamble Co., 391 East 6th Street, Cincinnati, OH 45202. Or telephone 1-800-262-1637.

Jell-O Gelatin

- **Style your hair.** A teaspoon of Jell-O dissolved in a cup of warm water makes an inexpensive setting lotion. Or use prepared Jell-O as you would any hair gel product.

- **Make marshmallows.** Gelatin is the main ingredient in any recipe for marshmallows.

- **Make wine Jell-O.** *The Joy of Cooking* suggests boiling one cup water, mixing with gelatin powder in a bowl until dissolved, then adding one cup red wine. Stir well, then refrigerate for four hours or until mixture gels. Serves four.

- **Wrestle in Jell-O.** Pour 2,347 boxes of Jell-O into an eight-foot-square padded box, add boiling water, and chill for two days.

- **Watch seedlings grow roots.** For a great science experiment for children, grow seeds in Jell-O and observe the root structures.

Invented
1897

The Name

May Davis Wait, the inventor's wife, came up with a name for the fruit-flavored gelatin by apparently combining the word *jelly* with *-o*, a popular suffix added to the end of a slew of food products at the time.

A Short History

In 1845, Peter Cooper, inventor of the Tom Thumb locomotive, patented the first clear powdered gelatin mix. Fifty years later, in Le Roy, New York, Pearl B. Wait, a carpenter who had been manufacturing cough medicine and laxative tea in his spare time, began experimenting with Cooper's clear gelatin, adding ingredients until he concocted a fruit flavor.

In 1899, unable to properly market his new packaged food, Wait sold his formula to Orator Francis Woodward, proprietor of the Genesee Pure Food Company. Woodward couldn't find a market for Jell-O either, until 1900, when he spent $336 to place an advertisement in the *Ladies' Home Journal*. In 1902, Woodward launched the first advertising campaign for Jell-O, proclaiming it "America's Most Famous Dessert" and introducing the charming little Jell-O Girl in 1904. By 1906, sales topped $1 million.

Ingredients

Sugar, gelatin, adipic acid (for tartness), disodium phosphate (controls acidity), fumaric acid (for tartness), red 40, artificial flavor, blue 1

Strange Facts

- Gelatin, a colorless protein derived from the collagen contained in animal skin, tendons, and bone, is extracted by treating hides and bone with lime or acid. The material is then boiled, filtered, concentrated, dried, and ground into granules that dissolve in hot water and congeal into a gel when the solution cools.
- As a food supplement, gelatin supplies the body with several amino acids lacking in wheat, barley, and oats.
- Norman Rockwell illustrated two early Jell-O advertisements and recipe books.

- According to the 1993 *Guinness Book of Records*, the world record for the largest single amount of Jell-O is held by Paul Squire and Geoff Ross, who made 7,700 gallons of watermelon-flavored pink Jell-O in a tank supplied by Pool Fab on February 5, 1981, at Roma Street Forum in Brisbane, Australia.
- In July 1950, the FBI arrested thirty-two-year-old electrical engineer Julius Rosenberg as a spy for the Soviet Union. According to the FBI, Rosenberg had torn a Jell-O box top in half, given a piece to his brother-in-law, David Greenglass, and told him that his contact at Los Alamos would produce the other half. The contact turned out to be spy courier Harry Gold, who received atomic energy data from Greenglass and paid him $500, allegedly giving the Soviet Union the secret of the atomic bomb. Although Rosenberg insisted on his innocence, he and his wife, Ethel, were sentenced to death in 1951, and after several appeals, in June 1953, the Rosenbergs became the first Americans ever executed for using Jell-O.
- Every April Fool's Day in Eugene, Oregon, the Maude Kerns Art Gallery holds the Jell-O Art Show, better known as "Jell-O-Rama," featuring works of local artists using Jell-O as a medium.

✳Distribution

- Jell-O is the best-selling gelatin in the United States.
- A box of Jell-O can be found in three out of four American pantries.
- Americans eat more than 690,000 boxes of Jell-O on an average day.
- Jell-O and Jell-O Sugar Free are available in twenty flavors, including cherry, strawberry, raspberry, lemon, lime, mango, apricot, orange, grape, peach, blackberry, berry blue, strawberry banana, wild strawberry, triple berry, and watermelon.

For More Information

Kraft Foods, Inc., Box JOGS-C, White Plains, NY 10625. Or telephone 1-800-431-1001.

Jif Peanut Butter

- **Shave.** Former senator Barry Goldwater of Arizona once shaved with peanut butter while on a camping trip. (For best results, avoid shaving with Jif Extra Crunchy.)

- **Remove bubblegum from hair.** Rub a dollop of Jif peanut butter into the bubblegum.

- **Remove airplane glue or cement glue from furniture.** Simply rub the dried glue with Jif peanut butter.

- **Grease a car or truck axle.** George Washington Carver developed axle grease from peanuts.

- **Make peanut soup.** Peanut butter is the main ingredient in any recipe for peanut soup.

- **Trap mice or rats.** Bait a trap with Jif peanut butter.

Invented
1956

The Name

Jif is short for *jiffy*, the amount of time it takes to make a peanut butter sandwich.

A Short History

For centuries, African tribes and the Incas ate a paste made from peanuts. In 1890, Dr. Ambrose W. Straub of St. Louis, MO, crushed peanuts into a paste for his geriatric patients with bad teeth. In 1903, Straub received the patent for a machine that ground peanuts into butter, unveiling his invention at the 1904 World's Fair in St. Louis. By 1914, there were several dozen brands on the market. Procter & Gamble introduced Jif in 1956, and today Jif is the top-selling peanut butter in America.

Ingredients

Roasted peanuts, sugar, and two percent or less of: molasses, partially hydrogenated vegetable oil (soybean), fully hydrogenated vegetable oils (rapeseed and soybean), mono- and diglycerides, and salt

Strange Facts

- Jif does not require refrigeration and will stay fresh for approximately three months after opening.
- A 28-ounce jar of Jif contains 1,218 peanuts.
- The Jif plant in Lexington, KY, is reportedly the largest peanut butter factory in the world.
- The peanut is a member of the pea family.
- Peanut butter sticks to the roof of your mouth because its high protein content draws moisture from your mouth.
- Peanut butter is the most commonly used form of the peanut. Half of America's 1.6-million-ton annual peanut crop is used to make peanut butter.
- As president of the United States, Gerald Ford had peanut butter on an English muffin for breakfast every morning.
- Jimmy Carter was the first peanut farmer elected president of the United States.

- According to *Americana* magazine, the average high school graduate has eaten 1,500 peanut butter and jelly sandwiches.
- The average jar of peanut butter is consumed in less than thirty days.
- Pound for pound, peanuts have more protein, minerals, and vitamins than beef liver.
- The Adults Only Peanut-Butter Lovers Fan Club publishes a newsletter called *Spread the News*, hosts annual conventions for peanut butter fanatics, and distributes peanut butter recipes.

Unusual Events

- Every October, Suffolk, VA, stages a peanut festival featuring the World's Only Peanut Butter Sculpture Contest, offering a prize for the best sculpture made entirely of peanut butter.

Distribution

- Americans eat 170 million pounds of Jif every year. That's enough to make two billion peanut butter sandwiches.
- Nearly 120 billion peanuts are used to make the amount of Jif peanut butter produced in one year.
- According to the Peanut Advisory Board, 83 percent of all Americans purchase peanut butter.
- One out of every ten peanuts grown in the United States for domestic consumption ends up in a jar of Jif.
- Procter & Gamble makes Jif Creamy, Jif Extra Crunchy, Simply Jif Creamy (low sugar and low salt), Simply Jif Extra Crunchy, and Jif Reduced Fat Creamy.

For More Information

- Procter & Gamble Co., P.O. Box 5561, Cincinnati, OH 45201. Or telephone 1-800-283-8915.
- National Peanut Council, 1500 King Street, Suite 301, Alexandria, VA 22314. Or telephone 1-703-838-9500.

Kingsford Charcoal Briquets

- **Prevent tools from rusting.** Placing a charcoal briquet in a toolbox helps absorb moisture, according to household-hints columnist Mary Ellen.

- **Freshen air in a closed space.** Placing a coffee can filled with charcoal briquets in a closet or chest helps absorb odors, according to *Reader's Digest*.

- **Deodorize your refrigerator.** A cup of charcoal briquets in the back of the refrigerator helps keep it smelling fresh and clean, according to Mary Ellen.

Invented
Early 1920s

The Name

Ford Charcoal was renamed Kingsford Charcoal Briquets after E. G. Kingsford, the relative who helped Henry Ford select the site for his charcoal plant.

A Short History

In the early 1920s, Henry Ford wanted to find a use for the growing piles of wood scraps from the production of his Model Ts. Ford learned of a process for turning the wood scraps into charcoal briquets, and one of his relatives, E. G. Kingsford, helped select the site for Ford's charcoal plant. Essentially, wood scraps are heated in ovens that contain little or no air, causing the hydrogen, nitrogen, and oxygen in the wood to escape, leaving behind black, porous wood char. The company town which sprang up around the site was named in Kingsford's honor, and in 1951, Ford Charcoal was renamed Kingsford Charcoal.

Ingredients

Wood char (contributes barbecue flavor), mineral char (to make the briquets burn longer), limestone (to give the briquets a white ash appearance when they're ready), sodium nitrate (to help the briquets ignite quickly), starch (binder)

Strange Facts

- Kingsford turns approximately one million tons of wood waste into a usable product—charcoal briquets—every year.
- *Fortune* magazine rated Kingsford Charcoal Briquets one of the best products made in Arnerica.
- Charcoal briquets for barbecuing should not be confused with activated charcoal, manufactured by other companies that remove most of the impurities from ordinary charcoal by treating it with steam and air heated to above 600°F. While wood, bone, and activated charcoal are all used to absorb colors, flavors, and odors from gases and liquids, activated charcoal—available in pet stores (for fish tank filters) and drug stores (in capsule form)—works best.
- Activated charcoal allegedly helps dry up acne pimples, according to Ben Harris, author of *Kitchen Medicines*, who suggests taking one-half teaspoon of activated charcoal three times a day after meals.

- In May 1959, the United States sent two young female monkeys, Able and Baker, into space in a *Jupiter* rocket. Monkey Able, dressed in a space suit, wore gauze and charcoal diapers.
- On July 20, 1969, Neil Armstrong, the first man on the moon spoke the first words on the moon: "That's one small step for man, one giant leap for mankind." The second thought he expressed was: "The surface is fine and powdery, it adheres in fine layers, like powdered charcoal, to the soles and sides of my foot."
- All automobile engines contain a canister filled with activated charcoal that absorbs evaporating gasoline fumes when the car's engine is off. The system is designed to prevent hydrocarbons from being released into the atmosphere by trapping and storing fuel vapor from the fuel tank, the carburetor, or the fuel injection system.
- The Kingsford Product Company remains the leading manufacturer of charcoal in the United States, converting more than one million tons of wood scraps into charcoal briquets each year.
- More than 77 percent of all households in the United States own a barbecue grill. Nearly half of those grill owners barbecue year round and, on the average, use their grills five times a month.

For More Information
The Kingsford Products Co., Oakland, CA 94623.

Kingsford's Corn Starch

- **Kill cockroaches.** Mix equal parts Kingsford's Corn Starch and plaster of Paris. Sprinkle the mixture in cracks and crevices. Cockroaches will eat the mixture and "petrify."

- **Cure athlete's foot.** Sprinkle Kingsford's Corn Starch on your feet and in your shoes to absorb moisture and reduce friction.

- **Relieve bad sunburn pain.** Add enough water to Kingsford's Corn Starch to make a paste, and apply directly to the burn.

- **Clean a carpet.** Sprinkle Kingsford's Corn Starch on the carpet, wait thirty minutes, then vacuum clean.

- **Clean bloodstains.** Immediately cover the spot with a paste of Kingsford's Corn Starch and cold water. Rub gently, place the object in the sun until dry to draw the blood into the corn starch, then brush off. Repeat if necessary.

- **Make spray starch for clothing.** Mix one tablespoon Kingsford's Corn Starch and one pint cold water. Stir to dissolve the corn starch completely. Fill a spray bottle and use as you would any starch. Be sure to shake vigorously before each use.

- **Substitute for baby powder and talcum powder.** Apply Kingsford's Corn Starch sparingly when diapering a baby. Corn starch is actually more absorbent than talcum powder, but apply lightly since it does cake more readily.

- **Help rubber gloves slip on easily.** Sprinkle Kingsford's Corn Starch inside the gloves.

- **Shine your car.** When buffing your car, sprinkle a tablespoon of Kingsford's Corn Starch on the wipe rag to remove excess polish easily.

- **Shampoo your hair.** Kingsford's Corn Starch can be used as a dry shampoo. Work into your hair, then brush out.

- **Prevent or kill mildew in damp books.** Sprinkle Kingsford's Corn Starch throughout the book to absorb the moisture from damp pages, wait several hours, then brush clean. If the pages are mildewed, brush the corn starch off outdoors to keep mildew spores outside the house.

- **Detangle knots.** Sprinkle a stubborn knot with a little Kingsford's Corn Starch.

- **Make fingerpaints.** Mix one-quarter cup Kingsford's Corn Starch with two cups cold water, boil until thick, pour into small containers, and color with food coloring.

- **Absorb excess polish from furniture.** After polishing furniture, sprinkle on a little Kingsford's Corn Starch and rub wood with a soft cloth.

- **Clean silver.** Make a paste with Kingsford's Corn Starch and water. Apply with a damp cloth, let dry, then rub off with cheesecloth.

- **Remove grease or oil stains from smooth fabric.** Apply Kingsford's Corn Starch to the spot, wait twelve hours, brush off, then launder as usual.

- **Make white clown makeup.** Mix two tablespoons Kingsford's Corn Starch with one tablespoon solid shortening. To tint it, add food coloring.

- **Give your dog a dry shampoo.** Rub Kingsford's Corn Starch into your dog's fur, then comb and brush out.

- **Clean stuffed animals.** Rub Kingsford's Corn Starch into the toy, let stand for five minutes, then brush off.

- **Prevent pastry dough from sticking to the cutting board and rolling pin.** Sprinkle the cutting board and rolling pin with Kingsford's Corn Starch—it's tasteless—before rolling out the dough.

- **Clean a deck of playing cards.** Place the deck of cards in a paper bag, adding four tablespoons Kingsford's Corn Starch, and shake briskly. Remove the cards from the bag and wipe clean.

- **Soothe skin irritations.** Apply a paste made of equal parts Kingsford's Corn Starch, zinc oxide, and castor oil.

- **Thicken gravy.** Corn starch has twice the thickening power of flour. When a gravy, sauce, soup, or stew recipe calls for flour, use half as much corn starch to thicken. One tablespoon of corn starch equals two tablespoons flour.

- **Relieve the pain and discomfort caused by hemorrhoids.** Ben Charles Harris, author of *Kitchen Medicines*, suggests mixing one tablespoon Kingsford's Corn Starch in enough water to make a paste, gradually adding more water to measure a pint, boiling the mixture for a few minutes, allowing it to cool, and then using it in an enema.

✳*Invented*
1842

158

The Name

Kingsford's Corn Starch was named after company founder Thomas Kingsford. Corn starch itself is named for the starch found in corn.

A Short History

All green plants manufacture starch through photosynthesis to serve as a metabolic reserve, but it wasn't until 1842 that Thomas Kingsford developed a technique for separating starch from corn. The corn-refining industry emerged fifty years later. In 1894, twenty corn starch and syrup producers grouped together as National Starch Manufacturing to prevent severe price competition and establish quotas, gaining 70 percent of the corn starch market, until their association disintegrated. By 1906, price wars forced New York Glucose to merge with Glucose Sugar Refining Company, forming Corn Products Refining Company (CPRC), the first stable corn-refining company, controlling 64 percent of the starch and 100 percent of the glucose output in the United States.

Over the years, CPRC faced a series of antitrust suits, forcing the company to sell portions of its business and eliminate "phantom freight" charges. By 1954, CPRC had only a 46 percent share of corn-grinding capacity, producing several brands, including Mazola, Karo, ARGO, and Kingsford's. In 1958, the corn refinery merged with Best Foods—producers of Hellmann's, Best Foods, Skippy, and Rit brands—and bought C. H. Knorr soups. In 1969, the company was renamed CPC International and, since 1988, acquired over fifty companies.

Ingredients

100 percent pure corn starch

Strange Facts

- Corn starch, the most important starch manufactured in the United States, can be hydrolyzed for the manufacture of D-glucose and corn syrup.

- Approximately one-third of the corn starch produced in America is sold for food purposes.

✴Distribution

- CPC operates twenty-nine plants in the United States, eight in Canada, thirty-eight in Europe, fourteen in Africa and the Middle East, thirty-four in Latin America, and eleven in Asia.
- In 1993, CPC International sold more than $1.1 billion worth of refined corn products worldwide.
- CPC International also makes Hellmann's mayonnaise, Best Foods, Mazola, Knorr soups, Skippy peanut butter, and Thomas' English Muffins.

For More Information

Best Foods, CPC International, Inc., International Plaza, P.O. Box 8000, Englewood Cliffs, NJ 07632-9976. Or telephone 1-800-344-2746.

Kiwi Shoe Polish

- **Stain wood.** Apply Kiwi Shoe Polish with a dry cloth.

- **Retouch walls.** Touch up scratches, scuff marks, and holes from picture hooks with a dab of the appropriate color Kiwi Shoe Polish.

- **Repair furniture finishes.** Cover up small scratches or discolorations on furniture or woodwork.

- **Use as oil paint on canvas.** Some artists use Kiwi Shoe Polish as paint in oil paintings.

Invented
1906

The Name

Inventor William Ramsay named the shoe polish Kiwi in honor of his wife, Annie Elizabeth Meek Ramsay, a native of Oamaru, New Zealand. The kiwi is the national bird of New Zealand, and "Kiwi" is a common nickname for a New Zealander, just as "Yankee" is a nickname for a citizen of the United States.

A Short History

In 1906, William Ramsay invented Kiwi Boot Polish and began marketing it in Melbourne, Australia. Ramsay would load boxes of his boot polish on his horse and wagon and sell the product to ranchers to protect their boots. During World War I and World War II, Kiwi Shoe Polish's popularity spread throughout the British Commonwealth and into the United States. A few years after World War II, the Australian company opened a manufacturing plant in Philadelphia, making only black, brown, and neutral shoe polish in tins.

In 1984, Consolidated Foods purchased Kiwi. The following year, Consolidated Foods changed its name to Sara Lee Corporation, after one of its most respected brand names, and Kiwi changed its name to Kiwi Brands.

Ingredients

Natural and synthetic waxes, solvents (to soften waxes and allow them to be spread on leather), oil-soluble dyes (to stain leather), pigments (to add color)

Strange Facts

- Nearly 80 percent of all corporate executives believe that well-cared-for shoes are very important to a person's success.
- New Zealand is the only place kiwi birds are found in the wild.
- Because the kiwi is the national emblem of New Zealand, pictures of the kiwi are found on money, stamps, and coins.
- The kiwi has wings but cannot fly. Its beak is a third the length of its body, and its nostrils are at the tip of that beak.
- A five-pound kiwi lays an egg that weighs just over a pound—a record in the bird kingdom.

Distribution

- Kiwi is the best-selling shoe polish in the world.
- Kiwi Brands also makes Kiwi Shine Wipes, Kiwi Clean Gleam, Kiwi Twist 'n Shine, Kiwi Scuff Zapper, Kiwi Wet Pruf, Kiwi Protect All, and Kiwi Sneaker Shampoo.

- Kiwi Brands' parent company, Sara Lee, makes Bali intimate apparel, Champion activewear, Coach leather goods, Hanes hosiery and apparel, L'eggs panty hose, Playtex intimate apparel, Ball Park frankfurters, and Endust no-wax dusting spray.

For More Information

Kiwi Brands, Douglassville, PA 19518-1239. Or telephone 1-610-385-3041. On the Internet, visit www.kiwicare.com.

Krazy Glue

- **Lessen the pain of paper cuts.** Apply Krazy Glue to paper cuts to relieve the pain. The Krazy Glue deprives the nerve endings of air, according to *The Doctors Book of Home Remedies II.*

- **Repair a broken fingernail.** Use a small drop of Krazy Glue to secure the nail in place, then coat with nail polish.

- **Remove ticks from inside the ear of a horse, cow, dog, or cat.** Put a drop of Krazy Glue on a broom straw, apply it to the tick, and pull it right out.

- **Reattach a broken heel or loose tassels.** Use a few drops of Krazy Glue and hold in place until secure.

- **Fix leaks in inflatable inner tubes, air mattresses, or air pillows.** Apply Krazy Glue to seal the hole or leaky valve stems.

- **Prevent bra pads from slipping.** Use Krazy Glue to attach Velcro to the inside cups of the bra and the outside of the pads.

Invented
1963

The Name

Krazy Glue is named for the glue's seemingly crazy strength, quick-setting properties, and longevity as an adhesive.

A Short History

In 1963, Toagosei Co., Ltd., a Japanese chemical company founded in 1942 in Tokyo, began producing the instant adhesive Aron Alpha. The product is distributed in the United States as Krazy Glue by Elmer's Products, Inc., a Borden Incorporated Company. Borden Inc., a dairy company founded in 1857 by Gail Borden Jr. in Burrville, Connecticut, had also become a glue manufacturer by 1929.

Ingredients

Modified ethyl cyanoacrylate

Strange Facts

- In the motion picture *What About Bob?* (1991), Dr. Leo Marvin (Richard Dreyfuss) describes the symbiotic Bob Wiley (Bill Murray) as "human Krazy Glue."
- If your fingers get stuck together with Krazy Glue, dissolve the bond with nail polish remover or acetone, or soften with warm soapy water.
- The winners of the 1996 "How Krazy Glue Saved the Day" contest, Don McMullan and Sharon Bennett of Clearwater, British Columbia, used Krazy Glue to get themselves down Robber's Pass when their eighteen-wheel semi-trailer's engine cooling fan separated from its rotating shaft hundreds of miles from the nearest service station in the middle of the night. They put six drops of Krazy Glue on the two metal pieces, held the parts together securely for three minutes, and were back on the road for another eighty thousand miles.
- Surgeons treat an arterial venous fistula, or entangled cluster of arteries, by injecting liquid acrylic agents into the abnormal blood vessels to seal off the excessive flow of blood. The material used, n-butyl cyanoacrylate, is similar to the ingredients in Krazy Glue.

- Physicians in Canada use an adhesive similar to Krazy Glue instead of stitches, lowering the possibility of bacterial infection and minimizing scarring.
- During her highly publicized disappearance for four days in April 1996, Margot Kidder, who costarred with Christopher Reeve in the Superman movies, lived inside a cardboard box with a homeless person in downtown Los Angeles while suffering a manic-depressive episode. According to *People* magazine, "Kidder had lost some caps on her front teeth that sometimes fell out and which she cemented back in place with Krazy Glue. 'When you're having a manic episode,' she says, 'you don't always remember to pack the Krazy Glue.'"
- Food stylists use Krazy Glue to keep food in place during photography sessions for advertisements, television commercials, and motion pictures.

Distribution

- Elmer's Products, Inc., which distributes Krazy Glue in the United States, also makes a variety of other consumer adhesives, including Elmer's Glue-All and Elmer's School Glue, as well as wood fillers and caulk.

For More Information

Elmer's Products, Inc., 180 East Broad Street, Columbus, OH 43215.

L'eggs Sheer Energy

- **Find a contact lens on the floor or carpet.** Cover your vacuum-hose nozzle carefully with a piece of L'eggs hose and a rubber band to keep the lens from being sucked in. Gently vacuum with the nozzle one inch above the floor.

- **Strain lumps from paint.** Stretch a L'eggs Sheer Energy panty hose across the paint can and pour.

- **Shine a wood floor.** Insert a folded bath towel into one leg of the stocking and hand buff the floor.

- **Apply wood stain, varnish, or polyurethane.** Old L'eggs make great substitutes for paint brushes. Ball up the panty hose and use it like a sponge or secure it to a stick with several rubber bands.

- **Clean dentures.** Cut a small piece of nylon from the L'eggs and polish dentures.

- **Scrub your back with soap.** Place a bar of soap inside one leg of a pair of L'eggs Sheer Energy at the knee, tie knots on both sides of it, hold one end of the stocking in each hand, and seesaw it across your back in the bathtub.

- **Prevent lint from sticking to clothes in the dryer.** Throw a pair of L'eggs into the dryer with your wet clothes.

- **Secure garbage bags inside your trash can.** Cut off the elastic top of a pair of L'eggs Sheer Energy and stretch the extra-large rubber band around the rim of the trash can to hold the plastic garbage bag in place.

- **Remove excess plaster after filling a hole.** Scrub with a balled-up pair of L'eggs.

- **Make a catnip ball.** Stuff the toe of a L'eggs stocking with catnip and knot it.

- **Clean dust from window screens.** Simply run a balled-up pair of L'eggs over the screen.

- **Wash bottles.** Wrap a section of a L'eggs around the bristles of a bottle brush, fasten with a rubber band, and scrub.

- **Secure mothballs.** Use a L'eggs stocking to hold mothballs in the closet.

- **Store plant bulbs, onions, or garlic.** Fill the foot of a pair of L'eggs Sheer Energy and hang it high to keep the contents dry.

- **Clean the sink, bathtub, and bathroom tiles.** Use a balled-up pair of L'eggs as a non-abrasive scouring pad.

- **Tie tomato plants to stakes.** The soft nylon of L'eggs Sheer Energy secures tomato stalks without causing any damage to the plant.

- **Clean your windows.** Use a balled-up pair of L'eggs.

- **Clean the dust from under the refrigerator.** Place one stocking leg over the end of a broomstick and secure with a rubber hand. Slide the broomstick under the refrigerator and move it back and forth.

- **Prevent soil from leaking out of a potted plant.** Place a pair of L'eggs Sheer Energy in the bottom of plant pots to provide drainage.

- **Remove dead insects from the hood of the car.** Use a damp balled-up pair of L'eggs to clean the car without scratching the finish.

Invented
1970

The Name

A clever combination of the words *legs* and *eggs*, with an apostrophe added to make the wordplay idiot-proof.

A Short History

At the 1939 World's Fair, Dupont introduced nylon stockings to the world. On May 15, 1940, they were available in stores. Nineteen years later, Glen Raven Mills of North Carolina introduced panty hose, eventually developing a seamless model just in time for the advent of the miniskirt in 1965. In 1970, Hanes creatively packaged panty hose in plastic eggs in supermarkets, drugstores, and convenience stores—places where they had never been available before. Sheer Energy was introduced in 1973 as the first L'eggs panty hose made with sheer spandex yarn. In 1991, L'eggs replaced the plastic egg with a cardboard package to reduce waste. While the plastic eggs were recyclable and used for arts-and-crafts projects, the new box, using 38 percent less material and made from recycled paper, allows 33 percent more containers to fit into the store display rack and is still rounded at the top like an egg.

Ingredients

PANTY: 90 percent nylon, 10 percent spandex; LEG: 80 percent nylon, 20 percent spandex; GUSSET: 55 percent cotton, 45 percent polyester

Strange Facts

- In the 1970s, when Peter Lynch, the most successful money manager in America, noticed his wife, Carolyn, bringing L'eggs panty hose home from the supermarket, his Fidelity Magellan fund bought stock in Hanes. The value of its shares rose nearly 600 percent.

- L'eggs supported the women of the 1994 and 1996 United States Olympic Teams.

*Distribution

- L'eggs is the best-selling panty hose in America.
- 97 percent of all supermarkets, drugstores, and convenience stores in the United States carry L'eggs panty hose.
- The full line of L'eggs products includes L'eggs Regular, L'eggs Control Top, L'eggs Classics, L'eggs Sheer Energy, L'eggs Sheer Elegance, L'eggs Silken Mist, L'eggs Active Support, L'eggs Everyday, L'eggs Just My Size, and L'eggs Silky Support Smooth Silhouettes.

For More Information

L'eggs Products, P.O. Box 2495, Winston-Salem, NC 27102. Or telephone 1-800-92-LEGGS.

Lipton Tea Bags

- **Deodorize your feet.** Boil three or four Lipton Flo-Thru Tea Bags in one quart of water for ten minutes. Add enough cold water to make a comfortable soak. Soak your feet for twenty to thirty minutes, then dry and apply foot powder. Do this twice a day until the odor is under control. Then continue twice a week to keep it under control. Tannin, which can be found in tea, is a drying agent.

- **Dye graying white fabrics.** If Clorox bleach won't whiten a graying white garment, soak the item in hot, strong-brewed Lipton tea until it is a shade darker than you desire. Then rinse in cold water and let dry.

- **Highlight brown hair.** Rinse red or brown hair with brewed Lipton tea for golden highlights.

- **Relieve sunburn pain.** Pat your sunburn with wet Lipton Flo-Thru Tea Bags.

- **Accelerate the germination of grass seeds.** Mix two tablespoons cold, strong-brewed Lipton tea into each pound of seed, cover, and set in the refrigerator for five days. Before sowing, spread the seed to dry for a day or two on newspapers on the garage or basement floor.

- **Deodorize stuffy rooms.** Mix one quart brewed Lipton tea and four tablespoons ReaLemon lemon juice, strain through a Mr. Coffee Filter, and store in empty spray bottles.

- **Soothe a sore throat or laryngitis.** Drink brewed Lipton tea with ReaLemon lemon juice or SueBee Honey.

- **Invigorate houseplants.** Water ferns and other houseplants once a week with a tepid, weak-brewed Lipton tea.

- **Polish black lacquer.** Wash black lacquer pieces with strong-brewed Lipton tea, then wipe dry with a soft cloth.

- **Help relieve diarrhea.** Drink plenty of Lipton tea and eat toast. The tannin in tea is reported to be helpful in cases of diarrhea, while its liquid replaces fluids lost by the body.

- **Soothe tired eyes.** Place Lipton Flo-Thru Tea Bags soaked in cool or lukewarm water over your eyes for at least fifteen minutes.

- **Soothe a burn.** Apply wet Lipton Flo-Thru Tea Bags directly to the burn, or secure in place with gauze.

- **Stop gums from bleeding after having a tooth pulled.** With your finger, press a cool, moist Lipton Flo-Thru Tea Bag against the cavity.

- **Fix a broken fingernail.** Cut a piece of gauze paper from a Lipton Flo-Thru Tea Bag to fit the nail, coat with Maybelline Crystal Clear Nail Polish, and press gently against the break. Then cover with colored nail polish.

- **Clean varnished woodwork.** Cold Lipton tea is a good cleaning agent for any kind of woodwork.

- **Tenderize meat.** Add equal parts strong-brewed Lipton tea and double-strength beef stock to a tough pot roast or stew. The tannin in tea is a natural meat tenderizer.

✴Invented
1890

✴The Name
Lipton tea is named after the founder of the company, Sir Thomas Lipton.

✴A Short History
Born in 1850 in Glasgow, Scotland, Sir Thomas Lipton sold cured meats, eggs, butter, and cheeses from a small store that grew into a chain of stores throughout Scotland and England. In 1888, Lipton entered the tea trade, and two years later entered the American market, pioneering packaged tea with the famous Flo-Thru bag. He was knighted in 1898 and made a baronet in 1902. A yachting enthusiast, Lipton made five unsuccessful attempts to win the Americas cup. His portrait, complete with nautical attire, adorns all Lipton tea packages. He died at the age of 81 in 1931.

✴Ingredients
Orange pekoe and pekoe cut black tea

✴Strange Facts
- According to an ancient Chinese legend, the first cup of tea was brewed by Emperor Shennong in 2737 B.C. when a few leaves from a tea plant accidentally fell into water he was boiling.
- Since tea plants grow more slowly in cooler air, yielding a better-flavored leaf, the best teas are grown at altitudes between 3,000 and 7,000 feet. Tea connoisseurs consider the tea grown on the slopes of the Himalayan mountains near Darjeeling, India, to be among the world's finest.
- Although tea is often considered a British custom steeped in tradition, tea was not introduced to England (or the American colonies) until British merchants formed the East India Company in 1600.

- During the Boston Tea Party on December 16, 1773, American colonists, disguised as Indians and protesting British taxes on imported tea, boarded three ships in Boston harbor and dumped into the water 342 chests of tea valued at 9,000 British pounds, an event that led to the Revolutionary War.

Distribution

- Lipton calls itself the "brisk" tea because it contains a blend of approximately twenty quality teas selected from around the world. Teas are chosen to provide the proper taste, color, and consistency.
- Tea is the most popular beverage in the world, and Lipton tea is the best-selling tea in America.
- According to the United States Department of Agriculture, in 1991, the average American consumed 2.8 gallons of tea, 6.5 gallons of coffee, 7.3 gallons of juice, 25.7 gallons of milk, and 43.2 gallons of soft drinks.
- India produces one-third of the world's tea, followed by China and Sri Lanka.
- Lipton also makes Decaffeinated Tea, Lemon Flavor Tea, and Tropical Flavor Tea.

For More Information

Thomas J. Lipton Company, 800 Sylvan Avenue, Englewood Cliffs, NJ 07632. Or telephone 1-800-697-7887.

Listerine

- **Cure acne.** Use a cotton ball to dab Listerine on blemishes.

- **Fertilize a lawn.** Jerry Baker, author of *The Impatient Gardener*, suggests mixing one cup Listerine, one cup Epsom salts, one cup liquid soap, and one cup ammonia in a one-quart jar, filling the rest of the jar with beer. Spray this on up to 2,500 square feet of lawn with a hose-attached sprayer in May and again in late June.

- **Use as a deodorant.** Listerine helps kill the bacteria that cause perspiration odor. Dab it under your arms.

- **Eliminate mildew odors.** Wipe with full-strength Listerine.

- **Disinfect wounds.** Listerine works as an astringent when poured on a laceration or abrasion.

- **Disinfect a washing machine at a Laundromat.** To avoid getting germs from another family, wipe off the surface of the machine with Listerine and add one-half cup Listerine to the wash cycle.

- **Prevent dandruff.** Wash your hair with Listerine.

Invented
1879

The Name

Listerine was named in honor of Sir Joseph Lister, the nineteenth-century British surgeon who pioneered sanitary operating room procedures.

A Short History

Impressed by Sir Joseph Lister's views on germs and his plea for "antiseptic surgery," Dr. Joseph Lawrence developed Listerine in his St. Louis laboratory as a safe and effective antiseptic for use in surgical procedures. The local Lambert Pharmacal Company manufactured Listerine exclusively for the medical profession and, in 1895, extended the sale and promotion of Listerine to the dental profession as an antibacterial mouthwash and gargle. In 1914, compelled by popular demand, Lambert made Listerine available to the general public.

Ingredients

ACTIVE: thymol 0.064 percent, eucalyptol 0.092 percent, methyl salicylate 0.06 percent, menthol 0.042 percent; INACTIVE: water, alcohol 26.9 percent, bentoic acid, poloxamer 40 percent, and caramel

Strange Facts

- Listerine is the only over-the-counter brand of mouthwash clinically proven to help prevent and reduce supragingival plaque accumulation and gingivitis when used in a conscientiously applied program of oral hygiene and regular professional care.

- Listerine should not be swallowed or administered to children under twelve years of age because it contains 26.9 percent pharmaceutical-grade alcohol.

Distribution

- Listerine is the best-selling brand of mouthwash in the United States.
- Listerine can be found in one out of every five homes in the United States.
- Listerine is available in regular, Cool Mint, and FreshBurst.

For More Information
Warner-Lambert Co., 201 Tabor Road, Morris Plains, NJ 07950. Or telephone 1-800-LISTERINE.

Lubriderm

FRESH SCENT

Lubriderm

SKIN
THERAPY
Moisturizing Lotion

For Normal to Dry Skin

Recommended by Dermatologists
Non-Greasy Feel

296 ml (10 fl oz)   07-0346-01

- **Shine shoes.** Rub a dab of Lubriderm on each shoe and buff thoroughly.

- **Shave.** If you run out of shaving cream, slather on Lubriderm.

- **Soothe a sunburn.** After soaking or using compresses, smooth on some bath oil. Then moisturize with Lubriderm.

- **Remove a ring stuck on a finger.** Apply Lubriderm around the ring band and slide the ring off.

- **Slip on rubber gloves.** Apply Lubriderm before putting on rubber gloves. The heat from washing dishes will also help the moisturizing skin cream melt in.

- **Prevent hangnails.** Moisturize your cuticles daily. Rub Lubriderm into the flesh surrounding your nails to keep the area soft.

- **Prevent dry skin in an air-conditioned or steam-heated room.** Use extra Lubriderm. Air-conditioning and steam heat dry skin.

- **Eliminate static cling.** Rub a dab of Lubriderm into your hands until it disappears, then rub your palms over your panty hose or slip.

Invented
1946

The Name

Lubriderm is apparently a clever combination of the word *lubricate* and the suffix *-derm*, derived from the Greek word *derma*, meaning skin.

A Short History

Texas Pharmacal developed Lubriderm Lotion in 1946 for dermatologists as a base for their own formulations of topical drugs to treat dermatological conditions involving dry skin. Lubriderm quickly gained a reputation as the dermatologist's choice as a compounding base, and demand for the moisturizer escalated. In the 1950s, Warner-Lambert bought Texas Pharmacal, and the product is now marketed by the Warner-Wellcome Consumer Health Care Group.

Ingredients

Water, mineral oil, petrolatum, sorbitol, lanolin, stearic acid, lanolin alcohol, cetyl alcohol, tri (PPG-3 myristyl ether) citrate, triethanolamine, methylparaben, methyldibromo glutaronitrile/phenoxyethanol, fragrance, ethylparaben, propylparaben, butylparaben, sodium chloride

Strange Facts

- Original Lubriderm Lotion, created for dermatologists, penetrates dry skin with pure moisturizing emollients to restore the skin's naturally healthy look and feel. The oil in Lubriderm Lotion is quickly absorbed into the dry upper layer of the skin, leaving it feeling clean and fresh.

- Lubriderm contains only one ingredient derived from animals. Lanolin, an occlusive agent found in Lubriderm, is derived from the wool of sheep. The sheep are shaved, and the lanolin is taken from the wool.
- Lubriderm is an oil-in-water emulsion. Since oil and water don't mix, Lubriderm Lotion is formulated with an emulsifier that holds the oil within the water. Oil in water allows dry skin to take up water better than water in oil. With water on the outside of the emulsion, some of this water evaporates, and the skin is cooled. The oil on the inside of the emulsion breaks down and forms a protective barrier over the skin surface, keeping the remaining supplemental water and the available natural moisture in the skin to provide moisturization.
- Clinical studies have shown that after continued use, the moisturizing benefits of Lubriderm Lotion last for days.

Distribution

- Warner-Lambert has operations in more than 130 countries.
- Lubriderm Dry Skin Care Lotion is available in Original Fragrance and Fragrance Free. Lubriderm is also available in Seriously Sensitive Lotion, Moisture Recovery Gel Creme, and Alpha Hydroxy Lotion and Creme.

For More Information

Warner-Lambert Company, 201 Tabor Road, Morris Plains, NJ 07950-2693. Or telephone 1-800-223-0182.

MasterCard

- **Scrape frost from a windshield.** If nothing else is available, use an old MasterCard to master the possibilities.

- **Open a locked door.** Slide an old MasterCard between the door and the frame to press the latch into the door. If the bevel faces the other way, cut the card into an L shape, insert it, and pull it toward you.

- **Scrape candle wax from a tabletop.** Use an old MasterCard to remove as much wax as possible. Then place a sheet of paper towel over the wax and press gently with a warm iron to absorb the remaining wax.

- **Clean your fingernails.** The corner of a MasterCard works as a manicure tool.

- **Scrape paint.** Use an old MasterCard to scrape off peeling paint.

- **Play guitar.** If you lose a guitar pick, use a corner of an old MasterCard.

Invented
1966

✳The Name

MasterCard was originally called MasterCharge. The word *master* implies predominance, while the word *charge* means to purchase on credit. The words *master* and *card* suggest the predominant credit card.

✳A Short History

Shopkeepers often let regular customers charge items to their account to be paid monthly, eventually letting them pay for large purchases in monthly installments. In the 1930s, oil companies offered motorists "courtesy cards" to use service stations across the country, and department stores began offering customers "revolving credit." In 1950, tarpaulin salesman Francis Xavier McNamara founded Diners Club, the first multipurpose credit card offered by an intermediary between the vendor and the buyer, popularized by an article in *The New Yorker*'s "Talk of the Town."

The Franklin National Bank in New York offered the first bank credit card in 1951. Numerous credit cards issued by independent banks quickly followed, but, by the mid-1960s, MasterCharge and BankAmericard (renamed MasterCard and Visa in the 1970s) dominated the field. Both MasterCard and Visa are credit associations that sign up banks that then offer cards to consumers.

✳Ingredients

Plastic, ink, magnetic strip, holographic image (color foil and ultraviolet ink)

✳Strange Facts

- An average of 200 million credit cards are used every day in the United States.
- Americans charged a total of $480 billion on credit cards in 1990. That's equal to $1 million every minute.
- The typical American credit card holder carries nine credit cards and owes over $2,000.

- In 1983, MasterCard became the first credit card company to introduce the laser hologram on its cards to combat counterfeiting.
- In 1988, MasterCard became the first payment card issued in the People's Republic of China.
- In 1990, Citibank, the largest issuer of credit cards in America, made over $610 million in profits on its Visa and MasterCard operations, according to Spencer Nilson, editor of *The Nilson Report*, an industry newsletter.
- According to *Consumer Reports*, 80 percent of all purchasing in the United States is done on credit.
- The magnetic strip on a MasterCard holds two or three tracks of information. The first track contains your name, expiration date, card type, and data such as your PIN and credit limit. The second track holds your account number, start date, and discretionary data. The third track holds information for ATM use.
- The first six digits of your account number indicate the company that issued the card. The second four digits identify region and branch information. The last five digits are your account number (the last digit being a check number for security purposes).

✳Distribution

- As of 1994, there were 238.9 million MasterCards in circulation worldwide. Of those, 135.6 million were held by Americans.
- MasterCard is accepted in more than 12.7 million locations in more than 220 countries and territories around the world.

For More Information

MasterCard International Incorporated, 888 Seventh Avenue, New York, NY 10106. Or telephone 1-212-649-4600.

Maxwell House Coffee

- **Dye fabric brown inexpensively.** Soak the fabric in a bucket of strong, black Maxwell House Coffee. This technique is also a good way to cover up an unremovable coffee stain on a white tablecloth.

- **Fertilize a garden or houseplants.** Work Maxwell House Coffee grounds into the topsoil.

- **Repair scratched woodwork.** Mix one teaspoon instant Maxwell House Coffee with two teaspoons water. Apply to the scratch with a cotton ball.

- **Start a charcoal fire.** Remove the top and bottom of an empty Maxwell House Coffee can and punch a few holes in the sides of the can. Stand the can in your barbecue grill, fill it with Kingsford charcoal briquets, add lighter fluid, and light. When the coals glow, remove the hot can with tongs and set in a safe place.

- **Prevent dampness in closets.** Fill an empty Maxwell House Coffee can with Kingsford charcoal briquets, punch holes in the plastic cover, and set on the floor in the back of the closet.

- **Repel ants.** Sprinkle dried Maxwell House Coffee grounds outside doors and cracks. Coffee deters ants.

- **Relieve a hangover.** Drink a couple of cups of Maxwell House Coffee. Coffee acts as a vasoconstrictor, reducing the swelling of blood vessels, the cause of headache.

- **Spread grass seed or fertilizer.** Punch holes in the bottom of an empty can of Maxwell House Coffee, fill with grass seed or fertilizer, cover with the plastic lid, and shake the can as you walk through your garden.

- **Transport live fishing bait.** Keep worms in a Maxwell House Coffee can filled with moist coffee grounds.

- **Keep toilet paper waterproof while camping.** Carry a roll of toilet paper inside an empty Maxwell House Coffee can.

- **Protect baby tomato plants.** Remove the tops and bottoms from Maxwell House Coffee cans, place a can over each plant, and step on the can to set it firmly in the soil. Remove cans when plants are a few weeks old.

- **Grow better melons.** Raise melons off the ground by resting them on top of upside-down empty Maxwell House Coffee cans pushed into the soil. The metal cans accumulate heat, making the fruit ripen earlier while also repelling insects.

- **Keep paintbrush bristles from bending while soaking in solvent.** Put solvent in an empty Maxwell House Coffee can, cut an X in the plastic lid, and push the brush handle up through the slit so that the brush hangs in the can rather than resting on its bristles.

- **Highlight brown or red hair.** Rinse your hair with Maxwell House Coffee for a rich and shiny color.

- **Deodorize the refrigerator and freezer.** Place a bowl filled with Maxwell House Coffee grounds on the back shelf.

- **Patch woodwork.** Mix dry instant Maxwell House Coffee with spackling paste until you achieve the desired brown tone, fill the crack or hole, and smooth with a damp cloth.

- **Clean a restaurant grill.** Pour leftover brewed Maxwell House Coffee over a warm or cold grill and wipe clean.

- **Wrap cookies and candies.** Cover an empty Maxwell House Coffee can with wrapping paper, fill with cookies or candy, cover with the plastic lid, then wrap.

- **Cover spots on black suede.** Sponge on a little black Maxwell House Coffee.

- **Make emergency lights.** Wrap reflector tape around a couple of empty Maxwell House Coffee cans and store in the trunk of your car for emergencies.

- **Make stilts.** String rope through holes punched in the closed ends of two empty Maxwell House Coffee cans.

- **Store nails, screws, bolts, and washers.** Maxwell House Coffee cans make perfect storage containers.

- **Improvise a gelatin mold.** Use an empty Maxwell House Coffee can.

- **Store cat box litter in the trunk of your car for emergencies.** Cat box litter, stored in empty Maxwell House Coffee cans, can be used for traction under the wheels of a car stuck in snow or ice.

- **Flavor spaghetti.** Add one-quarter to one-half teaspoon instant Maxwell House Coffee to spaghetti sauce. Coffee gives store-bought spaghetti sauce brown coloring and a less acidic flavor.

✳Invented
1892

✳The Name
Maxwell House Coffee is named after the Maxwell House hotel in Nashville, Tennessee.

A Short History

In 1873, Joel Owsley Cheek, a 21-year-old farm boy, left his home in Burkesville, Kentucky, to seek his fortune in Nashville. After a short stint as a traveling salesman for a wholesale grocery firm, he set up his own grocery firm and began experimenting to originate his ideal coffee blend, which he began selling in 1882. Among his clients was one of America's top-ranked hotels, the Maxwell House of Nashville. The elite hotel guests raved over the new "Maxwell House Coffee." In 1892, Cheek named his blend Maxwell House Coffee.

Legend has it that Theodore Roosevelt tasted the coffee while a guest at the Hermitage, Andrew Jackson's old Nashville home. When asked if he wanted another cup, Roosevelt purportedly responded, "Will I have another? Delighted! It's good to the last drop!" thus giving birth to the catchy slogan and the logo depicting a tilted coffee cup dripping one last drop.

In 1928, C. W. Post's cereal company acquired Cheek-Neal Company, changed the name to Maxwell House Products Company, and, the following year, acquired Clarence Birdseye's General Foods Company. Postum changed its name to General Foods Corporation, and, in 1985, was acquired by Philip Morris Companies, Inc. Three years later, Philip Morris Companies, Inc., acquired Kraft, Inc., and, in 1989, combined it with General Foods Corporation to form Kraft General Foods, Inc. In 1995, Kraft General Foods, Inc., shortened its name to Kraft Foods, Inc.

Ingredient

100 percent pure coffee

Strange Facts

- Maxwell House Coffee's slogan, "Good to the Last Drop," ignited a controversy over the proper use of the word *to*. Pundits asked, "What's wrong with the last drop?" A renowned English professor at Columbia University finally decreed that the word *to* is good usage and includes the last drop. The word *until* would preclude the last drop. The slogan was first used by Coca-Cola in 1908.

- Coffee, native to Ethiopia and cultivated and brewed in Arab countries for centuries, was not introduced into Europe until the seventeenth century.
- The average coffee tree, grown from seed, bears its first fruit after five to eight years and yields approximately one pound of coffee beans each year.
- While the coffee plant has many varieties, two species, *Coffea arabica* and *Coffea robusta*, provide 99 percent of the world's coffee.
- Americans now drink an average of 1.75 cups of coffee a day, nearly half of what they drank in 1962.

✳Distribution

- Maxwell House Coffee is also available in Maxwell House Lite, Maxwell House Master Blend, Maxwell House Filter Packs, Maxwell House Filter Pack Singles, and Maxwell House Filter Packs Decaffeinated.

For More Information

Kraft General Foods, Inc., P.O. Box 131, White Plains, NY 10625. Or telephone 1-800-432-6333.

Maybelline Crystal Clear Nail Polish

- **Stop a run in nylons.** Paint the snag immediately with Maybelline Crystal Clear Nail Polish.

- **Prevent the bottom edges of shaving cream cans from rusting.** Paint the bottom rim of the can with Maybelline Crystal Clear Nail Polish.

- **Thread a needle with ease.** Dip the end of the thread in Maybelline Crystal Clear Nail Polish, let dry, and thread.

- **Protect shirt buttons.** Dab the center of each button with Maybelline Crystal Clear Nail Polish to reinforce the threads so buttons stay on longer.

- **Prevent cut fabric from fraying.** Apply a thin coat of Maybelline Crystal Clear Nail Polish along seam edges to help prevent unraveling.

- **Laminate prescription labels.** Keep prescription labels legible by painting them with Maybelline Crystal Clear Nail Polish.

- **Repair a small dent in a window, car windshield, or wood floor.** Fill hole with a few drops of Maybelline Crystal Clear Nail Polish, let dry, then repeat until full.

- **Prevent the knots of small ribbons on lingerie from untying.** Dab the knots with Maybelline Crystal Clear Nail Polish.

- **Tighten loose dresser-drawer knobs.** Dip the end of the screw in Maybelline Crystal Clear Nail Polish, replace the knob, and let dry for a snug fit.

- **Prevent rust on toilet seat screws.** Paint the screws with Maybelline Crystal Clear Nail Polish.

- **Keep belt buckles shiny.** Paint Maybelline Crystal Clear Nail Polish on the buckle, let dry, and repeat four times.

Invented
1970s

The Name

T. L. Williams named his company in honor of his oldest sister, Mabel, who inspired him to produce an easy-to-use mascara, combining her name with the popular suffix *-line*.

The letter *y* was apparently added to make the spelling and pronunciation of the company name phonetic.

A Short History

In 3000 B.C., Chinese artists combined gum arabic, egg white, gelatin, and beeswax to create varnishes, enamels, and lacquers—which Chinese aristocrats started applying to their fingernails as a status symbol. The Maybelline Company, founded in 1915 by T. L. Williams, introduced Maybelline Cake Mascara in 1917, advertising in magazines and selling the mascara only by mail. In September 1932, Maybelline finally made mascara available in variety stores, followed by eye shadows and eye pencils. In the early 1960s, Maybelline introduced Ultra Lash, the first mass-market automatic mascara. In 1967, Williams sold his company to Plough, Inc., which became Schering-Plough Corp. in 1971. Maybelline introduced Great Lash mascara in 1973 and soon branched into other face, lip, and nail products—including a line of nail polishes. In 1992, Maybelline became a publicly held company.

✳Ingredients

Butyl acetate, ethyl acetate, nitrocellulose, polyester resin, sucrose acetate isobutyrate, isopropyl alcohol, camphor, acrylates copolymer, benzophenone-1, violet no. 2

✳Strange Facts

- The cosmetics industry in the United States includes face makeup (representing 35 percent of sales in 1992), eye cosmetics (30 percent), lip products (23 percent), and nail products (12 percent).
- Maybelline's Great Lash mascara has been the best-selling mascara in the United States since its introduction in 1973.

✳Distribution

- Maybelline markets cosmetics in the United States and 40 international markets (including Indonesia, Peru, Nicaragua, and Iceland) plus the Yardley line of soaps and bath-care products in the United States and Canada.
- In 1993, Maybelline's consolidated net sales were more than $346 million.
- In the United States, Maybelline is the number two cosmetics company, behind Cover Girl and ahead of Revlon.

For More Information

Maybelline, Inc., 3030 Jackson Avenue, Memphis, TN 38112-2018. Or telephone 1-901-324-0310.

McCormick/ Schilling Black Pepper

- **Stop small leaks in a car radiator.** Add a teaspoon of McCormick/Schilling Black Pepper to your radiator. The pepper sinks to the bottom, finds its way into small holes, and expands, filling them.

- **Repel moths.** Use McCormick/ Schilling Black Pepper as an alternative to mothballs. Fill a cheesecloth bag or the foot of a nylon stocking with pepper and use it as a sachet.

- **Stop colors from running.** Add a teaspoon of McCormick/Schilling Black Pepper to the first suds when you are washing cottons.

- **Keep dogs, raccoons, cats, and other animals away from your garden.** Sprinkle McCormick/Schilling Black Pepper around your hedges and flower beds.

- **Repel ants.** Sprinkle McCormick/Schilling Black Pepper in cracks and crevices.

- **Enhance the flavor of ice cream.** *McCormick/Schilling's New Spice Cookbook* recommends softening one quart vanilla or chocolate ice cream just enough to stir (without allowing it to melt), spooning it into a large bowl, and adding one tablespoon crushed green peppercorns, one teaspoon coarse ground black pepper, and one-quarter teaspoon coconut extract. Then eat.

Invented

A natural product, black pepper was most likely incorporated into the McCormick spice line during the 1896 acquisition of F. G. Emmett Spice Company.

The Name

McCormick & Company is named for company founder Willoughby McCormick.

A Short History

In 1889, twenty-five-year-old Willoughby McCormick founded McCormick & Company—crafting fruit syrups, root beer, and nerve and bone liniment in his Baltimore home—and hired three salesmen to peddle his wares door-to-door. A year later, the company was making food coloring, cream of tartar, and blood purifier. In 1896, McCormick bought the F. G. Emmett Spice Company of Philadelphia, firmly committing itself to the spice industry. By the turn of the century, McCormick was regularly trading with the East and West Indies, South Africa, Europe, and Central and South America. The company achieved coast-to-coast distribution in 1947 with the acquisition of A. Schilling & Co., producers of spices and extracts.

Strange Facts

- In 80 B.C., Alexandria, Egypt, became the greatest spice trading port of the eastern Mediterranean, with one of its entrances known as "Pepper Gate."
- In A.D. 410, Alaric the Visigoth demanded one and a half tons of pepper as ransom from Rome. Two years later, he started receiving three hundred pounds of pepper annually from the city.

- During the Middle Ages in Europe, pepper was counted out peppercorn by peppercorn.
- In the eleventh century, many towns kept their accounts in pepper. Taxes and rents were assessed and paid in pepper. A sack of pepper was worth a man's life.
- Between 1784 and 1873, the pepper trade furnished a huge portion of the import duties collected in Salem, Massachusetts, at one point financing 5 percent of the entire United States government's expenses.
- At the turn of the century, unscrupulous spice dealers would cut shipments of peppercorns with mouse droppings.
- The Russians sprinkle pepper on vodka.

Ingredients

Pure ground black pepper

Distribution

- McCormick is the world's largest spice company.
- The company's seasonings are sold under the McCormick brand name in the eastern U.S., the Schilling brand in the West, and under the Club House label in Canada.
- McCormick/Schilling also makes cream of tartar, food coloring, spices, seasoning, and vanilla extract.

For More Information

McCormick & Company, Inc., 18 Loveton Circle, Sparks, MD 21152. Or telephone 1-410-771-7301.

Miller High Life

- **Kill slugs.** Fill jar lids with half an inch of Miller High Life. Slugs love beer and drown in it.

- **Shampoo your hair.** Miller High Life is a terrific shampoo for oily hair, although shampooing your hair too frequently with beer can eventually dry out your scalp and lead to dandruff.

- **Marinate meats.** Marinating inexpensive cuts of meat in Miller High Life for approximately an hour before cooking increases the flavor and tenderness.

- **Lure insects away from an outdoor party or barbecue.** Place open cans of Miller High Life around the perimeter of the yard. Stinging insects, like wasps and yellow jackets, will be attracted to the beer instead of your guests.

- **Fertilize a lawn.** Jerry Baker, author of *The Impatient Gardener*, suggests mixing one cup Listerine, one cup Epsom salts, one cup liquid soap, and one cup ammonia in a one-quart jar, and then filling the rest of the jar with beer. Spray this on up to 2,500 square feet of lawn with a hose-attached sprayer in May and again in late June.

- **Set your hair.** Miller High Life works as a setting lotion. Shampoo your hair, towel dry, and then spray beer onto your hair, using a pump bottle before setting. It's excellent for oily hair.

- **Cook with Miller High Life.** Will Anderson, author of *From Beer to Eternity*, offers recipes for Beer Soup (requiring one quart beer), a Beer Sandwich (calling for three-quarters cup beer), and a Beer Omelet (made with one-half cup beer). The Miller Brewing Company offers a free recipe book, including recipes for Pot Roast with Beer (calling for one cup beer), Beer Burgers (needing three-quarters cup beer), and Beer Cookies (requiring one cup beer).

- **Bake bread.** Sprinkle three to five tablespoons sugar over three cups self-rising flour, add one can Miller High Life, and knead. Put the dough in a greased loaf pan, let stand for five minutes, then bake for forty-five minutes at 350°F. Rub butter over the top and bake for an additional five minutes. Serve warm.

Invented
1855

The Name

Miller beer was named after the company founder Frederick Miller. In 1903, when Miller's son, Carl, sought a new name for the light-colored pilsner, his wife's uncle, Ernst Miller, chanced upon a building down in New Orleans called High Life Cigars. The Miller Brewing Company paid $25,000 for the factory and the right to use the name. The word *beer* is believed to come from the Celtic word *beor*, used to describe the malt brew produced in the monasteries of North Gaul. In 1906, the company adopted "The Champagne of Bottled Beer" slogan to describe Miller High Life.

A Short History

No one knows exactly when people started brewing beer, but the earliest record of beer can be found on a Mesopotamian tablet (circa 7000 B.C.) inscribed with a cuneiform recipe for the "wine of the grain." Anthropologists believe Mesopotamians and Egyptians first developed the process of malting (making barley more suitable for brewing by germinating the barley grains, developing the enzymes that transform starch into fermentable sugars). Vikings brewed *bior* in Scandinavia, and Julius Caesar found the various tribes of the British isles drinking ale when he and his Roman legions landed. More than likely, Gaulish monks first used hops, which have a preservative and aromatic effect on beer.

After revolutionary upheavals ravaged Europe in 1848, hundreds of thousands of Germans immigrated to America, bringing with them a love of golden lager beer and the knowledge of how to brew it. A young German immigrant, Frederick Miller, formerly the brew master at Hohenzollern Castle in Germany, bought the small, five-year-old Plank Road Brewery west of Milwaukee in 1855. Miller produced 300 barrels of high-quality lager beer in his first year, storing the brew in a network of caverns in the hillside behind the brewery.

By Miller's death in 1888, the brewery was producing 80,000 barrels of beer annually. By 1954, under the leadership of Frederick C. Miller, the founder's grandson, Miller Brewing Company was the ninth largest brewery in the world, shipping two million barrels each year. When Philip Morris, the worldwide tobacco and consumer-packaged goods company, acquired the company in 1970, Miller was the nation's seventh largest brewer, producing 5.1 million barrels of beer that year. Philip Morris marketed Miller High Life with the popular "Miller Time" advertising campaign, and by the 1990s, Miller was brewing more than 40 million barrels per year, making it the second largest brewery in the United States, after Anheuser-Busch.

✳Ingredients

Malted barley, select cereal grains, pure water, choicest hops

✳Strange Facts

- During the Inca empire in Cuzco, Peru, beer made from maize was a luxury served by the state on ceremonial occasions.
- The Pilgrims landed at Plymouth Rock in December 1620, because, in the words of a diarist aboard the *Mayflower*, "We could not now take time for further search or consideration, our victuals being much spent, especially our beere."

- George Washington, Thomas Jefferson, and William Penn brewed beer on their estates.
- Miller Brewing, founded twenty-one years before the first Budweiser was brewed in 1876, is the world's third largest beer producer (after Anheuser-Busch and Heineken).
- In 1855, Frederick Miller established a beautifully landscaped twenty-acre beer garden in Milwaukee that attracted weekend crowds for bowling, dancing, fine lunches, and old-fashioned *gemutlichkeit*. The garden caught fire on July 4, 1891, and was ultimately torn down in 1909.
- In 1850, Frederick Charles Best and his brother dug tunnels in the hills behind the Plank Road Brewery to store beer in the days before refrigeration. When Frederick Miller bought the brewery five years later, he expanded the tunnels to a total of 600 feet—enough to store 12,000 barrels of beer. With the advent of refrigeration, the brewery abandoned the caves until 1952, when a portion of the caves was opened to tourists through the Miller Caves Museum.
- When company president Carl Miller took his adolescent daughter Loretta on a visit to the brewery, he sat her at the end of the bar in the dining room. Loretta held her hand up dramatically, inadvertently providing Miller with the inspiration for the High Life "Girl in the Moon." Carl's brother, Fred, sketched the High Life girl, using a photograph of Loretta. Between 1907 and 1911, the "Girl in the Moon" graced metal beer-serving trays used in beer gardens, hotels, bars, and restaurants. The trays and other "Girl in the Moon" promotional materials are now collector's items.
- Hollywood actor Arthur Franz portrayed Miller Brewing Company founder Frederick Miller in a 48-minute commercial film, *With This Ring*, produced in 1955. The movie, filmed in Hollywood, Milwaukee, and Sigmaringen, Germany, followed the story of a fictitious "brewer's ring" allegedly passed on from generation to generation over the 100-year history of the Miller Brewing Company.
- In 1983, Miller received the National Environmental Industry Award from the President's Council on Environmental Quality for excellence in air and water pollution control.
- As a founding member of Keep America Beautiful, the Miller Brewing Company has reduced the amount of aluminum in its cans by 45 percent, saving 100 million pounds of aluminum a year. In addition, recycled materials make up approximately 80 percent of its aluminum cans. Packing

materials are reused three to four times before they are sent to be recycled—keeping 750,000 pounds of corrugated cardboard out of the waste stream and reducing the company's need for new corrugated cardboard by 75 percent.

- Beer is 92 percent water.

Distribution

- In 1994, the Miller Brewing Company sold over $4 billion worth of beer.
- Miller also makes Löwenbräu, Meister Bräu, Milwaukee's Best, Molson, Red Dog, and Sharp's.
- Miller operates breweries in Milwaukee, Wisconsin; Eden, North Carolina; Albany, Georgia; Fort Worth, Texas; Trenton, Ohio; and Irwindale, California.
- Beer is the most popular alcoholic beverage in America, consumed regularly by more than 80 million Americans.
- Beer accounts for nearly 87 percent of all alcoholic beverages consumed in the United States. The average American drinks approximately 23 gallons of beer every year.
- According to New York's Simmons Market Research Bureau, 55.1 percent of all beer drinkers surveyed in 1985 were college educated, while 38.9 percent of all beer drinkers were high school dropouts.

For More Information

Miller Brewing Company, 3939 West Highland Boulevard, P.O. Box 482, Milwaukee, WI 53201-0482. Or telephone 1-800-MILLER6.

Miracle Whip Salad Dressing

- **Condition your hair.** Apply one-half cup Miracle Whip to dry hair once a week as a conditioner. Leave on for thirty minutes, then rinse a few times before shampooing thoroughly.

- **Remove a ring stuck on a finger.** Smear on some Miracle Whip and slide off the ring.

- **Give yourself a facial and tighten pores.** Miracle Whip helps moisten dry skin when applied as a face mask. Wait twenty minutes, then wash it off with warm water followed by cold water.

- **Remove white rings and spots from wood furniture.** Wipe on Miracle Whip, let stand for an hour, and polish the furniture.

- **Remove tar.** Spread a teaspoon of Miracle Whip on tar, rub, and wipe off.

- **Treat minor burns.** Rub Miracle Whip into the burn. Let it set, then wipe off.

- **Soothe sunburn and windburn pain.** Use Miracle Whip as a skin cream.

- **Remove dead skin.** Rub a dab of Miracle Whip into your skin and let it dry for a few minutes. While the skin is moist, massage with your fingertips. Dead skin will rub off your feet, knees, elbows, or face.

- **Remove chewing gum from hair.** Rub a dollop of Miracle Whip into the chewing gum.

✳Invented
1933

✳The Name

The word *miracle* presumably refers to the whip's endless uses rather than to any supernatural properties.

✳A Short History

In the eighteenth century, French Duc de Richelieu discovered a Spanish condiment made of raw egg yolk and olive oil in the port town of Mahón on the island of Minorca, one of the Balearic Islands. He brought the recipe for "Sauce of Mahón" back to France, where French chefs used it as a condiment for meats, renaming it *mayhonnaise*.

When mayonnaise arrived in the United States in the early 1800s, it was considered a haute French sauce, too difficult to prepare. The invention of the electric blender and the advent of bottled dressings catapulted mayonnaise into the mainstream as a sandwich spread. In 1912, Richard Hellmann, a German immigrant who owned a delicatessen in Manhattan, began selling his premixed mayonnaise in one-pound wooden "boats," graduating to glass jars the following year.

To compete with Hellmann's mayonnaise, J. L. Kraft and Bros. Co., a cheese wholesaling business started in Chicago by James Lewis Kraft in 1903, purchased several regional salad dressing companies during the 1920s and introduced Kraft brand mayonnaise in 1930.

During the Depression, when mayonnaise became a luxury item, Kraft introduced Miracle Whip—a spoonable dressing that combined the best features of both mayonnaise and boiled dressing—at the 1933 Chicago World's Fair. The Kraft exhibit attracted millions of visitors, and within seven months, Miracle Whip, advertised on the Kraft Music Hall radio program, became the best-selling salad dressing in America.

✶Ingredients

Soybean oil, water, vinegar, sugar, egg yolks, starch, food starch-modified, salt, mustard flour, spice, paprika, natural flavor

✶Strange Facts

- In 1991, Kraft sold enough Miracle Whip to make 3.8 billion servings of potato salad.
- Miracle Whip contains less fat and 30 percent fewer calories than mayonnaise.
- The Miracle Whip Chocolate Cake, developed by consumers during World War II food rationing, has been the most requested recipe from the Kraft Kitchens.
- Kraft celebrated the fiftieth anniversary of Miracle Whip in 1983 at the Waldorf-Astoria in New York City with a five-foot-high cake in the shape of a Miracle Whip salad dressing jar—complete with the famous red, white, and blue label.

✶Distribution

- Miracle Whip has been the best-selling salad dressing in the United States since 1933.
- Kraft introduced Miracle Whip Light reduced-calorie salad dressing in 1984 and Miracle Whip Free nonfat dressing in 1991.

For More Information

Kraft Foods, Inc., One Kraft Court, Glenview, IL 60025. Or telephone 1-800-543-3733.

Mr. Coffee Filters

- **Filter broken cork from wine.** If you break the cork when opening a wine bottle, filter the wine through a Mr. Coffee Filter.

- **Clean windows and mirrors.** Mr. Coffee Filters are lint-free, so they'll leave your windows sparkling.

- **Protect china.** Separate your good dishes by putting a Mr. Coffee Filter between each dish.

- **Cover bowls or dishes when cooking in the microwave.** Mr. Coffee Filters make excellent covers.

- **Protect a cast-iron skillet.** Place a Mr. Coffee Filter in the skillet to absorb moisture and prevent rust.

- **Apply shoe polish.** Ball up a lint-free Mr. Coffee Filter.

- **Recycle frying oil.** After frying, strain oil through a sieve lined with a Mr. Coffee Filter.

- **Weigh chopped foods.** Place chopped ingredients in a Mr. Coffee Filter on a kitchen scale.

- **Hold tacos.** Mr. Coffee Filters make convenient wrappers for messy foods.

- **Stop the soil from leaking out of a plant pot.** Line a plant pot with a Mr. Coffee Filter to prevent the soil from leaking through the drainage holes.

- **Prevent a Popsicle from dripping.** Poke one or two holes as needed in a Mr. Coffee Filter, insert the Popsicle, and let the filter catch the drips.

Invented

1972

The Name

Inventor Vince Marotta, determined to give his coffeemaker a simple, catchy name, came up with Mr. Coffee off the top of his head.

A Short History

In the 1960s, Vince Marotta presided over North American Systems in Pepper Pike, OH, building shopping malls and housing developments. When business slowed in 1968, Marotta fell ill, and while recuperating in bed, he realized how fed up he was with percolated coffee and decided to develop a better way to make coffee. He contacted the Pan American Coffee Bureau and discovered that South American coffee growers believed that the best way to extract the oil from coffee beans was to pour water, heated to 200°F, over the ground beans. Marotta hired engineer Irv Schultze to devise a bimetal actuator to control the temperature of the water. Observing how restaurants used a white cloth in their large coffee percolators to capture loose grounds and eliminate sediment, Marotta decided to use a paper filter in his coffeemaker.

Marotta showed up at the 1970 Housewares Convention in Chicago with a prototype for Mr. Coffee. On the spot, he hired Bill Howe, a buyer with Hamilton Beach, to represent his product. Howe invited 100 buyers up to Marotta's hotel room for coffee, and, within two years, Mr. Coffee was selling 42,000 coffee machines a day. According to Marotta, the paper filters—"the blade to the razor"—were cut and fluted by a paper company from an existing paper stock. Marotta sold the Mr. Coffee Company in 1987, and the company went public in 1990.

Ingredients

Virgin paper pulp

Strange Facts

- In 1972, Marotta single-handedly convinced Joe DiMaggio to be the spokesman for Mr. Coffee's television commercials, which DiMaggio did for the next fifteen years.
- Mr. Coffee machines outsell both Black & Decker and Proctor-Silex coffee machines by nearly two to one.

Distribution

- Mr. Coffee is the best-selling coffeemaker in the world.
- Since 1972, more than 50 million Mr. Coffee machines have been sold.
- More than 10 billion Mr. Coffee paper filters are sold every year.

For More Information

Mr. Coffee, Inc., Bedford Heights, OH 44146. Or telephone 1-800-321-0370.

Morton Salt

- **Soften a new pair of jeans.** Add one-half cup Morton Salt to detergent in the washing machine.

- **Repel fleas.** Since salt repels fleas, wash doghouses with salt water to prevent fleas.

- **Remove rust from household tools.** Make a paste using two tablespoons Morton Salt and one tablespoon ReaLemon. Apply the paste to rust with a dry cloth and rub.

- **Dissolve soap suds in the sink.** Sprinkle Morton Salt on soap bubbles to make them pop.

- **Clean coffee and tea stains from china cups.** Mix equal amounts Morton Salt and white vinegar.

- **Stop pipes from freezing or thaw frozen pipes.** Sprinkle Morton Salt down waste pipes in cold weather.

- **Clean dust off silk flowers.** Put the flowers in a large paper bag, pour in two cups Morton salt, close the bag, and shake. Salt knocks the dust off the flowers. Remove the flowers from the bag and shake off the excess salt.

- **Remove dandruff.** Shake one tablespoon Morton Salt into dry hair. Massage gently and shampoo.

- **Prevent grass from growing in crevices.** Sprinkle Morton Salt in the cracks. Salt is a corrosive that kills plants.

- **Absorb spilled cooking grease or a broken egg.** Pour Morton Salt immediately on the spill, let sit for twenty minutes, then wipe up.

- **Prevent colors from fading in the wash.** Add one cup coarse Morton Salt to detergent in the washing machine.

- **Keep slugs away.** Sprinkle Morton Salt on the sidewalk close to the grass. When slugs try to approach your house, the salt will kill them by reverse osmosis. This works well in keeping slugs away from pet food, too.

Invented
1912

The Name

Morton Salt is named for company founders Joy and Mark Morton. An advertising agency developed the famous umbrella girl trademark, depicting a little girl standing in the rain with an umbrella over her head and holding a package of salt tilted backward with the spout open and the salt running out. In 1914, Joy Morton's son, Sterling Morton II, then president of the company, suggested the slogan "When It Rains It Pours" to convey the message that Morton Salt would pour easily even in damp weather.

A Short History

In 1879, Joy Morton, one of four sons born to J. Sterling Morton, acting governor of the Nebraska Territory, invested $10,000 to become a partner in E. I. Wheeler & Company, a Chicago company acting as an agent for Onondaga Salt. Following Wheeler's death in 1885, Morton acquired his partner's interest and, with his brother Mark, formed Joy Morton & Co., which soon became one of the largest producers of salt and the only nationwide salt company. In 1910, the partnership, which had acquired several other salt companies, became the Morton Salt Company. In 1912, Joy Morton developed Morton's Table Salt, a new, free-running salt packed in a blue-and-white cardboard canister with an aluminum pouring spout, invented by J. R. Harbeck.

Ingredients

Salt, sodium silicoaluminate, dextrose, potassium iodide

Strange Facts

- The first written reference to salt is found in the story of Lot's wife, who was turned into a pillar of salt when she disobeyed the angels and looked back at Sodom.
- The expression "He is not worth his salt" originated in ancient Greece, where salt was traded for slaves.
- Roman soldiers were paid "salt money," salarium agentum, the origin of the English word salary.
- The superstition that spilling salt brings bad luck may have its origins in Leonardo da Vinci's *Last Supper*, which depicts an overturned salt cellar in front of Judas Iscariot. The French believed that throwing a pinch of salt over the shoulder would hit the devil in the eye, preventing any further foul play.
- The timeless Morton Umbrella Girl has been updated with new dresses and hairstyles five times since she first appeared in 1914. She was updated in 1921, 1933, 1941, 1956, and 1968.
- Salt has an estimated 14,000 specific industrial applications, including general food seasoning, curing of animal hides, the preparation of saline solutions, the manufacture of chlorine gas (to make plastics, insecticides, synthetic fibers, and dyes), and the manufacture of sodium hydroxide (to make rayon, explosives, cosmetics, and pharmaceuticals).
- Salt inhibits the growth of bacteria, yeast, and molds, working as a natural preservative in butter, margarine, salad dressings, sausages, cured meats, and various pickled products. Salt also plays a key role in the leavening of bread, the development of the texture and rind of natural cheeses, the bleached color of sauerkraut, and the tenderness of vegetables.

★Distribution

- In 1994, Morton International sold more than $541 million worth of salt worldwide, manufacturing an extensive line of Highway/Ice Control Salt, Grocery Salt, Water Conditioning Salt, Food/Chemical Processing Salt, and Agricultural Salt.
- Morton International is the number one salt company in North America and the only nationally distributed salt in the United States.

For More Information

Morton International, Inc., Morton Salt, Chicago, IL 60606-1597. Or telephone 1-312-807-2000.

Nestea

UnSweetened

Nestea® 100% Tea

Iced Tea Mix
3 OZ (g)

- **Soothe sunburn pain.** Empty a jar of Nestea into a warm bath. Soak in the tea. The tannic acid will relieve the sunburn pain.

- **Clean a varnished floor, woodwork, or furniture.** Cold Nestea makes an excellent cleaning agent for wood.

- **Remove corns.** Soak the corn in warm Nestea for 30 minutes each day for a week or two until the tannic acid in the tea dissolves the corn.

- **Repair scratched woodwork.** Mix one level teaspoon Nestea with two teaspoons water. Use a cotton ball to apply the paste to the scratched surface.

- **Make a natural air freshener.** Mix up one quart Nestea and add four tablespoons lemon juice. Strain through a Mr. Coffee Filter. Pour into empty spray bottles.

- **Tenderize meat.** Mix Nestea and use one part tea to one part double-strength beef stock as the liquid in a pot roast or stew. The tannin in the tea tenderizes meat.

Invented
1948

The Name

Nestea is an ingenious combination of the first syllable of the company name *Nestlé* (after company founder Henrí Nestlé) and the word tea. The German word *nestlé* means "little nest," and the Nestlé logo was inspired from this meaning.

A Short History

In 1867, amid public concern over infant mortality, Henrí Nestlé of Vevey, Switzerland, developed Farine Lactée, an infant formula made from concentrated milk, sugar, and cereal. Eight years later Nestlé sold his company—then doing business in sixteen countries—for one million francs. In 1905, a year after the company began selling chocolate, Nestlé merged with the Anglo-Swiss Condensed Milk Company of central Switzerland under the Nestlé name. In 1938, Nestlé, then doing business with Brazilian coffee growers, introduced Nescafé instant coffee, which was distributed to American troops during World War II. That same year Nestlé introduced the Nestlé Crunch bar, followed by Nestlé Quik drink mix in 1948 and Taster's Choice coffee in 1966.

The concept of iced tea, first introduced at the 1904 St. Louis World's Fair by a merchant trying to sell warm tea on a hot summer day (by simply pouring the tepid brew over ice), did not become popular until 1948, when Nestlé scientists introduced Nestea hot tea mix. In 1956, Nestlé scientists introduced Nestea iced tea mix, the first 100 percent instant tea soluble in both hot and cold water, popularized in television commercials with the slogan "Take the Nestea Plunge." Nestlé also owns L'Oréal, Libby's, Carnation, Hills Brothers, Vittel, Buitoni, Butterfinger, Baby Ruth, and more than 40 Stouffer's Hotels. In 1991, the Nestlé Beverage Company and the Coca-Cola Company formed Coca-Cola/Nestlé Refreshments Company to market ready-to-drink iced coffee, chocolate, and tea beverages worldwide.

✳Ingredient

100 percent tea

✳Strange Facts

- Today, Nestlé is the largest packaged food manufacturer, coffee roaster, and chocolate maker in the world, operating 438 factories in 63 countries.
- Nestlé is the largest company in Switzerland, yet more than 98 percent of its revenue comes from outside the country.
- While tea is the world's most popular beverage, Americans consume more than 80 percent of their tea iced.

✳Events

The Tea Council of the United States has designated June "National Iced Tea Month."

✳Distribution

- Americans currently drink nearly 35 billion glasses, or seven gallons per person, of iced tea every year, according to Nestea spokesperson Andrea Cook.
- The full line of Nestea iced tea mix products includes Nestea Iced Tea Mix, Nestea 100 Percent Tea, Nestea 100 Percent Tea with Lemon, Nestea Sugarfree Iced Tea Mix, Nestea Ice Teasers, Nestea Tea Bags, Nestea Ready-to-Drink, and Nestea Instant Herb Teas.

For More Information

Nestlé Beverage Company, 345 Spear Street, San Francisco, CA 94105. Or telephone 1-800-637-8535.

Oral-B Mint Waxed Floss

- **Truss poultry for cooking.** Fill the cavity with stuffing, cross the two legs, and tie legs together with Oral-B Mint Waxed Floss. If necessary, sew the cavity closed.

- **Repair the mesh screening on playpens.** Sew up the rip with Oral-B Mint Waxed Floss.

- **Cut a birthday cake.** Oral-B Mint Waxed Floss cuts cake into neat slices.

- **Lift cookies from a cookie sheet.** Slide a strand of Oral-B Mint Waxed Floss between fresh-baked cookies and the cookie sheet.

- **Repair a tent or backpack.** When hiking or camping, Oral-B Mint Waxed Floss makes a durable, strong thread for tough repairs.

- **Sew buttons on heavy coats.** Use Oral-B Mint Waxed Floss as a durable thread.

- **Hang pictures, sun catchers, or wind chimes.** Oral-B Mint Waxed Floss is stronger and more durable than ordinary string.

- **String beaded necklaces.** Oral-B Mint Waxed Floss is thin enough for small beads, yet stronger than thread.

- **Slice cheese.** Oral-B Mint Waxed Floss cuts neatly through cheese for clean slices.

Invented
1994

The Name

Dental floss is a simple combination of the words *dental* and *floss*, stemming from the Latin word *dentalis* and the Danish word *vlos*.

A Short History

The early Egyptians used thread as dental floss, but Johnson & Johnson received the first patent for a woven silk dental floss in 1876. In 1896, Johnson & Johnson made dental floss commercially available in waxed and unwaxed silk. In 1940, at the recommendation of Dr. Charles Bass, Johnson & Johnson switched from silk to nylon. In the 1940s, periodontist Robert Hutson invented Oral-B toothbrushes, the first multitufted, soft-nylon-bristle toothbrushes. In 1984, Gillette branched into dental products with the purchase of Oral-B.

Ingredients

Nylon, plastic, wax, mint

Strange Facts

- Merriam-Webster, Inc., added the verb *floss* to its dictionary in 1974.
- According to Johnson & Johnson, roughly 55 percent of all flossers floss one or more times daily. Of those individuals, 14 percent floss before breakfast, 26 percent floss between breakfast and lunch, 19 percent floss between lunch and dinner, 32 percent floss after dinner, and 67 percent floss just before going to bed.
- Approximately 80 percent of all dental floss consumers prefer waxed floss products.

- Women tend to floss more than men, and people over fifty years of age tend to floss more than children and young adults.

✳Distribution

- Consumers purchase more than 3.5 billion yards of dental floss every year.
- Oral-B is the world's leading producer of dental care products.
- In 1995, Oral-B sold over $441 million worth of products.

For More Information

Oral-B Laboratories, Redwood City, CA 94065. Or telephone 1-415-598-5000.

Oral-B
Toothbrush

- **Clean the grout between bathroom tiles.** Use a clean, old Oral-B Toothbrush to scrub the grout clean.

- **Make a spatter painting.** Place a piece of paper inside a small cardboard box and place leaves, stencils, or flowers on the paper. Cover the opening of the box with a sheet of metal screening secured in place with rubber bands. Dip the Oral-B Toothbrush in paint and scrub it over the screen, allowing the paint to spatter over the paper. Remove the screen and various objects, and let the painting dry.

- **Stake up small plants.** Use the handles from old Oral-B Toothbrushes.

- **Give a manicure or pedicure.** A clean, old Oral-B Toothbrush dipped in soapy water is both gentle and effective for cleaning fingernails and toenails.

- **Neutralize car battery acid to facilitate cleaning.** Use an old toothbrush to scrub encrusted battery terminals clean with a paste made from three parts baking soda to one part water.

- **Clean typewriter keys.** Scrub the keys with a clean, old Oral-B Toothbrush dipped in alcohol.

- **Unblock small appliance vents.** Gently clear lint and dust from the vent with a clean, old Oral-B Toothbrush.

- **Clean artificial flowers and plants.** Use a clean, old Oral-B Toothbrush and soapy water.

- **Clean crevices.** Use a clean, old Oral-B Toothbrush with silver polish to remove tarnish from silver.

- **Groom your eyebrows.** Use a clean, old Oral-B Toothbrush.

- **Clean combs.** Dip a clean, old Oral-B Toothbrush in alcohol and scrub the teeth of the comb.

- **Clean the blade of an electric can opener.** Unplug the can opener and use a clean, old Oral-B toothbrush dipped in alcohol to clean the blade.

- **Clean a food grater.** Scrub the grater with a clean, old Oral-B toothbrush dipped in dishwashing liquid.

- **Clean a motor.** Dip a clean, old Oral-B Toothbrush in kerosene or mineral spirits to remove gunk from crevices.

Invented

1940s

The Name

Oral-B is a combination of *oral* hygiene and the letter *B*, which stands for the word *better*.

A Short History

The nylon-bristle toothbrush is a descendant of the "chew stick," a twig with a frayed end of soft fibers that was rubbed against the teeth to clean them. Chew sticks have been found in Egyptian tombs dating to 3000 B.C. The first bristled toothbrush, made from bristles plucked from the backs of hog's necks and fastened to bamboo or bone handles, originated in China in 1498. Traders from the Orient introduced Europeans to the practice of brushing their teeth, and the few Europeans who adopted the practice opted for horsehair toothbrushes, though most preferred the Roman toothpick. After Du Pont chemists discovered nylon in the 1930s, the company marketed the first nylon-bristle toothbrush in 1938.

In the 1940s, periodontist Robert Hutson invented Oral-B Toothbrushes, the first multitufted, soft-nylon-bristle toothbrushes. In 1984, Gillette acquired Oral-B, enabling Oral-B to make its toothbrushes available in virtually every country in the world.

Ingredients

Nylon, plastic

Strange Facts

- In 1937, the year before Du Pont introduced the first nylon-bristle toothbrush, the United States imported 1.5 million pounds of hog bristles for toothbrushes.
- According to the American Dental Association, 80 percent of all Americans fail to replace their toothbrush until after the bent bristles are no longer fit for cleaning teeth.
- Oral-B Toothbrushes incorporate the features recommended by dental professionals: a long narrow neck designed for more effective brushing of back teeth; a thumb grip for better maneuverability; a rounded head for greater comfort; and polished, end-rounded bristles to help protect gums and tooth enamel.
- Oral-B Indicator bristles fade as the brush wears out.

Distribution

- Oral-B is the world's leading producer of dental care products.
- Oral-B Toothbrushes are used by more dentists and hygienists worldwide than any other toothbrushes.

- Oral-B Toothbrushes are available in straight and angled handles, and in a variety of head sizes and bristle textures.
- In 1995, Oral-B sold over $441 million worth of products.

For More Information

Oral-B Laboratories, Redwood City, CA 94065. Or telephone 1-415-598-5000.

Pam No Stick Cooking Spray

- **Speed up a sled.** Spray Pam No Stick Cooking Spray on the bottom of a sled or an inner tube before taking it out in the snow.

- **Dry nail polish.** After polishing your nails, spray with Pam No Stick Cooking Spray.

- **Prevent cut grass from sticking to the blades of a lawn mower.** Spray the cutting blade of the lawn mower with Pam No Stick Cooking Spray before cutting the lawn.

- **Lubricate bicycle chains and roller-skate wheels.** Spray with Pam No Stick Cooking Spray.

- **Prevent tomato sauce stains on plastic containers.** Spray the insides of the containers with Pam No Stick Cooking Spray before filling the containers with any food containing tomatoes.

- **Season a cast-iron pot or skillet.** Wash in warm, soapy water after each use, wipe thoroughly dry, coat the inside with Pam No Stick Cooking Spray, then wipe clean with a sheet of paper towel.

- **Make salt stick to air-popped popcorn.** Spray the popcorn with Pam No Stick Cooking Spray, then salt it.

- **Help snow or dirt slide off a shovel.** Spray Pam No Stick Cooking Spray on the snow or garden shovel.

- **Prevent a key from sticking in the lock.** Spray the lock and/or the key with Pam No Stick Cooking Spray.

- **Clean soap scum from a shower door.** Spray Pam No Stick Cooking Spray on a soft cloth, and wipe clean.

- **Make cleaning a grater less grating.** Before using the grater, spray it with Pam No Stick Cooking Spray to make cleanup easier.

- **Make defrosting the freezer easier.** After defrosting the freezer, spray it with Pam No Stick Cooking Spray.

- **Prevent dishwasher runners from sticking.** Spray the runners with Pam No Stick Cooking Spray.

- **Prevent squeaky door hinges.** Spray with Pam No Stick Cooking Spray.

- **Make cleaning the broiler pan easier.** Spray the pan with Pam No Stick Cooking Spray before cooking.

- **Prevent Saran Wrap from sticking to a pie or cake.** Spray the underside of the plastic wrap with Pam No Stick Cooking Spray.

- **Make cleaning artificial snow from windows easier.** Before decorating windows with artificial snow, spray the glass lightly with Pam No Stick Cooking Spray.

- **Prevent waffles from sticking to a waffle iron.** Spray Pam No Stick Cooking Spray on the waffle iron.

- **Prevent dough from sticking to a table.** Spray the surface with Pam No Stick Cooking Spray.

- **Prevent car doors from freezing shut.** Spray the rubber gaskets with Pam No Stick Cooking Spray. The vegetable oil seals out water without harming the gasket.

*Invented
1957

*The Name

Pam is believed to be named after the daughter of company cofounder Arthur Meyerhoff. Coincidentally, the archaic meaning of the word *pamper* is "to indulge with rich food."

*A Short History

In 1959, Arthur Meyerhoff and Leon Rubin started Pam Products, Inc., in Chicago, but business wasn't too successful. Two years later, Rubin received a patent for a nonstick cooking oil consisting of lecithin dissolved in an organic solvent and dispensed from an aerosol container. Meyerhoff and Rubin founded Gibraltar Industries to market this new Pam cooking spray, introducing the product on local Chicago television cooking shows. Sales began taking off after Carmelita Pope, a well-known Chicago personality, endorsed Pam and demonstrated its many uses.

In 1971, Gibraltar Industries merged with American Home Products, makers of Chef Boyardee foods and a leader in women's health care products. American Home Products acquired the patent for Pam and began marketing the product through its Boyle-Midway Division, which introduced Butter Flavor Pam in 1984 and Olive Oil Pam in 1989. The following year, American Home Products assumed responsibility for the Pam cooking spray business.

*Ingredients

Canola oil, grain alcohol from corn (added for clarity), lecithin from soybeans (prevents sticking), and propellant

★Strange Facts

- A 1.25-second spritz of Pam No Stick Cooking Spray compares to a tablespoon of butter, margarine, or canola oil. A tablespoon of butter contains 11.5 grams of fat, a tablespoon of margarine contains 11 grams of fat, a tablespoon of canola oil contains 14 grams of fat, and a 1.25-second spritz of Pam No Stick Cooking Spray contains only 1 gram of fat.
- Pam No Stick Cooking Spray, the original and number-one–selling aerosol nonstick cooking spray in the United States, is all natural and does not contain any sodium or cholesterol.
- American Home Products replaced the fluorocarbons in Pam No Stick Cooking Spray with other edible oils to meet environmental standards.

★Distribution

- American Home Products sold $152 million worth of food products in 1993.
- American Home Products makes the estrogen drug Premarin, the most prescribed drug in America, and the contraceptive implant Norplant. The company also makes Advil, Anacin, Chap Stick, Chef Boyardee, Crunch 'n Munch, Denorex, Gulden's, Jiffy Pop, Preparation H, and Robitussin.

For More Information
American Home Food Products, Inc., Five Giralda Farms, Madison, NJ 07940. Or telephone 1-800-PAM-4YOU.

Pink Pearl Eraser

- **Clean piano keys.** Use a Pink Pearl Eraser to remove marks from the ivory keys.

- **Fix a wobbly table.** Cut a Pink Pearl Eraser to fit the bottoms of the table legs and affix with nails or glue.

- **Remove scuff marks from floors.** Simply use a Pink Pearl Eraser.

- **Prevent framed pictures from tilting or scratching the wall.** Glue at least two Pink Pearl Erasers to the bottom edge of the back of the frame.

- **Improvise a pincushion.** In a pinch, keep needles, pins, and safety pins stuck in a Pink Pearl Eraser.

- **Erase fingerprints from woodwork.** Gently rub with a Pink Pearl Eraser.

- **Prevent throw rugs from skidding.** Glue thin slices of a Pink Pearl Eraser to the bottom of the rug at the four corners.

- **Clean cotton upholstery.** Rub lightly with a Pink Pearl Eraser.

- **Store small drill bits.** Twist the bits point-first into a large Pink Pearl Eraser.

- **Clean golf balls.** Pack a Pink Pearl Eraser in your golf bag.

- **Clean gold.** The Pink Pearl Eraser gently scours gold-plated items such as pens and jewelry without damaging the material.

Invented

Circa 1890

The Name

Eberhard Faber commonly named its erasers after its pencils. At the time, Eberhard Faber already had a trademark on a pencil called the "Pearl" that was manufactured exclusively for F. W. Woolworth Company. Since the eraser was pink in color and the company already had rights to the "Pearl" name, Eberhard Faber decided to call it the "Pink Pearl" eraser.

A Short History

In 1848, Eberhard Faber, great-grandson of Casper Faber, who first produced and marketed lead pencils in Nuremberg, Bavaria, in 1761, came to America to establish an import business that included Faber Pencils. In 1861, he started his own pencil factory in New York City. Upon Eberhard Faber's death in 1879, the business was passed down to his twenty-year-old son, John, who demonstrated his business savvy by promptly having his name legally changed to Eberhard Faber II. Eberhard II headed the company until his death in 1946. His nephew, Eberhard III, would have become the next president had he not died a year earlier trying to save the life of his son, Eberhard Faber IV, who was being pulled out to sea by an undertow (Eberhard IV was saved by his uncle, Duncan Taylor). Instead, Eberhard III's widow, Julia Faber, became the major owner of the firm, and ten years later, the company moved to Wilkes-Barre, Pennsylvania. In 1971, Eberhard Faber IV became president and chief executive officer of the company. In 1987, Faber-Castell Corporation purchased Eberhard Faber, and the following year the company's facilities were moved to Lewisburg, Tennessee. In 1994, Newell Co. bought Faber-Castell and merged with Sanford Corporation.

✳Ingredients

Synthetic rubber, factice (a soybean-based filler), and pumice

✳Strange Facts

- Eberhard Faber founded the United States's first pencil factory in New York City in 1861 on the present site of the United Nations building. After being destroyed by a fire in 1872, the pencil plant was relocated to Brooklyn's Greenpoint section.
- Pumice, a volcanic ash from Italy, helps the rubber erase and gives it more erasing power. The unique formulation of rubber and factice gives the Pink Pearl its distinctive aroma and also makes it softer than any other eraser in the world.
- Eberhard Faber was the first company to put erasers on pencils. The idea caught on in the United States immediately, but it has never caught on in Europe. Europeans claim they shun the practice because pencils with erasers encourage schoolchildren to be careless. Students (and just about everyone else in Europe) use separate erasers.
- A poor or abrasive eraser actually loosens and removes the paper fibers. A well-formulated eraser like the Pink Pearl erases by cleaning the paper surface.

✳Distribution

- In 1996, Eberhard Faber sold more than 4.7 million Pink Pearl Erasers. Laid end to end, that's enough erasers to reach from Washington, D.C., to Philadelphia.
- Sanford, the company that owns Eberhard Faber, is the world's largest manufacturer of pencils.

For More Information

Sanford, 551 Spring Place Road, Lewisburg, TN 37091. Or telephone 1-800-323-0749.

Quaker Oats

- **Relieve itching from chicken pox.** Pour one-half cup Quaker Oats in a blender and blend into a powder on medium-high speed, then sift. Put two tablespoons into a warm bath and soak in the oatmeal for 30 minutes.

- **Give your hair a dry shampoo.** Apply dry Quaker Oats to your hair, work it through with your fingers, and brush it out to remove the oils.

- **Give yourself a moisturizing facial.** Make a paste from Quaker Oats, lemon juice, and honey. Apply to face, let sit for ten minutes, then rinse with warm water.

Invented
1877

The Name

In 1887, Henry D. Seymour, one of the founders of a new American oatmeal milling company, purportedly came across an article on the Quakers in an encyclopedia and was struck by the similarity between the religious group's qualities and the image he desired for oatmeal. A second story contends that Seymour's partner, William Heston, an ancestor of Quakers, was walking in Cincinnati one day and saw a picture of William Penn, the English Quaker, and was similarly struck by the parallels in quality.

A Short History

Oatmeal's popularity as a breakfast food soared when Ferdinand Schumacher, a German immigrant running a grocery store in Akron, OH, prepared oatmeal in such a way as to reduce cooking time, packing his prepared oatmeal in convenient glass jars. Schumacher's success inspired the launch of dozens of other oatmeal companies, including the Quaker Mill Company, founded in 1877 in Ravena, OH. Merchants bought oatmeal in nondescript barrels, selling it to customers by scooping it into brown paper bags. In 1880, Henry Crowell, president of the American Cereal Company, visualized the advantages of selling packaged products directly to consumers, packaging Quaker Oats in the now-famous cardboard canister and launching an advertising campaign.

Ingredient

100 percent natural rolled oats

Strange Facts

- The name Quaker Oats inspired several lawsuits. The Quakers themselves unsuccessfully petitioned the U.S. Congress to bar trademarks with religious connotations.
- Explorer Robert Peary carried Quaker Oats to the North Pole, and explorer Admiral Richard Byrd carried Quaker Oats to the South Pole.
- A gigantic likeness of the Quaker Oats man was placed on the White Cliffs of Dover in England, requiring an act of Parliament to have it removed.
- In 1990, when the Quaker Oats Company used Popeye the Sailor Man in oatmeal ads, the Society of Friends objected, insisting that Popeye's reliance on physical violence is incompatible with the religion's pacifist principles. The Quaker Oats Company quickly apologized and ended the campaign.

- In 1988, when nutritionists claimed that oat bran reduced cholesterol, sales for the Quaker Oats Company jumped 600 percent. In July 1992, a major report in the *Journal of the American Medical Association*, sponsored by the Quaker Oats Company, concluded that oat bran lowers blood cholesterol by an average of just 2 to 3 percent. On the bright side, the report claimed that a 1 percent reduction in cholesterol nationwide could lead to a 2 percent decrease in deaths from heart disease.

Distribution

- In 1994, the Quaker Oats Company sold more than $403 million worth of hot cereals (Old Fashioned Quaker Oats, Quick Quaker Oats, and Instant Quaker Oatmeal), nearly six times its closest competitor, private-label brands.
- Old Fashioned Quaker Oats and Quick Quaker Oats are the best-selling "long-cooking" cereals in the United States.
- Instant Quaker Oatmeal is the best-selling "instant" hot cereal. In fact, Instant Quaker Oatmeal is the number three selling breakfast cereal in America.

ReaLemon

- **Remove ink spots from cloth.** While ink is wet, apply ReaLemon liberally to the spot, then wash garment in normal cycle with regular detergent in cold water.

- **Get rid of dandruff.** Apply one tablespoon ReaLemon to your hair. Shampoo, then rinse with water. Rinse again with a mixture of two tablespoons ReaLemon with two cups water. Repeat every other day until dandruff disappears.

- **Write with invisible ink.** Use a cotton swab as a pen to write in ReaLemon on a piece of white paper. Once it dries, hold the paper near a hot lightbulb. The writing will turn brown.

- **Eliminate blackheads.** Apply some ReaLemon over blackheads before going to bed. Wait until morning to wash off the juice with cool water. Repeat for several nights until you see a big improvement in the skin.

- **Create blond highlights**. Rinse your hair with one-quarter cup ReaLemon in three-quarters cup water.

- **Deodorize a cutting board.** Wash with ReaLemon to rid a cutting board of the smell of garlic, onions, or fish.

- **Remove fruit or berry stains from your hands.** Rinse hands with ReaLemon juice.

- **Remove rust and the mineral discolorations from cotton T-shirts and briefs.** Use one cup ReaLemon in the washing machine.

- **Clean a microwave oven.** Add four tablespoons ReaLemon to one cup water in a microwave-safe four-cup bowl. Boil for five minutes in the microwave, allowing the steam to condense on the inside walls of the oven. Then wipe clean.

- **Whiten, brighten, and strengthen fingernails.** Soak fingernails in ReaLemon for ten minutes, brush with a mixture of equal parts white vinegar and warm water, then rinse well.

- **Stop bleeding and disinfect minor wounds.** Pour ReaLemon on a cut or apply with a cotton ball.

- **Relieve poison ivy.** Applying ReaLemon over the affected areas should soothe itching and alleviate the rash.

- **Clear up facial blemishes.** Dab ReaLemon on the spot a few times a day.

- **Eliminate odors in your humidifier.** Add four teaspoons ReaLemon to the water.

- **Relieve rough hands or sore feet.** Apply ReaLemon, rinse, then massage with Star Olive Oil.

- **Clean brass, copper, and stainless steel kitchen sinks**. Make a paste from ReaLemon and salt, scrub gently, then rinse with water.

- **Relieve a cough.** Mix four tablespoons ReaLemon, one cup honey, and one-half cup Star Olive Oil. Heat five minutes, then stir vigorously for two minutes. Take one teaspoon every two hours.

- **Train a dog to stop barking.** Squirt some ReaLemon in the dog's mouth and say "Quiet."

- **Relieve constipation.** Before breakfast, drink four tablespoons ReaLemon in one cup warm water. Sweeten with honey.

Invented
Early 1940s

The Name

Company founder Irvin Swartzberg combined the words *real* and *lemon* and capitalized the shared letter *l* to form the clever hybrid ReaLemon.

A Short History

Irvin Swartzberg founded the Puritan-ReaLemon Company in Chicago and began developing lemon juice products in 1934. His highly perishable products varied in strength and flavor because the lemons were not of uniform quality. In the early 1940s, after years of experimentation, Swartzberg produced a bottled lemon juice that was always consistent in flavor and strength by concentrating the juice of fresh lemons and then adding water. He also enhanced his product with filtration and preservation processes.

Ingredients

Water, lemon juice concentrate, lemon oil, .025 percent sodium benzoate (preservative), .025 percent sodium bisulfite (preservative)

Strange Facts

- Three to four tablespoons ReaLemon equal the juice of one lemon.
- Cutting down on sodium? Use ReaLemon instead of salt on vegetables, fish, chicken, pasta, or rice.

✦Distribution

- ReaLemon is the best-selling lemon juice in the United States and the only nationally distributed brand of bottled lemon juice.

For More Information

Borden, Inc., Columbus, Ohio 43215. Or telephone 1-800-426-7336.

Reddi-wip

- **Lighten coffee.** Use a tablespoon of Reddi-wip as a substitute for milk or cream in a cup of coffee.

- **Shave.** Apply Reddi-wip to wet skin as a substitute for shaving cream.

- **Condition your hair.** Apply one-half cup Reddi-wip to dry hair once a week as a conditioner. Leave on for thirty minutes, then rinse a few times before shampooing thoroughly.

- **Make a sour cream substitute.** Mix three or four drops of lemon juice with one cup Reddi-wip and let sit for thirty minutes.

- **Give yourself a moisturizing facial.** Reddi-wip helps moisten dry skin when applied as a face mask. Wait twenty minutes, then wash it off with warm water followed by cold water.

- **Soothe a burn on the roof of your mouth from hot pizza.** Fill your mouth with Reddi-wip to coat the lesion. Press the Reddi-wip gently against the roof of your mouth with your tongue. Repeat if necessary.

- **Remove makeup.** Wet face with lukewarm water, spread a handful of Reddi-wip on face, rinse clean with lukewarm water, and blot dry.

- **Improve marital relations.** Give new meaning to the phrase "dessert topping."

✳Invented

1948

✳The Name

Reddi-wip calls your attention to the fact that the whipped cream is ready to use because it's already whipped.

✳A Short History

In 1941, 28-year-old Aaron "Bunny" Lapin, a Washington University drop-out selling shirts and socks in his father's clothing emporium in St. Louis, Missouri, went to Chicago to visit his brother-in-law, Mark Lipsky, who was in the milk business. In Lipsky's outer office sat a man trying to sell a product called "Sta-Whip," a substitute whipping cream made of light cream and vegetable fat, held together with a secret chemical stabilizer. Whipping cream, which contains a minimum of 30 percent butterfat, was not made during World War II because war-time restrictions prohibited the manufacture of cream containing more than 19 percent butterfat. At Lapin's suggestion, his brother-in-law bought the rights to the Sta-Whip formula and handed over the business to Lapin.

Lapin returned to St. Louis and made a deal with Valley Farm Dairy. The dairy would make Sta-Whip, Lapin would sell it, and they'd split the profits.

Lapin convinced local bakeries to try making whipped cream cakes with Sta-Whip, and within two weeks, Lapin was making more money with his substitute whipping cream than he was in the clothing store. He then sold his first franchise to Louis Lang, a veteran dairy man in St. Louis, who made the product, sold it in bulk to bakers and in containers to housewives, and paid Lapin royalties.

To avert the slump in whipping cream sales during the summer months, Lapin had a "gun" designed which drug store soda fountain jerks could use to squirt Sta-Whip on ice cream sodas.

To prevent a container of Sta-Whip from spoiling before it could all be used, Lapin decided to develop a disposable pressure-propelled can to dispense Sta-Whip. Fortunately, the process had already been developed. In 1931, Charles Goetz, a senior chemistry major at the University of Illinois, worked part-time in the Dairy Bacteriology Department improving milk sterilization techniques. Convinced that storing milk under high gas pressure might inhibit bacterial growth, Goetz began experimenting—only to discover that milk released from a pressurized vessel foamed. Realizing that cream would become whipped cream, Goetz began seeking a gas that would not saturate the cream with its own bad flavor. At the suggestion of a local dentist, Goetz succeeded in infusing cream with tasteless, odorless, nonflammable nitrous oxide, giving birth to aerosol whipped cream and aerosol shaving cream.

In 1947, Lapin persuaded the Knapp-Monarch Co., an appliance manufacturer in St. Louis, to can his whipped cream—renamed Reddi-wip—and to develop a special nozzle to trap the gas that whips the cream inside the can, forcing out only whipped cream. The next year, Lapin set up Reddi-wip as a corporation, and by 1951, the company was doing $7 million in business.

☆Ingredients

An ultrapasteurized blend of cream, skim milk, whey, sugar, corn syrup, mono- and diglycerides, natural and artificial flavors, carrageenan, whipping gas—nitrous oxide

☆Strange Facts

- In the 1950s, Reddi-wip, Inc. tried to develop aerosol ketchup, aerosol shampoo, aerosol mayonnaise, aerosol mustard, and aerosol iodine.
- Reddi-wip, Inc. sponsored the Arthur Godfrey radio show.
- Company founder Aaron Lapin was nicknamed "Bunny" by his classmates at the University of Washington after they learned that his last name means "rabbit" in French.

- In 1988, at an erotic art exposition in Moscow, a woman was covered in whipped cream and men in the audience were invited to lick it off, according to *Time* magazine.

✳Distribution

- Reddi-wip is available in Instant Real Whipped Light Cream, Deluxe Instant Real Whipped Heavy Cream, Fat Free Whipped Topping, and Non-Dairy Whipped Topping.

For More Information

Visit Reddi-wip on the internet at www.beatricecheese.com. Or write Beatrice Cheese, Inc., Waukesha, WI 53186. Or telephone 1-414-782-2750.

Reynolds Cut-Rite Wax Paper

- **Make hangers glide along a clothes rod.** Rub a sheet of Reynolds Cut-Rite Wax Paper over the clothes rod and hangers will glide back and forth more easily.

- **Preserve autumn leaves.** Place the leaves between two sheets of Reynolds Cut-Rite Wax Paper, then place the wax paper between two sheets of brown paper. Press with a warm iron to seal, then trim the paper around the leaves.

- **Prevent shoe polish from smearing.** Let the shoe polish dry, then rub with a sheet of Reynolds Cut-Rite Wax Paper to remove the excess polish. Use a second sheet of Cut-Rite Wax Paper as a work surface to prevent the shoe polish from spattering the floor.

- **Prevent a mess when whipping cream with an electric beater.** Cut two small holes in the middle of a sheet of Reynolds Cut-Rite Wax Paper, slip the stem of the beaters through the holes, and attach to the machine.

Lower the beaters into the mixing bowl, keeping the wax paper over the bowl, and turn on the machine.

- **Save stamps.** Keep stamps between sheets of Reynolds Cut-Rite Wax Paper to prevent them from sticking together.

- **Prevent spatters in the microwave.** Cover spaghetti and meatballs, chili, or other saucy foods with Reynolds Cut-Rite Wax Paper.

- **Make a crayon sun-catcher.** Using a small pencil sharpener, shave crayons onto a sheet of Cut-Rite Wax Paper. Fold the wax paper in half, covering all the shavings. Press with a warm iron until the crayon shavings melt. When cool, thread string through the top of the wax paper and hang in a window.

- **Improvise a diaper changing pad.** A sheet of Cut-Rite Wax Paper can be used as an easy-to-tote changing mat.

- **Save ingredients when measuring.** When measuring flour, sugar, baking mix, or other dry ingredients, crease a sheet of Cut-Rite Wax Paper down the middle, open it up, and place it on the kitchen countertop. Spoon the ingredient into a dry measuring cup, and level it off with a knife or spatula, letting the excess fall on the wax paper. Pick up the wax paper, and pour the excess back in its canister.

- **Never grease a cake pan again.** Place each pan on a sheet of Cut-Rite Wax Paper, trace around the bottom of the pan, cut out the wax paper circle, and place it in the pan. After baking and cooling, loosen the sides of the cake with a knife. Invert the cake onto a cooling rack, remove the pan, and peel off the wax paper for a smooth surface that's ready to frost.

- **Store candles.** Roll candles in a sheet of Cut-Rite Wax Paper before placing them in a drawer or storage box to protect them from getting scuffed.

- **Resurface a metal sliding board.** Rub a sheet of Reynolds Cut-Rite Wax Paper on the metal slide.

- **Prevent a skin from forming in paint cans.** Place the paint can lid on a sheet of Reynolds Cut-Rite Wax Paper, trace around the lid, and cut a pattern from the wax paper. Lay the wax paper directly on the surface of the paint in the can and replace the lid. The wax paper will keep oil- or water-based paints fresh for months.

- **Shine kitchen appliances and counters.** Buff appliance exteriors and counter tops with a sheet of Reynolds Cut-Rite Wax Paper.

- **Fix a stuck metal zipper.** To make a metal zipper work smoothly, run a sheet of Reynolds Cut-Rite Wax Paper up and down the teeth.

- **Seal a wooden salad bowl.** Wash and dry the wooden salad bowl thoroughly, then rub the entire bowl with a sheet of Reynolds Cut-Rite Wax Paper.

- **Clean and shine a floor between waxings.** Put a piece of Reynolds Cut-Rite Wax Paper under the mop head and clean.

Invented
1927

The Name

Reynolds Metals was named after company founder Richard S. Reynolds Sr. The Reynolds logo, used since 1935, was inspired by Raphael's version of *St. George and the Dragon*. The legend of England's patron saint, depicted in several noted paintings, symbolizes the crusading spirit.

A Short History

Early in his career, Richard S. Reynolds worked for his uncle, tobacco king R. J. Reynolds. In 1919, the young Reynolds started his own business, the U.S. Foil Co., supplying tin-lead wrappers to cigarette and candy companies. When the price of aluminum dropped in the 1920s, Reynolds switched to the new lightweight, noncorrosive metal. In 1924, U.S. Foil bought the company that made Eskimo Pies, the ice cream product wrapped in foil. Four years later, Reynolds purchased Robertshaw Thermostat, Fulton Sylphon, and part of Beechnut Foil, adding the companies to U.S. Foil to form Reynolds Metals. Foreseeing a need for aluminum if the United States became involved in World War II, Reynolds Metals began mining bauxite (aluminum ore) in Arkansas in 1940 and opened its first aluminum plant near Sheffield, Alabama, the following year. Reynolds Metals pioneered the development of aluminum siding in 1945 and Reynolds Wrap Aluminum Foil in 1947. In 1982, the company introduced Reynolds Plastic Wrap.

Ingredients

Paper and wax

Strange Fact

- Each year Reynolds Metals sells enough Cut-Rite Wax Paper to circle the globe more than fifteen times.

Distribution

- Reynolds Metals also makes Reynolds Wrap Aluminum Foil, Reynolds Plastic Wrap, Reynolds Oven Bags, and Reynolds Freezer Paper.
- Reynolds Metals is the second largest aluminum company in the United States (behind Alcoa), and the third largest aluminum company in the world (behind Canada's Alcan Aluminum).

For More Information

Reynolds Metals Company, 6601 West Broad Street, P.O. Box 27003, Richmond, VA 23261-7003. Or telephone 1-804-281-2000.

- **Remove rust spots from chrome car bumpers.** Rub the bumper with a crumpled-up piece of Reynolds Wrap dipped in Coca-Cola.

- **Keep dogs and cats off furniture.** Place pieces of Reynolds Wrap on the furniture. The sound of rustling foil frightens pets.

- **Clean pots and pans when camping.** A crumpled-up piece of Reynolds Wrap makes an excellent pot scrubber.

- **Fix battery-operated toys or appliances.** If the batteries in a Walkman or a toy are loose as the result of a broken spring, wedge a small piece of Reynolds Wrap between the battery and the spring.

- **Speed up your ironing.** Place a piece of aluminum foil under the ironing board cover to reflect the heat from the iron.

- **Make decorative trays or holiday decorations.** Cut cardboard into desired shape and size and cover with Reynolds Wrap.

- **Catch messy oven drips.** Tear off a sheet of Reynolds Wrap a few inches larger than baking pan. Place foil on the oven rack below the food being baked. (To prevent damage to the oven, do not use foil to line the bottom of the oven.)

- **Avoid paint splatters.** Mold Reynolds Wrap around doorknobs when painting.

- **Polish chrome.** Use a piece of crumpled-up Reynolds Wrap to polish the chrome on strollers, high chairs, and playpens.

- **Improvise a funnel.** Double over a piece of Reynolds Wrap and roll into the shape of a cone.

- **Secure plant cuttings.** Place Reynolds Wrap across the top of a glass jar filled with water. Poke holes in the foil and insert the cuttings securely in place. The foil also prevents the water from evaporating too quickly.

- **Make a disposable palette.** Mix paints on a piece of Reynolds Wrap.

- **Clean tarnished silverware.** Line a metal cake pan with Reynolds Wrap and fill with enough water to cover the silverware. Add two tablespoons baking soda per quart of water. Heat the water above 150°F. Place the tarnished silverware in the pan so it touches the aluminum foil. Do not let the water boil. The hydrogen from the baking soda combines with the sulfur in the tarnish, removing the stains.

- **Clean a barbecue grill.** After barbecuing, place a sheet of Reynolds Wrap on the hot grill. The next time you use the barbecue, peel off the foil, crinkle it into a ball, and rub the grill clean, easily removing all the burned food.

- **Re-adhere a linoleum floor tile.** Put a piece of Reynolds Wrap on top of the tile and run a hot iron over it several times to melt the glue underneath. Place several books on top of the tile until the glue dries completely.

- **Prevent steel wool from rusting.** Wrap the pad in Reynolds Wrap and store it in the freezer.

- **Clean starch off an iron.** Run the iron over a piece of Reynolds Wrap.

- **Store wet paint brushes.** Wrap the wet brushes in Reynolds Wrap and store them in your freezer. When you're ready to paint again, defrost the brushes for an hour or more.

- **Store leftover paint.** To prevent a layer of skin from forming over the paint surface, set the paint can on top of a sheet of Reynolds Wrap, trace around it, cut out a disc of foil, and place it on the paint surface before sealing the can closed.

Invented

1947

The Name

Reynolds Wrap aluminum foil was named after the founder of Reynolds Metals Company, Richard S. Reynolds, Sr. The Reynolds logo, used since 1935, was inspired by Raphael's version of *St. George and the Dragon*. The legend of England's patron saint, depicted in several noted paintings, symbolizes the crusading spirit.

A Short History

Richard S. Reynolds worked for his uncle, tobacco king R. J. Reynolds, manufacturing the thin sheets of tin and lead foil then used to wrap cigarettes. In 1919, the young Reynolds started his own business, the U.S. Foil Co., supplying tin-lead wrappers to cigarette and candy companies. When the price of aluminum dropped in the 1920s, Reynolds switched to the new lightweight, noncorrosive metal. Reynolds Metals started producing aluminum siding, boats, cookware, and kitchen utensils. In 1947, Richard S. Reynolds introduced a .0007-inch-thick aluminum foil capable of conducting heat quickly and sealing in moisture.

Ingredients

Aluminum

✴Strange Facts

- About 500 million pounds of aluminum foil and foil containers are used in the United States every year. That's equal to eight million miles of aluminum foil.
- To recycle sheets of Reynolds Wrap aluminum foil used for cooking, simply rinse well to remove food particles. For the Reynolds Aluminum Recycling Center nearest you, call 1-800-344-WRAP.

✴Distribution

- Reynolds Wrap can be found in three out of four American households.
- As the only nationally distributed brand of aluminum foil, Reynolds Wrap is also the best-selling aluminum foil in America.

For More Information

Consumer Products Division, Reynolds Metals Company, Richmond, VA 23261. Or telephone 1-800-433-2244.

Saran Wrap

- **Create a miniature greenhouse to help seeds germinate.** Lay a sheet of Saran Wrap over four Popsicle sticks inserted into a seed tray. The Saran Wrap creates a tiny greenhouse, providing enough humidity to keep the growing medium moist for germination. If too much moisture collects on the inside of the plastic, remove it for a few hours.

- **Protect a book cover.** Use a sheet of Saran Wrap to protect a dust jacket.

- **Temporarily repair a window.** Tape Saran Wrap over a small hole to keep out wind, rain, or snow.

- **Hold a screw in position.** Push the screw through a small piece of Saran Wrap, fit the screwdriver into the groove in the head, gather up the edges of the Saran Wrap and hold back over the blade of the screwdriver, and screw.

- **Prevent a layer of skin from forming inside a paint can.** Place a sheet of Saran Wrap over the open paint can before tapping the lid closed with a hammer.

✦ Invented
1953

✦ The Name

Saran, the trademark name for vinylidene chloride polymer, was made up by Dow chemists, who added the word *Wrap* to clarify the new plastic's purpose.

✦ A Short History

Swiss chemist and businessman Jacques Brandenberger invented cellophane and spent the next ten years developing the machinery to mass-produce his invention. In 1908, he patented the manufacturing process, and in 1911, he began selling cellophane, named from *cell*ulose (the wood pulp derivative used to make the film) and the Greek word *diaphanes* ("transparent"). Coating cellophane with polyvinylidene chloride gives the film the lowest gas and moisture transmission.

   Meanwhile, in Midland, Michigan, Herbert Dow had developed a process in 1897 to use electricity to extract bromides and chlorides from underground brine deposits. He founded Dow Chemical, and the company's first product was chlorine bleach. In the 1940s, Dow research yielded synthetic plastics, leading to the introduction of Saran Wrap, the company's first major consumer product, in 1953. Plastics and silicone products boosted sales, catapulting Dow to the forefront of U.S. companies with sales topping $1 billion in 1964. Today polyvinylchloride and polypropylene films have replaced cellophane in almost every use where heat is not present.

✦ Ingredient

Plastic film

✦ Strange Facts

• When Carl Reiner asked Mel Brooks as the 2,000-Year-Old Man to name the greatest invention in the history of the world, Brooks replied, "Saran Wrap."

- The unique composition of Saran Wrap provides the highest temperature tolerance and resistance to hot fats and oils, making it the best product for use in a microwave oven. It is strong enough to go directly from the freezer to the microwave without melting or tearing. (Always turn back one corner of the plastic wrap to let excess steam escape during cooking. And never use any plastic wrap to microwave foods with a high sugar content. These foods can be extremely hot and may cause plastic wrap to melt.)
- Rumor contends that a piece of Saran Wrap can be used as an impromptu condom. It does not work. Plastic film does not withstand the friction of sexual intercourse, nor does it provide an adequate barrier against sperm.

✳Distribution

- Dow operates 68 manufacturing plants in the United States and 115 plants in thirty-one foreign countries.
- Dow, the nation's number-two chemical company (after Du Pont), also makes Ziploc Storage Bags, Handi-Wrap, Spray 'n Wash, and Dow Bathroom Cleaner.

For More Information

DowBrands L.P., P.O. Box 68511, Indianapolis, IN 46268-0511. Or telephone 1-800-428-4795.

Scotchgard

- **Make ski pants.** Spray a pair of old jeans with Scotchgard. Be sure to wear long underwear for warmth.

- **Protect white gloves.** Spray with Scotchgard before you wear them.

- **Preserve sewing patterns.** Spray a new pattern with Scotchgard to prevent rips, tears, and wrinkles.

- **Waterproof an umbrella.** Spray the fabric on an umbrella with Scotchgard so water runs off with a quick shake, allowing the umbrella to dry faster.

- **Waterproof tents, backpacks, and sleeping bags.** Stay dry during a camping trip by spraying your gear with Scotchgard.

- **Protect mattresses from bed wetters.** Spray mattresses with Scotchgard to resist moisture.

- **Keep schoolbooks and supplies dry inside a student's backpack.** Spray the outside of a student's backpack with Scotchgard.

- **Protect neckties from spills.** Spray ties with Scotchgard so spills roll right off.

☀Invented
1956

☀The Name

Scotchgard is a combination of the words *Scotch*, meaning "Scotsman," and a misspelling of *guard*, meaning "to protect."

☀A Short History

In 1902, 3M was started by five businessmen in Two Harbors, Minnesota, to sell corundum to manufacturers of grinding wheels. When that failed, the company moved to Duluth and converted an old flour mill to a sandpaper factory, eventually moving to St. Paul in 1910. The company introduced Scotch brand masking tape in 1925, followed by Scotch brand cellophane tape in 1930.

In 1944, 3M bought the rights to a process for producing fluorochemical compounds. The company's researchers could not find any practical uses for the process or its reactive, fluorine-containing by-products—until a laboratory assistant accidentally spilled a sample of the substance on one of her tennis shoes. The assistant could not wash the stuff off with water or hydrocarbon solvents, and the stained spot on her tennis shoe also resisted soiling. Two 3M chemists, Patsy Sherman and Sam Smith, realized that this substance might be used to make textiles resist water and oil stains, and went to work to enhance the compound's ability to repel liquids, giving birth to Scotchgard.

Dr. Richard Smith, the son of Sam Smith, led a team of scientists working to eliminate the ozone-depleting chemical methyl chloroform in the product his father developed. In 1994, 3M introduced the new water-based Scotchgard.

☀Ingredients

Naphthol spirits, carbon dioxide, heptane, fluoroalkyl polymer, petroleum distillate, trichloroethane

✳Strange Fact

- 3M voluntarily phased out most uses of chlorofluorocarbons (CFCs) and other Class I ozone-depleting chemicals in its operations worldwide by the end of 1992, four years before the United States government mandate for 1996.

✳Distribution

- In 1977, there were nearly thirty formula variations for Scotchgard for protecting materials including furniture fabrics, wall coverings, luggage, and carpets.

For More Information

3M Home & Commercial Care Products, P.O. Box 33068, St. Paul, MN 55133. Or telephone 1-800-364-3577.

Scotch Packaging Tape

- **Cork a wine or champagne bottle.** Wipe the lip of the bottle dry and seal tightly with a small piece of Scotch Packaging Tape.

- **Remove splinters.** Place Scotch Packaging Tape over the splinter and gently peel off.

- **Remove fuzz, lint, and pet hair from clothing and furniture.** Wrap a strip of Scotch Packaging Tape around your hand, adhesive side out, and pat.

- **Hold wires in place while soldering.** Use Scotch Packaging Tape.

- **Clean a metal file.** Put a piece of Scotch Packaging Tape over the length of the file, press firmly, then peel off. The shavings will stick to the tape.

- **Provide first aid in an emergency.** Bandage wounds with torn sheets and Scotch Packaging Tape, or make emergency splints with two-by-fours and Scotch Packaging Tape.

- **Kill ants.** Use a strip of Scotch Packaging Tape to pick up an advancing line of ants.

- **Repair clothes in an emergency.** Scotch Packaging Tape will hold fabric together until you can find a needle and thread.

- **Tag the pull cord that opens the drapes.** Wrap a half-inch piece of Scotch Packaging Tape at eye level around the right cord.

- **Remove dust balls from under a bed or couch.** Wrap Scotch Packaging Tape, adhesive side out, to the end of a broomstick, and slide it under the furniture.

- **Detain crooks.** Wrap a captured thief or burglar securely to a chair with Scotch Packaging Tape, call 911, and wait for the police.

- **Remove a broken windowpane.** Wearing gloves, crisscross Scotch Packaging Tape on both sides of the broken glass, tap the inside edges with a hammer until the pane breaks free, then peel off the tape to remove any shards.

- **Secure the lid on a barbecue grill for transportation purposes.** Simply use Scotch Packaging Tape.

- **Repair torn book covers.** Adhere the cover back to the binding with Scotch Packaging Tape.

- **Organize cables and extension cords.** Tape the cords together with Scotch Packaging Tape.

- **Prevent picnic tablecloths from blowing away.** Tape the corners to the table with Scotch Packaging Tape.

- **Reinforce game and puzzle boxes.** Fortify the corners of boxes with Scotch Packaging Tape.

- **Attach loose speakers to a boom box.** Use Scotch Packaging Tape.

- **Label suitcases.** Write your name and address on two index cards and use Scotch Packaging Tape to tape one card inside the suitcase and another on the outside.

- **Hang any item on a pegboard.** Fold a piece of Scotch Packaging Tape over the edge of any small object, punch a hole in the tape, and hang on a peg.

- **Repair a broken taillight.** Use Scotch Packaging Tape to hold the translucent red plastic in place.

- **Fix a frayed shoelace tip.** Wrap the frayed end with a small strip of Scotch Packaging Tape.

- **Repair a disposable diaper.** If the adhesive tab doesn't stick, tape the diaper together with Scotch Packaging Tape.

⋆Invented
1940

⋆The Name

The name Scotch tape actually resulted from an ethnic slur foisted upon manufacturers of the tape—although the product does not have any connection with Scotland or the Scottish.

In 1925, the automobile industry, eager to satisfy Americans' craving for two-tone cars, had difficulty making a clean, sharp edge where one color met another. Richard Drew, a 25-year-old laboratory employee primarily involved with abrasives used to make sandpaper at the Minnesota Mining and Manufacturing Company (better known as 3M), developed a two-inch-wide strip of paper tape coated with a rubber-based adhesive. To cut costs, he had the masking tape coated with only a strip of glue one-quarter-inch wide along each edge, instead of coating the entire two-inch width.

Unfortunately, the tape failed to hold properly, and the painters purportedly told the 3M salesman, "Take this tape back to those Scotch bosses of yours and tell them to put adhesive all over the tape, not just on the edges." The 3M Company complied, but when the salesman returned to the automobile paint shop, a painter derogatorily asked him if he was still selling that "Scotch" tape, launching a trade name based on an ethnic slur denoting stinginess. The name, like the improved tape, stuck.

A Short History

In 1929, the Flaxlinum Company asked 3M to develop a water- and odor-proof tape to seal the wrapping on insulation slabs in railroad refrigeration cars. Drew coated Du Pont's new moisture-proof cellophane with a rubber-based adhesive, which, while not strong enough for insulation slabs, was marketed to the trade as Scotch Tape—"the only natural, transparent, quick seal for 'Cellophane.'" Since then, the 3M Company has developed more than nine hundred kinds of pressure-sensitive tapes from Drew's invention, including Scotch Packaging Tape.

Ingredients

Polypropylene, adhesive

Strange Fact

- 3M produced a gold reflective Scotch tape that was used in a lunar landing vehicle as insulation against the temperature extremes of space.

Distribution

- Scotch brand tapes also include Scotch Transparent Tape, Scotch Mailing Tape, and Scotch Strapping Tape.

For More Information

3M Consumer Stationery Division, P.O. Box 33594, St. Paul, MN 55133. Or telephone 1-800-364-3577.

Scotch Transparent Tape

- **Trim bangs.** Place a piece of Scotch Transparent Tape across the bangs and cut the hair just above the tape.

- **Help keep long-stemmed flowers standing upright in a vase.** Criss-cross Scotch Transparent Tape across the mouth of the vase.

- **Avoid losing small parts when fixing an appliance.** Before dismantling the item, tape a strip of Scotch Transparent Tape, adhesive side up, on your worktable. Place the parts on the tape in the order you remove them, so they are ready to be reassembled.

- **Make sewing snaps on clothing a snap.** Tape the snaps, hooks, and eyes to the garment, sew them on right along with the Scotch Transparent Tape, then pull the tape off.

- **Fix a broken eyeglass lens temporarily.** Use a small piece of Scotch Transparent Tape at the top and bottom of the crack.

- **Restring a necklace of beads of graduated sizes.** Tape a strip of Scotch Transparent Tape, adhesive side up, on a desktop. Arrange beads in order on the tape, then restring.

- **Attach a sewing pattern to fabric.** Use Scotch Transparent Tape to tape the pattern to the material, then cut the pattern, leaving a reinforced edge.

- **Prevent a plaster wall from crumbling when driving a nail into it.** Make a small X over the spot with two strips of Scotch Transparent Tape, then drive in the nail.

- **Caddie nails.** Place nails between layers of Scotch Transparent Tape so they are readily available.

- **Prevent knickknacks from scratching highly polished table tops.** Line the bottoms of the objects with Scotch Transparent Tape.

- **Fix a frayed shoelace tip.** Wrap the frayed end with a small strip of Scotch Transparent Tape.

- **Protect labels on prescription medicines.** Cover the label with Scotch Transparent Tape.

- **Stop a run in panty hose.** In an emergency, place a piece of Scotch Transparent Tape over the snag.

- **Prevent small children from poking objects into electrical outlets.** Cover the sockets with Scotch Transparent Tape.

- **Save recipes clipped from magazines.** Simply use Scotch Transparent Tape to attach the clipped recipes to index cards.

- **Keep seed markers in the garden legible.** Cover the seed markers with Scotch Transparent Tape.

- **Sew in a zipper.** Baste the seam closed, press open, tape the zipper face down along the basted seam on the wrong side of the fabric (allowing the tape to hold the zipper flat). Sew on a machine, then remove the tape and basting.

- **Straighten bent stems in your garden.** Make a splint with a Popsicle stick and Scotch Transparent Tape.

- **Kill ants.** Wrap a long strip of Scotch Transparent Tape around your hand, adhesive side out, to pick up an advancing line of ants.

✳Invented
1929

✳The Name

The name Scotch tape resulted from an ethnic slur foisted upon manufacturers of the tape—although the product does not have any connection with Scotland or the Scottish.

In 1925, the automobile industry, eager to satisfy Americans' craving for two-tone cars, had difficulty making a clean, sharp edge where one color met another. Richard Drew, a 25-year-old laboratory employee at the Minnesota Mining and Manufacturing Company (better known as 3M), developed a two-inch-wide strip of paper tape coated with a rubber-based adhesive. To cut costs, the masking tape was coated with a strip of glue one-quarter-inch only wide along the edges, instead of covering the entire two-inch width.

Unfortunately, the tape failed to hold properly, and the painters purportedly told the 3M salesman to "Take this tape back to those Scotch bosses of yours and tell them to put adhesive all over the tape, not just on the edges." The 3M Company complied, but when the salesman returned to the automobile paint shop, a painter derogatorily asked him if he was still selling that "Scotch" tape, launching a trade name based on an ethnic slur denoting stinginess. The name, like the improved tape, stuck.

✳A Short History

In 1929, the Flaxlinum Company of St. Paul asked 3M to develop a moisture-proof, transparent tape to seal the wrapping on insulation slabs in railroad refrigerator cars. Richard Drew, the inventor of masking tape, coated Du Pont's new moisture-proof cellophane with a pressure-sensitive rubber-based adhesive, which, while not strong enough for insulation slabs, was marketed as Scotch Cellulose Tape to the trade in 1930 as "the only natural, transparent, quick seal for 'Cellophane.'"

In the meantime, the process for heat-sealing cellophane had been developed, virtually eliminating the need for Scotch tape. But Americans, caught in the midst of the Depression, soon discovered that Scotch tape could be used to mend torn pages of books, fix broken toys, and seal open cans of evaporated milk.

Because the end of Scotch tape tends to stick to the roll, camouflaged by its transparency, in 1932 John A. Borden, a 3M sales manager, invented the tape dispenser with a ledge to keep the end of the tape away from the roll and incorporated a serrated edge to cut the tape.

✳Ingredients

Cellophane, adhesive

✳Strange Facts

- After cows ate the resin-coated fabric on the rudder section of a 1946 Taylor craft airplane, the plane's owner, Edward Bridwell, used Scotch Transparent Tape to repair it.
- Ornithologists have used Scotch Transparent Tape to cover cracks in the soft shells of fertilized pigeon eggs, allowing the eggs to hatch.
- Landlords in Bangkok, Thailand, have used Scotch Transparent Tape to repair cracks in the walls of tenants' apartments.
- During the Depression, banks first used Scotch Transparent Tape to mend torn currency.
- During World War II, 3M stopped selling Scotch Transparent Tape to civilians because the military wanted it all. At least one American munitions factory used transparent tape as a conveyor belt to move bullets.
- Also during World War II, England's Ministry of Home Defense used more than ten million yards of Scotch Transparent Tape on windows to minimize flying glass during air raids.
- In 1961, 3M engineers perfected the tape so that it would never yellow or ooze adhesive. Scotch Magic Transparent Tape, with its matte finish backing, disappears when applied. It is also water resistant, and you can write on it.
- Scotch tape has been used as an anticorrosive shield on the Goodyear blimp.
- The Scottish tartans used to designate Scotch tapes were exclusively designed for the 3M Company by New York color consultant Arthur Allen in the 1940s.

⋆Distribution

- Scotch tape, the best-selling tape of any kind in the world, is found in virtually every home and office in the United States.
- Scotch-brand tapes also include Scotch Packaging Tape, Scotch Magic Tape, and Scotch Double Stick Tape.
- Today, 3M makes more than 300 different types of tapes.

For More Information

3M Consumer Stationery Division, Box 33594, St. Paul, MN 55133. Or telephone 1-800-364-3577.

Silly Putty

THE ORIGINAL

NOTHING ELSE IS...

Silly Putty®

WARNING:
CHOKING HAZARD- Small parts.
Not for children under 3 yrs.

- **Align and test CAT scanners.** Silly Putty's specific gravity is similar to human flesh.

- **Clean ink and ribbon fiber from typewriter keys.** Roll Silly Putty into a ball and press into the typewriter keys.

- **Collect cat fur and lint.** Flatten Silly Putty into a pancake and pat the surface.

- **Lift dirt from car seats.** Mold Silly Putty into whatever shape best fits into crevices.

- **Strengthen hands and forearm muscles.** Squeeze Silly Putty for ten minutes every day in each hand.

- **Fix a wobbly table.** Place a piece of Silly Putty under a leg.

- **Stop a small machine part from rattling.** Wrap Silly Putty as a buffer between two pieces of rattling metal.

- **Calm your nerves.** Playing with Silly Putty has therapeutic value in reducing emotional pressure and calming nerves.

✳ Invented
In the 1940s

✳ The Name

Toy store proprietor and former advertising copywriter Paul Hodgson came up with the name Silly Putty off the top of his head while playing with the pink polymer.

✳ A Short History

In the 1940s, when the United States War Production Board asked General Electric to synthesize a cheap substitute for rubber, James Wright, a company engineer assigned to the project in New Haven, CT, developed a pliant compound dubbed "nutty putty" with no real advantages over synthetic rubber. In 1949, Paul Hodgson, a former advertising copywriter running a New Haven toy store, happened to witness a demonstration of the "nutty putty" at a party. He bought 21 pounds of the putty for $147, hired a Yale student to separate it into half-ounce balls, and marketed the putty inside colored plastic eggs as Silly Putty. When it outsold every other item in his store, Hodgson mass-produced Silly Putty as "the toy with one moving part," selling up to 300 eggs a day. *The New Yorker* featured a short piece on Silly Putty in "Talk of the Town," launching an overnight novelty in the 1950s and 1960s.

✳ Ingredients

Boric acid, silicone oil

✳ Strange Facts

- In 1961, Silly Putty attracted hundreds of Russians to the United States Plastics Expo in Moscow.
- The astronauts on *Apollo 8* played with Silly Putty during their flight and used it to keep tools from floating around in zero gravity.

- **Tighten a screw.** Wrap a few steel strands from an S.O.S Steel Wool Soap Pad around the threads of a screw.

- **Plug up mouse holes.** Plug small cracks and holes with S.O.S Steel Wool Soap Pads.

⊀Invented
1913

⊀The Name

Mrs. Edwin Cox, the inventor's wife, named the soap pads S.O.S., for "Save Our Saucepans," convinced that she had cleverly adapted the Morse code international distress signal for "Save Our Ships." In fact, the distress signal S.O.S. doesn't stand for anything. It's simply a combination of three letters represented by three identical marks (the *S* is three dots, the *O* is three dashes). The period after the last *S* was eventually deleted from the brand name in order to obtain a trademark for what would otherwise be an international distress symbol.

⊀A Short History

In 1917, Edwin Cox, a struggling door-to-door aluminum cookware salesman in San Francisco, developed in his kitchen a steel wool scouring pad caked with dried soap as a free gift to housewives to get himself invited inside their homes to demonstrate his wares and boost sales. A few months later, demand for the soap-encrusted pads snowballed. Cox quit the aluminum cookware business and went to work for himself.

⊀Ingredients

Steel wool, soaps, all-purpose detergents

⊀Strange Facts

- To prevent an S.O.S Steel Wool Soap Pad from rusting, wrap it in aluminum foil and place it in the freezer.

- S.O.S boxes are made from 100 percent recycled paperboard, with a minimum 35 percent post-consumer content.

✳Distribution

- For 75 years, S.O.S has been America's best-selling steel wool soap pads.
- S.O.S Steel Wool Soap Pads are also available in Lemon Fresh Scent and Junior pads.

For More Information

The Clorox Company, 1221 Broadway, Oakland, CA 94612. Or telephone 1-510-271-7000.

SPAM Luncheon Meat

- **Polish furniture.** SPAM purportedly makes good furniture polish, according to the *New York Times Magazine.*

- **Steam-proof mirrors.** SPAM can be used to keep the condensation off the bathroom mirror when showering, also according to the *New York Times Magazine.*

- **Go fishing.** SPAM makes excellent bait, according to Ann Kondo Corum, author of *Hawaii's SPAM Cookbook.*

Invented

1937

The Name

SPAM, possibly a contraction of *spiced ham,* was named by actor Kenneth Daigneau, the brother of R. H. Daigneau, a former Hormel Foods vice president. When other meatpackers started introducing similar products, Jay C. Hormel decided to create a catchy brand name to give his spiced ham an unforgettable identity, offering a $100 prize to the person who came up with a new name. At a New Year's Eve party in 1936, Daigneau suggested the name SPAM.

A Short History

Jay C. Hormel, son of the company's founder, was determined to find a use for several thousand pounds of surplus pork shoulder. He developed a distinctive canned blend of chopped pork and ham known as Hormel spiced ham that didn't require refrigeration. SPAM luncheon meat was hailed as the "miracle meat," and its shelf-stable attributes attracted the attention of the United States military during World War II. By 1940, 70 percent of Americans had tried it, and Hormel hired George Burns and Gracie Allen to advertise SPAM on their radio show. On March 22, 1994, Hormel Foods Corporation celebrated the production of its five billionth can of SPAM.

Ingredients

Chopped pork shoulder, chopped pork ham, salt, water, sugar, and sodium nitrate

Strange Facts

- If laid end to end, five billion cans of SPAM would circle the earth 12.5 times.
- Five billion cans of SPAM would feed a family of four three meals a day for 4,566,210 years.
- One hundred million pounds of SPAM were issued as a Lend-Lease staple in the rations to American, Russian, and European troops during World War II, fueling the Normandy invasion. GIs called SPAM "ham that failed the physical." General Dwight D. Eisenhower confessed to "a few unkind words about it—uttered during the strain of battle."
- Former British prime minister Margaret Thatcher, as a young woman of eighteen working in her family's grocery store, remembers SPAM as a "wartime delicacy."
- In *Khrushchev Remembers*, Nikita Khrushchev credited SPAM with keeping the Russian Army alive during World War II. "We had lost our most fertile, food-bearing lands—the Ukraine and the Northern Cau-

casians. Without SPAM, we wouldn't have been able to feed our army."

- In the 1980s, David Letterman suggested SPAM-on-a-Rope for his *Late Night* audience "in case you get hungry in the shower."
- When Vernon Tejas made his solo winter ascent of Mount McKinley in 1988, he took a picture of himself with a can of SPAM at the summit.
- Hormel Foods board chairman R. L. Knowlton presented a can of SPAM to Mikhail Gorbachev in June 1990 and another can of SPAM to Boris Yeltsin in June 1992.
- The Pentagon sent approximately $2 million worth of SPAM to United States troops during the Gulf war.
- South Koreans consider SPAM an upscale food. The *Wall Street Journal* reported that a Seoul executive in search of the perfect present bought SPAM, explaining, "It is an impressive gift."
- Anthropologist Jane Goodall and her mother once made 2,000 SPAM sandwiches for Belgian troops fleeing from their African colony.

✴Recipes

- SPAM can be grilled, panfried, broiled, sautéed, and baked or added to ethnic dishes, sandwiches, pasta salads, pizzas, casseroles, stir-fry dishes, appetizers, and soups.
- The Ala Moana Poi Bow in Honolulu serves SPAM musubi and SPAM, eggs, and rice.
- The Green Midget Cafe, created by Monty Python's Flying Circus, serves "egg and SPAM; egg, bacon, and SPAM; egg, bacon, sausage, and SPAM; SPAM, bacon, sausage, and SPAM; SPAM, egg, SPAM, SPAM, bacon, and SPAM; SPAM, SPAM, SPAM, egg, and SPAM; SPAM, SPAM, SPAM, SPAM, SPAM, SPAM, baked beans, SPAM, SPAM, SPAM, and SPAM; or lobster thermidor aux crevettes with a Mornay sauce garnished with truffle pâté, brandy, and a fried egg on top and SPAM."
- Mr. Whitekeys' Fly by Night Club in Spenard, AK, offers Cajun SPAM, SPAM nachos, and pasta with SPAM and sundried tomatoes in cream sauce.
- The winning recipes from the 1992 State Fair Best of SPAM Recipe Competition included SPAM Mousse, SPAM Golden Harvest Corn Chowder, and SPAM Cheesecake.

- A SPAMBURGER, "the only hamburger actually made with ham," can be made by grilling, panfrying, or broiling a slice of SPAM and then layering the slice with lettuce, tomato, mayonnaise, and cheese on a hamburger bun.
- Hormel Foods' cookbook, *The Great Taste of SPAM*, includes recipes for SPAM Stew with Buttermilk Topping, SPAM Fajitas, and SPAM Strudels with Mustard Sauce.

✳Unusual Events

- Sixty-eight state and regional fairs hold Hormel Foods–sanctioned SPAM recipe contests each year.
- In Hawaii, Maul Mall hosts an annual SPAM cook-off.
- Austin, TX, has been home to the SPAMorama barbecue and cooking contest since 1974.
- Seattle, WA, hosts a yearly SPAM luncheon meat celebration.
- The SPAM Jamboree, held every Fourth of July weekend in Austin, MN, is the only SPAM event Hormel officially sponsors.
- At the 1983 SPAMposium, 33 self-proclaimed SPAMophiles gathered from across the nation to deliver scholarly papers and demonstrations, including making explosives from SPAM.

✳Distribution

- Americans consume 113 million cans of SPAM a year.
- The average Hawaiian eats twelve cans of SPAM a year, followed by the average Alaskan with six cans, and then Texans, Alabamians, and Arkansans with three cans apiece.

For More Information

Hormel Foods Corporation, 1 Hormel Place, Austin, MN 55912-3680. Or telephone 1-800-523-4635.

Spray 'n Wash

- **Remove chewing gum from hair.** Spray the gum with Spray 'n Wash, rub between fingers, comb out, then shampoo.

- **Clean shower tiles and doors.** Spray with Spray 'n Wash, wait three minutes, then wipe clean with a sponge.

- **Remove varnish from hands.** Spray hands with Spray 'n Wash, rub, then wash with soap and water. Spray 'n Wash usually works better than turpentine, without burning the skin.

- **Clean bathroom fixtures.** Spray generously with Spray 'n Wash, then shine with a cloth.

- **Remove spots from indoor-outdoor carpeting.** Spray spots generously with Spray 'n Wash, wait five minutes, then hose down.

★Invented
1970

The Name

Spray 'n Wash denotes the way this product is used. Consumers simply *spray* a garment soiled with a tough stain *and* then throw it in the *wash*.

A Short History

Herbert H. Dow founded the Dow Chemical Company with the discovery of salt deposits in northern Michigan, expanding into the research, development, and manufacture of industrial chemicals. Dow started manufacturing consumer products in 1953 with the introduction of Saran Wrap, followed by Handi-Wrap in 1960, Dow Oven Cleaner in 1963, Scrubbing Bubbles in 1966, and the Ziploc Storage Bag and Spray 'n Wash in 1970. Spray 'n Wash was introduced in an aerosol can, and in 1974, was made available in liquid form. Spray 'n Wash Stain Stick® was introduced in 1990.

Ingredients

Water, surfactant, enzymes, fragrance, stabilizers, preservative, dye

Strange Facts

- Spray 'n Wash is nonflammable and biodegradable, has an environmentally safe propellant, and does not contain phosphorus or chlorinated solvents.
- In 1995, Spray 'n Wash was reintroduced to the marketplace with new ergonomically designed bottles, more effective formulations, and an improved trigger sprayer.
- In 1994, Dow became the exclusive supplier of rigid Styrofoam-brand insulation for Habitat for Humanity, a nonprofit organization that has built over 30,000 homes with the help of the hard-working, low-income families who buy the homes. As of this writing, Habitat for Humanity ranks as the seventeenth largest home builder in the United States.
- Since 1990, Dow, in partnership with Huntsman Chemical and the U.S. National Park Service, has brought recycling to seven national parks. In

1995, nearly two million pounds of aluminum, glass, and plastics were collected in the parks, reducing the solid waste sent to landfills.
- In 1991, the U.S. Environmental Protection Agency announced the 33/50 program, challenging companies to voluntarily reduce emissions of seventeen chemical pollutants by 33 percent by 1992, and by 50 percent by 1995. By the end of 1993, Dow had achieved a 47 percent global reduction—cutting global emissions from over 4,500 tons every year to just under 2,500 tons per year.

Distribution

- Dow operates 130 manufacturing sites in 30 countries, and employs approximately 53,700 people around the world.
- In 1994, DowBrands sold more than $845 million worth of consumer products.

For More Information

DowBrands L.P., P.O. Box 68511, Indianapolis, IN 46286. Or telephone 1-800-428-4795.

Star Olive Oil

- **Shave.** If you run out of shaving cream, slather on Star Olive Oil.

- **Slow a dog from shedding.** Pour one tablespoon Star Olive Oil on your dog's food while the dog is shedding.

- **Clean pearls.** Rub a dab of Star Olive Oil over pearls, cleaning each pearl individually. Wipe dry with a chamois cloth.

- **Polish lacquered metal.** Use a few drops of Star Olive Oil on a soft cloth.

- **Relieve a cough.** Mix three to four tablespoons lemon juice, one cup honey, and one-half cup Star Olive Oil. Heat for five minutes, then stir vigorously for two minutes. Take one teaspoon every two hours.

- **Soothe frostbite.** Warm some Star Olive Oil and gently dab on frostbitten skin.

- **Relieve a scalded throat.** Take two teaspoons Star Olive Oil to coat and soothe the throat.

- **Rejuvenate dry skin.** Lubricate with Star Olive Oil.

- **Condition your hair.** Warm up Star Olive Oil, massage it into your hair and scalp, wrap your head in a towel, and sit under a dryer. Later, shampoo as usual.

- **Relieve jellyfish or man-of-war stings.** Apply Star Olive Oil for immediate relief, then seek medical attention.

- **Soothe an earache.** Warm and insert a few drops Star Olive Oil into the affected ear, plug with cotton, and apply a hot water bottle.

- **Relieve bursitis.** Heat Star Olive Oil and massage into the shoulder or upper arm daily.

- **Rejuvenate a palm or fern plant.** Add two tablespoons Star Olive Oil at the root of the plant once a month.

- **Relieve constipation.** Take one to three tablespoons Star Olive Oil as a mild laxative.

Invented

3300 B.C.

The Name

Olive oil is the oil squeezed from an olive. Company founder Angelo Giurlani originally gave his olives the brand name *Stella*, the Italian word for *star*, but later changed the name to Star to give the company a more American flavor and increase sales.

A Short History

Olive oil is a fragrant, edible oil obtained by pressing and crushing fresh olives. As early as 3300 B.C., villages on the Aegean Islands were trading olive oil with the Greek mainland and Crete. Today, Italy is the world's leading producer of olive oil, followed by Spain and Greece. In 1898, Angelo Giurlani and his brothers, all Italian immigrants, founded A. Giurlani & Bro. Inc., to import, pack, and distribute olive oil. In 1987, the company changed its name to Giurlani USA.

Ingredients

100 percent olive oil

Strange Facts

- Olive Oyl is the name of Popeye the Sailor Man's girlfriend.
- According to the Talmud, around 165 B.C.E. a small jar of olive oil burned in the temple of Jerusalem for eight days, astonishing the Maccabees (the Jewish army that had just recaptured the city from the Syrians). The Jewish holiday of Chanukah celebrates that wonder.
- In ancient Egypt and Greece, women were advised to insert olive oil into their vaginas for contraceptive purposes. Olive oil was thought to prevent sperm from entering the uterus. It doesn't.

Distribution

- Star Olive Oil is available in Original and Extra Light in Flavor.
- Star also imports, packs, and distributes Spanish olives, wine vinegars, capers, cocktail onions, specialty peppers, sundried tomatoes, anchovies, and maraschino cherries.

For More Information

Giurlani USA, 4652 East Date Avenue, Fresno, CA 93725. Or telephone 1-209-498-2900.

SueBee Honey

- **Condition hair and prevent split ends and frizzies.** Mix one tablespoon SueBee Honey and two teaspoons Star Olive Oil. Warm the mixture (but not too hot), dip your fingers into it, and rub it into the strands of hair. Soak a towel in hot water, wring out completely, and wrap around your head for twenty minutes. Then shampoo as usual, lathering well to remove the olive oil.

- **Give yourself a facial.** Mash a banana and add one tablespoon SueBee Honey. Cover your face with the mixture, let sit fifteen minutes, then rinse with warm water.

- **Dress wounds and burns.** Apply SueBee Honey to the injury. Honey is hygroscopic and absorbs water, creating an environment in which disease-producing microorganisms, deprived of their moisture, cannot live.

- **Soothe a sore throat.** Take one teaspoon of SueBee Honey at bedtime, letting it trickle down your throat.

- **Cure a hangover.** Honey is a concentrated source of fructose. Eating SueBee Honey on crackers helps your body flush out whatever alcohol remains in the body.

- **Relieve a cough due to a cold.** Dissolve one tablespoon SueBee Honey and one tablespoon ReaLemon in a small glass of warm water and sip it. For a stronger solution, combine equal parts SueBee Honey and ReaLemon, and take one teaspoon at bedtime. Both mixtures may help loosen phlegm.

- **Make a bath toy.** Use an empty SueBee honey bear in the bathtub.

- **Make a glue dispenser.** Fill a SueBee honey bear with Elmer's Glue-All and tint with food coloring to make colorful glues.

- **Substitute honey for sugar when cooking.** Use SueBee Honey in place of granulated sugar for up to one half of the sugar. With experimentation, honey can be substituted for all the sugar in some recipes. For baked goods, add about one-half teaspoon baking soda for each cup of honey used, reduce the amount of liquid in the recipe by one-quarter cup for each cup of honey used, and reduce the oven temperature by 25°F to prevent overbrowning. For easy removal, spray measuring cup with Pam No Stick Cooking Spray before adding honey.

- **Make children sleepy at bedtime and help prevent small children from wetting the bed.** A teaspoon of honey at bedtime will act as a sedative to a child's nervous system and will attract and hold fluid in a child's body during the hours of sleeping. When a child over one year is given honey, the blood and tissue calcium begins to increase. The calcium unites with excess phosphorus to form a compound that makes bones, teeth, hair, and fingernails. The sedative effect on the nervous system of a child may be observed within an hour. Honey should not be fed to infants under one year of age. Honey is a safe and wholesome food for older children and adults.

- **Help heal erysipelas.** Generously cover the affected area with honey, then cover with cotton for 24 hours. Repeat if necessary.

✳Invented
Between 10 and 20 million B.C.

The Name

SueBee is a combination of the misspelled word *Sioux*, the Indian tribe for which Sioux City, Iowa, is named, and the word *Bee*, the insect that makes honey.

A Short History

Honey is the sweet liquid produced by bees from flower nectar. The source of the nectar determines the color and flavor of the honey. Most honey in the United States is produced from clover or alfalfa, yielding light-colored and delicately flavored honeys. Other common honeys are made from basswood, buckwheat, eucalyptus, fireweed, orange blossom, sage, tulip poplar, tupelo, and wildflower. Honeycombs are harvested and placed in honey extractors that whirl the honeycombs around, forcing the honey out. After the honey is extracted, it is pasteurized, strained, filtered, and vacuum-packed into jars, poured into squeezable bottles, or "spun" and packed in serving tubs.

In 1921, in Sioux City, Iowa, five men pooled $200 and three thousand pounds of honey to create the Sioux Honey Association. Today, hundreds of members market their honey worldwide through the Association, which oversees the consistent flavor and premium quality of SueBee Honey.

Ingredient

U.S. Grade A white pure honey

Strange Facts

- In ancient times, women were advised to put honey in their vaginas for contraceptive purposes. The stickiness was thought to prevent sperm from entering the uterus. It doesn't.
- Anthropologists believe that ancient Egyptians used honey in embalming and to feed to sacred animals.
- Honey is alluded to in the Sumerian and Babylonian cuneiform writings, the Hittite code, the sacred writings of India, the Vedas, and in Chinese

manuscripts. In the Bible, Israel is called "the land of milk and honey." Egyptian tomb reliefs from the third century B.C. depict workers collecting honey from hives, and archaeologist T. M. Davies discovered a 3,300-year-old jar of honey in an Egyptian tomb.

- In ancient Greece, mead, an alcoholic beverage made with honey, was considered the drink of the Greek gods.

- Honey contains more nutrients than refined sugars, including traces of thiamin, riboflavin, niacin, pantothenic acid, vitamin B_6, vitamin C, calcium, copper, iron, magnesium, manganese, phosphorus, potassium, sodium, and zinc.

- Since honey absorbs and retains moisture, it is commonly used in the baking industry to keep baked goods moist and fresh. Honey's high sugar content and acidity make it an excellent food preservative and sweetener. Honey's unique properties also enhance salad dressings, sauces, candies, dairy products, spreads, fillings, cereals, cured meats, beverages, and snack foods.

- Vegans are strict vegetarians who eat only foods from plants, avoiding all animal flesh and animal products, including milk, cheese, eggs, and honey.

- The proverb "More flies are taken with a drop of honey than a ton of vinegar" first appeared in *Gnomologia* by Thomas Fuller in 1732.

- Beekeepers are called apiarists.

- The queen bee is the only sexually developed female in the hive. Worker bees (sexually undeveloped females) select a two-day-old larva to be the queen. She emerges from her cell eleven days later to mate in flight with approximately eighteen drone bees (males), receiving several million sperm cells, which last her two-year life span. The queen starts to lay eggs about ten days after mating. A productive queen can lay three thousand eggs in a single day.

- The honeybee's distinctive buzz is actually the sound of its wings stroking 11,400 times per minute.

- "If you want to gather honey," said President Abraham Lincoln, "don't kick over the beehive."

- The scotch liqueur Drambuie is made with honey.

- "The only reason for being a bee that I know of is making honey," said Winnie the Pooh in *The House at Pooh Corner* by A. A. Milne. "And the only reason for making honey is so I can eat it."

- Store honey at room temperature away from direct sunlight. Refrigeration speeds crystallization. To avoid sticky drips, place honey jars and bottles on a saucer or disposable coaster.

- Honey never spoils. Crystallization does not affect the taste or purity of honey. If honey crystallizes, just pop it in warm water or in the microwave in a microwave-safe container on high for one to three minutes, stirring every thirty seconds.

*Distribution

- SueBee Honey is the only nationally advertised brand of honey in the United States, and the Sioux Honey Association is the largest honey marketing organization in the world.
- In 1994, more than 217 million pounds of honey were produced in the United States, valued at $111 million.
- The International Trade Commission estimates that there are about 211,600 beekeepers in the United States. An estimated 200,000 are hobbyists with less than twenty-five hives. The approximately 2,000 commercial beekeeping operations in the United States (with over three hundred hives each) produce about 60 percent of the nation's honey.
- Many commercial beekeepers rent out their colonies during the year to pollinate crops for farmers. The U.S. Department of Agriculture estimates that about 2.8 million acres of almonds, apples, melons, plums, avocados, blueberries, cherries, cucumbers, pears, cranberries, kiwi, and other major crops in the United States depend on insect pollination from honeybees.
- Utah is known as the beehive state, despite the fact that in 1994, North Dakota led the nation in honey production with more than 32 million pounds, followed by South Dakota, California, and Florida with more than 19 million pounds each.
- The National Honey Board's honey bear logo appears on over 390 food products that contain high levels of pure honey used according to the board's strict standards.
- Every year the average American consumes 1.1 pounds of honey. That's one honey bear per person. To make one pound of honey, a hive of bees must tap two million flowers, flying over 55,000 miles. The average worker honeybee makes one-twelfth teaspoon of honey in her lifetime, flying about fifteen miles per hour and visiting between fifty and one hundred flowers in each collection trip.
- SueBee makes Clover Honey, Sunflower Honey, Natural Pure Honey, Orange Honey, Sage Honey, Spun Honey, Aunt Sue's Raw Honey,

Squeeze Bears, Premium Barbecue Sauce, and Louisiana Style Premium Barbecue Sauce. SueBee Honey also packages a variety of Private Label products including Clover Maid, Super G, Fred Meyer, Grand Union, Stop & Shop, Western Family, Village Park, National, and North American.

- For a free copy of the National Honey Board's new 96-page honey-inspired cookbook, *Sweetened with Honey*, send your name and address, along with a check or money order for $2.50 to cover postage and handling to: National Honey Board, Dept. C, P.O. Box 7760, Marshfield, WI 54449. Allow four to six weeks for delivery.

For More Information

- Sioux Honey Association, P.O. Box 388, Sioux City, IA 51102. Or telephone 1-712-258-0638.
- National Honey Board, 390 Lashley Street, Longmont, CO 80501-6010. Or telephone 1-800-553-7162.

Tabasco Pepper Sauce

- **Control spider mites, whiteflies, aphids, and thrips on houseplants.** Purée two teaspoons Tabasco pepper sauce and three cloves garlic in a blender; add three cups water and two tablespoons biodegradable liquid detergent, then strain into a spray bottle and coat the leaves of the plant.

- **Combat the common cold.** Mix ten to twenty drops Tabasco pepper sauce in a glass of tomato juice. Drink several of these decongestant tonics daily to help relieve congestion in the nose, sinuses, and lungs. Or gargle with ten to twenty drops Tabasco pepper sauce mixed in a glass of water to clear out the respiratory tract.

- **Prevent cats from scratching dark woodwork.** Rub the area with Tabasco pepper sauce and buff thoroughly. The faint smell of Tabasco pepper sauce repels cats.

- **Make spicy popcorn.** Add a few drops of Tabasco pepper sauce to the cooking oil before adding the popcorn kernels.

- **Make a Bloody Mary.** Combine one quart tomato juice, one cup vodka, one tablespoon fresh lime or lemon juice, one tablespoon Worcestershire sauce, one teaspoon salt, and one-quarter teaspoon Tabasco pepper sauce in a two-quart pitcher. Stir well, chill, and serve over ice, garnished with a slice of lime.

- **Make a Cola Volcano.** Mix one or two drops Tabasco pepper sauce to a glass of Coca-Cola, stir well, and add ice.

- **Cook with Tabasco pepper sauce.** *The Tabasco Cookbook* by Paul McIlhenny with Barbara Hunter suggests recipes for Frog Legs Piquant, Cheese Scones, and Spiced Peaches—all with Tabasco pepper sauce.

- **Relieve a toothache.** Apply a dab of Tabasco pepper sauce to the gum.

Invented
1868

The Name

Tabasco, a name of Central American Indian origin, was chosen by creator Edmund McIlhenny because he liked the sound of the word.

A Short History

In 1862, when Union troops entered New Orleans, Edmund McIlhenny, a successful banker, fled with his wife, Mary Avery McIlhenny, to Baton Rouge and then to Avery Island, an island of solid salt approximately 140 miles west of New Orleans and the site of America's first salt mine. In 1863, Union forces invaded the island and destroyed the salt mines, and the McIlhennys fled to Texas.

After the Civil War, Edmund McIlhenny returned to Avery Island to find his wife's family plantation plundered but some capsicum hot peppers surviving. Determined to turn the peppers into income, McIlhenny made a pepper sauce by mixing crushed peppers and salt in crockery jars and letting the concoction age for thirty days. He then added "the best French wine vinegar" and let the mixture age for another thirty days. He strained the sauce, filled several small cologne bottles, and sent the sauce to friends. In 1868, McIlhenny sent 350 bottles of his pepper sauce, under the trademark Tabasco, to a carefully selected group of wholesalers, and a year later, he sold several thousand bottles at a dollar each. The company is family-run to this very day.

✳Ingredients

Vinegar, aged red pepper, salt

✳Strange Facts

- Tabasco pepper sauce is made from a species of pepper called *Capsicum frutescens*, known for centuries in Latin America and first recorded in 1493 by Dr. Chauca, the physician on Columbus's voyage.
- Capsicum peppers contain an alkaloid called capsaicin, a spicy compound found in no other plant.
- In 1912, pharmacologist Wilbur Scoville devised an organoleptic test to rate the hotness of peppers. The mildest bell peppers rate zero; habaneros peppers score 200,000 to 300,000 units. Tabasco pepper sauce scores between 9,000 to 12,000 units on the Scoville scale.
- Tabasco pepper sauce is still made much the same way Edmund McIlhenny first developed the sauce. Ripe peppers are harvested, crushed, mixed with Avery Island salt, and aged in white oak barrels for up to three years. The peppers are then drained, blended with strong, all-natural vinegar, stirred for several weeks, strained, bottled, and shipped.
- Harvard University's Hasty Pudding Club produced *Burlesque Opera of Tabasco* in 1893 with the approval of Edmund McIlhenny's son, John Avery McIlhenny, who bought the rights to the production and had it staged in New York City.
- In 1898, Lord Horatio Herbert Kitchener's troops brought Tabasco pepper sauce on their invasion of Khartoum in the Sudan.
- In the 1920s, Fernand Petiot, an American working at Harry's Bar in Paris, created the Bloody Mary. Tabasco pepper sauce was added to the recipe in the 1930s at the King Cole Bar in New York's St. Regis Hotel.
- In 1932, when the British government began an isolationist "Buy British" campaign, Parliament banned the purchase of Tabasco pepper sauce, popular in England since 1868 and available in the House of Commons dining rooms. The resulting protest from members of Parliament was dubbed "the Tabasco Tempest," and inevitably Tabasco pepper sauce returned to parliamentary tables. To this day Queen Elizabeth uses Tabasco pepper sauce on her lobster cocktail.

- During the Vietnam War, McIlhenny Company sent thousands of copies of the *Charley Ration Cookbook*, filled with recipes for spicing up C-rations with Tabasco pepper sauce, wrapped around two-ounce bottles of Tabasco pepper sauce in waterproof canisters.
- Former president George Bush is a Tabasco pepper sauce devotee, sprinkling the sauce on tuna fish sandwiches, eggs, and fried pork rinds. After receiving the Republican nomination for President in 1988, Bush handed out personalized bottles of Tabasco pepper sauce as presents for members of his family who dined with him at Arnaud's Restaurant in New Orleans. "I love hot sauce," Bush told *Time* magazine in 1992, "I splash Tabasco all over."
- During Operation Desert Storm, a miniature bottle of Tabasco pepper sauce was included in one out of every three ration kits sent to troops in the Gulf. The United States military now packs Tabasco pepper sauce in every ration kit.
- Over 100,000 people visit Avery Island each year to see Tabasco pepper sauce being made and visit the Tabasco Country Store. Each visitor receives a miniature bottle of Tabasco pepper sauce and a handful of recipes.
- For a free catalogue filled with Tabasco and McIlhenny Farms products, assorted cookbooks, giftware, and Cajun specialties, telephone 1-800-634-9599.

Distribution

- McIlhenny Company sells more than 100 million bottles of Tabasco pepper sauce a year.
- Tabasco pepper sauce bottles are labeled in nineteen languages and shipped to more than one hundred countries.
- Americans use more Tabasco pepper sauce than any other nation, followed by the Japanese, who sprinkle it on pizza and spaghetti.
- McIlhenny Company produced all its peppers on Avery Island until the late 1960s. Now, more than 90 percent of the pepper crop is grown and harvested under the company's direct supervision in Honduras, Colombia, Venezuela, Dominican Republic, Costa Rica, and Ecuador.
- Food critic Craig Claiborne claims that "Tabasco sauce is as basic as mother's milk."

For More Information
McIlhenny Company, Avery Island, LA 70513-5002. Or telephone 1-800-634-9599.

Tang Drink Mix

- **Clean toilet bowls.** Put Tang in the toilet bowl and let it sit for one hour. Brush and flush. The citric acid in Tang removes stains from porcelain.

- **Clean your dishwasher.** Put Tang in the detergent cup and run the machine through its normal cycle. The citric acid in Tang removes grunge and soap scum from the inside of a dishwasher.

- **Shampoo your hair.** The citric acid in Tang cuts through sebum oil in hair.

- **Spice up your baking.** Add Tang to your cake and cookie mixes for an "orange zest."

- **Make a space-age screwdriver.** Mix Tang with vodka.

- **Cook with Tang.** The Kraft Consumer Center offers a free packet of recipes, including Orangey Pancakes (made with one-half cup of Tang), Whipped Orange Butter (requiring two tablespoons of Tang), Oriental Barbecue Sauce (using one-third cup of Tang), and Herbed Orangey

Dressing (made with three tablespoons Tang and one envelope of Good Seasons Classic Herb Salad Dressing Mix).

✳ Invented
1959

✳ The Name

Tang is short for *tangy* and also suggests the flavor of tangerine.

✳ A Short History

Following the introduction of instant coffee and powdered milk, General Foods decided to create a breakfast beverage from a powder that required no refrigeration, mixed with water into single servings, and provided the taste of real orange juice and all the same vitamins. Scientists at the Post Division of General Foods struggled to infuse the powder with stable, water-soluble forms of vitamin A, develop an orange coloring, and prevent the powder from caking in the jar.

✳ Ingredients

Sugar, fructose, citric acid (provides tartness), calcium phosphate (prevents caking), potassium citrate (controls acidity), ascorbic acid (vitamin C), orange juice solids, natural flavor, titanium dioxide (for color), xanthan and cellulose gums (provide body), yellow 5, yellow 6, niacinamide, artificial flavor, vitamin A palmitate, vitamin B_6, riboflavin (vitamin B_2), BHA (preserves freshness), folic acid

✳ Strange Facts

- In 1965, Tang accompanied the astronauts on the Gemini spaceflights, and Tang has been on all United States spaceflights through to the *Apollo 11* moon landing in 1969, helping Tang garner a reputation as a nutritionally balanced futuristic food.

- On *Saturday Night Live*, Mrs. Loopner (Jane Curtin) and her daughter, Lisa Loopner (Gilda Radner), drank Tang by the pitcher. Beldar Conehead (Dan Aykroyd) consumed mass quantities of the orange powder dry and straight from the jar.

✳Distribution

- Tang holds an 85 percent share in the instant breakfast drink category.

For More Information

Kraft Foods, Inc., Box 6Q-TJA, White Plains, NY 10625. Or telephone 1-800-431-1002.

Tidy Cats

- **Create emergency traction for automobiles.** Keep a bag of Tidy Cats in your car trunk in case you get stuck in the ice or snow. When poured under the tire, it provides excellent traction.

- **Soak up car oil and transmission fluid.** Tidy Cats works as an absorbent to pick up transmission leaks from garage floors. Pour a thick layer of unused Tidy Cats over the puddle, wait 24 hours, and sweep up with a broom. Scrub clean with a solution of detergent and hot water.

- **Deodorize a garbage can.** Cover bottom of garbage can with one inch unused Tidy Cats to absorb grease and moisture.

- **Prevent mildew in bathtub.** Pour unused Tidy Cats in a flat box and place in your bathtub to prevent mildew when you leave your house for a long time. (Keep the bathroom door closed if you have cats so that they can't use it.)

- **Deodorize a stale refrigerator.** Pour unused Tidy Cats in a flat box, place it on the middle shelf, and shut the door for five days.

- **Provide traction on driveways and sidewalks that are covered with snow.** Sprinkle unused Tidy Cats on the snow-covered walk to prevent slipping and falling.

- **Prevent musty, damp odors in a closed summer house.** Fill shallow boxes with unused Tidy Cats. To soak up musty, lingering odors, place one in each room before closing up the house.

- **Deodorize sneakers.** Fill the feet of knee-high hose with unused Tidy Cats, tie the ends, and place inside sneakers overnight.

- **Prevent grease fires in barbecue grills.** Cover bottom of grill with a three-quarter-inch layer of unused Tidy Cats to reduce fires.

Invented
1971

The Name

Ed Lowe coined the name Kitty Litter® and sold his first cat box filler exclusively through pet stores beginning in 1947. Twenty years later, when grocery stores finally agreed to carry Kitty Litter, Lowe repackaged his product as Tidy Cats (so the grocery stores could charge a lower price for the cat box filler while the pet stores could continue charging a premium price for Kitty Litter). Lowe came up with the name Tidy Cats from the way Kitty Litter helps keep a cat box tidy.

A Short History

In 1947, Edward Lowe went into business with his father and one employee to supply sawdust and absorbent clay to local Michigan and northern Indiana industries, including Bendix, Whirlpool, and Studebaker. In the winter of 1947, Ed Lowe's clay was first used as cat box filler with the introduction of Kitty Litter Brand, sold through pet stores. In 1971, Lowe introduced Tidy Cats for exclusive sale through grocery stores, creating the first nationally advertised cat box filler. In 1977, Lowe introduced the first microencapsulated deodorant system, followed by the first dual-deodorant system in 1985 and the first cat box filler that fights odor-causing bacteria in 1989.

*Ingredients

Ground clay, deodorizing system, baking soda

*Strange Facts

- Tidy Cats reacts to the pH level of cat urine but is also sensitive to the presence of ammonia odors.
- Ed Lowe's autobiography, *Tail of the Entrepreneur*, published in 1994, tells the inspiring story of the Kitty Litter empire.
- A parasite sometimes found in cat feces can cause toxoplasmosis in pregnant women and those with suppressed immune systems. Special care should be taken in handling used cat box filler. Keep box away from food preparation areas and wash hands thoroughly after handling to reduce risk of infection. For more information, consult your physician.

*Distribution

- Tidy Cats ranks as the best-selling cat box filler in the United States.

For More Information

Purina Pet Products, Checkerboard Square, St. Louis, MO 63164. Or telephone 1-800-835-6369.

Turtle Wax

- **Lubricate furniture drawers and windows.** Apply Turtle Wax on the casters of drawers and windows so they slide open and shut easily.

- **Make bumper stickers easy to remove.** Apply Turtle Wax to the spot before applying the bumper sticker, thus assuring that the bumper sticker will peel away with much greater ease within a month.

- **Polish leather shoes.** Dab on Turtle Wax and shine with a clean, soft cloth.

- **Make a swing set sliding board more slippery.** Cover with two coats of Turtle Wax, polishing between applications.

- **Polish Formica or plastic tabletops.** A coat of Turtle Wax rejuvenates dulled plastic tabletops and counters.

- **Prevent snow from sticking to a shovel.** Cover the shovel with two thick coats of Turtle Wax.

- **Remove the white rings from furniture.** Apply Turtle Wax to the ring with your finger.

- **Prevent playing cards from sticking together.** Wax the backs of the cards with Turtle Wax and rub with a soft cloth.

- **Help dust and dirt slide off a dustpan.** Put a coat of Turtle Wax on the dustpan.

- **Clean and refinish your bathtub.** Rub Turtle Wax into the tub, tiles, and faucets with a soft cloth, and polish immediately with a clean cloth or an electric buffer before the wax dries.

- **Prevent tools from rusting.** Lightly coat tools with Turtle Wax.

Invented
1945

The Name

While driving from Beloit, Wisconsin, company founder Benjamin Hirsch, the developer of Plastone car polish, stopped at a place named Turtle Creek, rested by a stream, and was struck by his reflection in the water. Realizing that his car polish provided a wax coating as tough as a turtle shell and as reflective as Turtle Creek, he renamed his product Turtle Wax.

A Short History

In 1945, with just $500, ex-magician Benjamin Hirsch set up shop in a small Chicago storefront at 2207 Chicago Avenue, where he developed Plastone Liquid Car Polish by mixing batches in a bathtub. His wife and partner, Marie, would bottle the polish, and Ben would sell it. His best sales technique was to wax parked cars while waiting for the owners to return. In the early 1950s, after a sales call in Beloit, Wisconsin, Ben took a stroll along Turtle Creek, and shortly after, Liquid Plastone Car Polish became Turtle Wax with the hard shell finish. Today, the Hirsches' daughter, Sondra, and her husband, Denis Healy, run the company.

Ingredients

Silicones, polishing agents, water, thickeners, petroleum distillates, preservatives, coloring

★Strange Fact

- Turtle Wax, Inc., is frequently offered supplies of turtles. Former company president Carl Schmid would refuse these offers politely and point out that the turtles in Turtle Wax are like the horses in horseradish.

★Distribution

- Turtle Wax is the world's largest-selling car wax.
- Turtle Wax also makes car polishes, car washes, protectants, velour cleaner, upholstery cleaner, carpet cleaner, spot remover, wheel cleaners, chrome polish, rubbing compound, polishing compound, bug and tar remover, and de-icer.

For More Information

Turtle Wax, Inc., 5655 West 73rd Street, Chicago, IL 60638. Or telephone 1-708-563-3600.

20 Mule Team Borax

- **Preserve flowers.** Mix one part 20 Mule Team Borax and two parts cornmeal. Fill the bottom one inch of an empty airtight canister with the mixture. Place the flower on the mixture, then gently cover the flower with more mixture, being careful not to crush the flower or distort the petals. Flowers with a lot of overlapping petals, such as roses and carnations, are best treated by sprinkling mixture directly into the blossom before placing them into the box. Seal the canister and store at room temperature in a dry place for seven to ten days. When the flowers are dried, pour off the mixture and dust the flowers with a soft artist's brush. Borax removes the moisture from blossoms and leaves, preventing the wilting that would normally result.

- **Shine china.** Add one-half cup 20 Mule Team Borax to a sinkful of warm water, rinse fine china, then rinse again in clean water.

- **Deodorize cat litter.** Mix one-and-a-half cups 20 Mule Team Borax to every five pounds of cat litter to reduce and control odor in the cat box.

- **Clean hairbrushes and combs.** Mix a quarter cup 20 Mule Team Borax and a tablespoon of Dawn dishwashing detergent in a basin of warm water. Soak hairbrushes and combs in the solution, rinse clean, and dry.

- **Clean a metal coffeepot.** Fill the percolator with water and add one teaspoon 20 Mule Team Borax and one teaspoon detergent powder. Boil the water, let the mixture sit for a few minutes, then rinse clean.

- **Clean chocolate from clothing.** Sponge the spot with a solution of one tablespoon 20 Mule Team Borax and one cup warm water. Flush with water. If that doesn't work, make a paste with borax and water, work into the stain, let set for one hour, flush well with warm water, and launder as usual.

- **Make children's clothing flame retardant.** Mix together nine ounces 20 Mule Team Borax and four ounces boric acid in one gallon water. If the article is washable, soak in the solution after the final rinsing, then dry. If the garment is not washable, spray with the solution. This solution, recommended by fire departments, may wash out of clothing and should be used after each washing or dry cleaning.

- **Make your own household cleanser for walls and floors.** Add one-half cup 20 Mule Team Borax, one-half teaspoon Dawn dishwashing liquid, and one teaspoon ammonia to two gallons warm water.

- **Make your own automatic dishwashing soap.** Use equal parts 20 Mule Team Borax and washing soda.

- **Gently clean porcelain and aluminum cookware.** Sprinkle 20 Mule Team Borax on pots and pans, rub with a damp dishcloth, and rinse thoroughly.

- **Reduce water spots on glasses and dishes.** Add one tablespoon 20 Mule Team Borax to the dishwasher.

- **Clean spills and stains on carpet and upholstery.** Blot up the spill, sprinkle 20 Mule Team Borax to cover the area, let dry, and vacuum. Before treating, make sure the carpet dye is colorfast by testing an unexposed area with a paste of 20 Mule Team Borax and water. For wine and alcohol stains, dissolve one cup 20 Mule Team Borax in one quart water. Sponge in the solution, wait thirty minutes, shampoo the spotted area, let dry, and vacuum.

- **Deodorize garbage disposals.** Sprinkle two to three tablespoons 20 Mule Team Borax in the drain, let it stand for fifteen minutes, then flush with water with the disposal on. Borax helps deodorize garbage disposals by neutralizing acidic odors.

- **Neutralize urine odors from mattresses and mattress covers.** Dampen the spot, rub in 20 Mule Team Borax, let dry, then vacuum or brush clean.

- **Neutralize pet urine and sour spilled milk odors.** Dampen the spot, rub in 20 Mule Team Borax, let dry, then vacuum or brush clean.

- **Boost laundry detergent.** Add one-half cup 20 Mule Team Borax to each wash load along with the recommended amount of detergent. For large capacity and front-loading machines, add three-quarters cup. Borax acts as a water conditioner, boosting the cleaning power of detergent by controlling alkalinity, deodorizing the clothes, and aiding the removal of stains and soil.

- **Wash diapers and baby clothes.** Flush out dirty diapers and soak as soon as possible in a diaper pail filled with warm water and one-half cup 20 Mule Team Borax. Presoak for at least thirty minutes before washing in warm water, adding one-half cup Borax with the recommended amount of detergent. Wash linens, bibs, slips, and cotton crib liners in hot water, adding one-half cup 20 Mule Team Borax and detergent. Borax helps get rid of odors, reduce staining, and make diapers more absorbent.

- **Wash delicate hand washables.** Dissolve one-quarter cup 20 Mule Team Borax and two tablespoons detergent in a basin of warm water. Soak hand washables for ten minutes, rinse in clear, cool water, blot with a towel, lay flat (woolens) or hang to dry (away from sunlight and direct heat).

- **Eliminate bathtub rust stains.** Scrub the stains with a paste made from 20 Mule Team Borax and ReaLemon lemon juice.

- **Soften soap and rinse waters.** Add one tablespoon 20 Mule Team Borax per quart of water.

- **Clean and deodorize a refrigerator.** Mix one tablespoon 20 Mule Team Borax in one quart warm water. Wash spilled food with a sponge and soft cloth. Rinse with cold water.

- **Keep the water in a humidifier free from odor.** Dissolve one tablespoon 20 Mule Team Borax per gallon of water before adding to the unit. Use this treatment once or twice a year.

- **Wash windows.** Mix one-quarter cup 20 Mule Team Borax, one-half cup ammonia, and two gallons water to add more sparkle when cleaning windows.

- **Reduce ash and eliminate smoke problems from candlewicks in home-made candles.** Dissolve one tablespoon table salt and three tablespoons 20 Mule Team Borax in one cup warm water. Soak heavy twine in the solution for at least twenty-four hours. Allow the twine to dry thoroughly before using to make candles.

Invented
1891

The Name

20 Mule Team Borax is named for the twenty-mule teams used to transport borax from the mines in Death Valley during the late nineteenth century. The word *borax* derives from the Arabic *buraq* or *baurach*, which means to glitter or shine.

A Short History

Borax, a naturally occurring mineral composed of sodium, boron, oxygen, and water, was mined in 2000 B.C. from salt lakes in Tibet and Kashmir. It has been used in pottery glazes since the Middle Ages and was brought to Europe by Arabs. Borax is generally found embedded deep in the ground, along with clay and other substances. In 1881, borax deposits were discovered in Death Valley, California. W. T. Coleman, a San Francisco–based sales agent for borax producer F. M. "Borax" Smith, promptly acquired the discovery site and other nearby properties, including one near Furnace Creek where he established the Harmony Borax Works. Beginning in 1883, famous 100-foot-long twenty-mule teams hauled Coleman's borax

165 miles across the desert from Death Valley to the nearest train depot in Mojave. The twenty-day round trip started 190 feet below sea level and climbed to an elevation of over 2,000 feet before it was over.

In 1890, "Borax" Smith acquired Coleman's borax properties and established the Pacific Coast Borax Company, using Coleman's "Twenty-Mule Team" as the brand name for its "99½% pure" borax. In 1886, Smith joined with a British chemical firm to form Pacific Coast Borax and Redwood's Chemical Works, Ltd., which formed Borax Consolidated, Ltd. London-based RZT Corporation (formerly Rio Tinto-Zinc), the world's largest mining concern, acquired Borax in 1968. Twenty years later, 20 Mule Team Borax, Borateem bleach, and Boraxo brand soap were sold to the Dial Corporation.

✳Ingredient

Borax

✳Strange Facts

- Despite changes in packaging, 20 Mule Team Borax has remained unchanged for over 100 years.
- In some cases, the twenty-mule teams of Death Valley actually consisted of eighteen mules and two horses.
- Between 1883 and 1889, the twenty-mule teams hauled more than twenty million pounds of borax out of Death Valley. During this time, not a single animal was lost nor did a single wagon break down.
- Today it would take more than 250 mule teams to transport the borax ore processed in just one day at Borax's modern facility in the Mojave Desert.
- Although the mule teams were replaced by railroad cars in 1889, twenty-mule teams continued to make promotional and ceremonial appearances at events ranging from the 1904 St. Louis World's Fair to President Woodrow Wilson's inauguration in 1916. They won first place in the 1917 Pasadena Rose Parade and attended the dedication of the San Francisco Bay Bridge in 1937.
- In 1940, MGM produced *Twenty Mule Team*, a popular movie that was promoted by a forty-city mule-team tour. The film starred Wallace Beery, Leo Carrillo, and Anne Baxter.

- Borax is used in the manufacture of glass and ceramic glazes, fire-retardant textiles and wood, and photographic developers.
- Since boron is important in the calcium cycle of plants, borax is often added to boron-poor soils as a fertilizer.
- Borax deposits in Death Valley were abandoned when richer deposits were found elsewhere in the Mojave Desert, turning mining settlements into ghost towns that now help make the region a tourist attraction.
- Borax retards flames because it melts at a low temperature and blocks the diffusion of oxygen to the burning surface.
- According to legend, borax was used by Egyptians in mummification.
- In the furniture business, the word *borax* signifies cheap, mass-produced furniture.
- Adding borax to hard water precipitates mineral salts.
- 20 Mule Team Borax was once proclaimed a "miracle mineral" and was used to aid digestion, keep milk sweet, improve the complexion, remove dandruff, and even cure epilepsy.
- Borax sponsored *Death Valley Days*, first on radio and later on television. This program became the longest-running serial in American broadcasting history.

✷Distribution

- Borax conducts mining operations at Boron in California's Mojave Desert and at four sites in the Argentine Andes.
- Most of the world's supply of borates comes from Boron, California, and from Turkey.
- Borax's mine in Boron supplies more than half of the world's borax.
- The Dial Corporation operates thirteen manufacturing plants in the United States and one in Mexico.
- The Dial Corporation also makes Dial Soap, the best-selling deodorant soap in the United States.

For More Information
- The Dial Corp., Consumer Information Center, 15101 North Scottsdale Road, Scottsdale, AZ 85254. Or telephone 1-800-528-0849.
- U.S. Borax Inc., 26877 Tourney Road, Valencia, CA 91355-1847. Or telephone 1-805-287-5400.

Uncle Ben's Converted Brand Rice

- **Remedy intestinal disorders.** Eating plain Uncle Ben's Converted Brand Rice will help cure diarrhea, according to *Prevention* magazine.

- **Prevent moisture from clumping up salt.** Add a few grains of uncooked Uncle Ben's Converted Brand Rice to the salt shaker to absorb excess moisture.

- **Make a maraca for children.** Put a handful of uncooked Uncle Ben's Converted Brand Rice inside a clean, empty milk carton, and seal the carton shut with Scotch Packaging Tape. Let the child decorate the milk carton with glitter, plastic jewels, and shapes cut from construction paper.

- **Clean stains from a thermos bottle.** Pour in a tablespoon of uncooked Uncle Ben's Converted Brand Rice and a cup of warm water. Shake vigorously, then rinse.

Invented
1943

The Name

In the 1940s, rice farmers in Houston, Texas, rated their rice against the rice grown by a local farmer named Uncle Ben. Frank Brown, a maître d' in a Houston restaurant, posed for the portrait of Uncle Ben.

A Short History

During the processing necessary to produce white rice, the bran layer—containing a large part of the nutritive value of rice—is removed. In England, scientists discovered a special steeping and steaming process to force the bran nutrients, under pressure, into the rice grain *before* the bran is removed, locking the nutrients inside the grain.

In the early 1940s, George Harwell, a successful Texas food broker, received permission to introduce the process developed in England to the United States—but only if he could build a plant immediately. Because the new process improved the nutritional, cooking, and storage qualities of a food that had remained unchanged for more than five thousand years, Harwell convinced the United States government that this unique product merited war priorities. In 1943, Harwell and his partners shipped the first carload of Converted Brand Rice to an army quartermaster depot.

Until the end of World War II, Converted Brand Rice was produced for use solely by military personnel. Then in 1946, Harwell's company, Converted Rice, Inc., brought this special rice to American consumers for the very first time, using the familiar portrait of Uncle Ben as its trademark. Consumer response was so great that in just six years Uncle Ben's Converted Brand Rice became the number-one packaged long-grain rice sold in the United States.

Ingredients

Long-grain parboiled rice enriched with iron (ferric orthophosphate) and thiamine (thiamine mononitrate)

Strange Facts

- The original Uncle Ben was a black rice farmer known to rice millers in and around Houston for consistently delivering the highest quality rice for milling. Uncle Ben harvested his rice with such care that he purportedly received several honors for full-kernel yields and quality. Legend holds that other rice growers proudly claimed their rice was "as good as Uncle Ben's." Unfortunately, further details of Uncle Ben's life (including his last name) were lost to history.

- In the 1980s, the company dropped Uncle Ben from the rice boxes for two years. Sales plummeted, and the company quickly reinstated Uncle Ben's portrait on the boxes.
- The world's leading producer of rice is China. The world's leading exporter of rice is Thailand, followed by the United States. The world's leading importer of rice is Iran.
- Adding one tablespoon of butter, margarine, or oil to the water before adding the rice will prevent the rice from becoming sticky.
- To reheat cooked rice, put it in a coffee filter placed in a vegetable steamer and heat over boiling water.
- Rice is thrown at weddings as a symbol of fertility.
- Rice is grown on more than 10 percent of the earth's arable surface.
- Rice is the mainstay for nearly 40 percent of the world's population.
- Uncle Ben's Converted Brand Rice retains up to 85 percent of the natural B-complex vitamins, giving it more natural food value than ordinary white rice.
- In 1995, Houston Rockets basketball star Hakeem Olajuwon agreed to be a spokesperson for Uncle Ben's.

✸Distribution

- Uncle Ben's is the world's leading parboiled rice brand.
- Uncle Ben's rices include Uncle Ben's Converted Brand Original Rice, Uncle Ben's Brand Instant Rice, Uncle Ben's Brand Boil-in-Bag Rice, Uncle Ben's Brown Rice, Uncle Ben's Long Grain and Wild Rice, Uncle Ben's Country Inn Recipes Rice Dishes, and Uncle Ben's Country Inn Recipes Pasta and Sauce Dishes.

For More Information

Uncle Ben's, Inc., P.O. Box 1752, Houston, TX 77251. Or telephone 1-713-674-9484.

Vanilla Extract

- **Perfume yourself.** A dab of Mc-Cormick/Schilling Pure Vanilla Extract behind each ear makes a delightful fragrance.

- **Eliminate paint odor.** Mix two teaspoons McCormick/Schilling Pure Vanilla Extract per gallon of paint.

- **Flavor Alka-Seltzer.** Add a few drops of McCormick/Schilling Pure Vanilla Extract and one teaspoon sugar to a glass of Alka-Seltzer to improve the taste.

- **Eliminate odors in the refrigerator.** Pour a few drops of McCormick/Schilling Pure Vanilla Extract on a cotton ball and place it on a saucer in the refrigerator.

- **Deodorize a cooler.** Wash out the cooler with a solution of three-quarters cup Clorox bleach per gallon of hot water, then saturate a cloth with McCormick/Schilling Pure Vanilla Extract and wipe down the insides.

Invented
Unknown

The Name

Vanilla extract is the extract from the vanilla bean, prepared by chopping the beans into small pieces and then percolating them with alcohol and water.

A Short History

Vanilla beans, the fruit of a unique species of orchid with aerial roots, fruit pods, and fragrant flowers, is native to the tropical rain forests of Mexico and Central America. Indigenous natives discovered that the tasteless and odorless vanilla bean, when dried by months of tropical heat and humidity, produced a rich taste and aroma. When Aztecs conquered the Indian nations of southeastern Mexico in the 1500s, they named the vanilla bean *tlilxochitl*. In 1520, Aztec emperor Montezuma served Spanish explorer Hernán Cortez a thick, syrupy mixture of cocoa beans, ground corn, honey, and black vanilla pods in a golden goblet. Cortez conquered the Aztecs, killed Montezuma, and brought vanilla to Europe, where it achieved great popularity. Today, vanilla beans are grown primarily in Madagascar, Indonesia, Tahiti, and Mexico.

Ingredients

Vanilla bean extractives in water, alcohol (35 percent), and sugar

Strange Facts

- The word *vanilla* stems from the Latin word *vagina*, perhaps because vanilla fruit pods vaguely resemble a sheath or possibly because vanilla was considered an aphrodisiac.
- Vanilla is the world's most popular flavor.
- The vanilla bean requires approximately nine months to reach maturity, growing six to ten inches long like an overgrown string bean. Harvested beans are immersed in a hot-water bath, then put into wooden boxes and covered with blankets to lock in the heat, where they will "sweat" for 24 to 72 hours, beginning the enzymatic change that produces vanillin. Finally, the beans are placed on blankets and dried in the sun for three to

four months to complete the curing process. The cured beans—wrinkled and chocolate colored—are tied in bundles, packed in boxes, and shipped to McCormick, where they are weighed, chopped, and percolated in large stainless steel containers much like coffee percolators. After the vanilla is aged for several weeks, it is bottled and shipped to stores.

- The Totonac Indians of Mexico discovered how to hand-pollinate the vanilla orchid, which flowers for only one day.
- Vanilla is the second most expensive flavoring in the world to produce, preceded only by saffron.
- Queen Elizabeth I loved vanilla so much that she eventually refused all foods prepared without it.
- Thomas Jefferson, having acquired a taste for vanilla in France, was the first person to import it to the United States.
- The vanilla orchid is the only orchid known to bear edible fruit.

✳Distribution

- McCormick products are distributed under the Schilling label in the western United States.
- Vanilla is the foremost flavor in ice cream, puddings, cakes, chocolates, baked goods, syrups, candies, liqueurs, tobacco, and soft drinks. Vanilla tincture is also used in perfumes.

For More Information

McCormick & Company, Inc., P.O. Box 208, Hunt Valley, MD 21030-0208.

Vaseline Petroleum Jelly

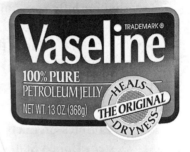

- **Lure trout.** Coat small pieces of sponge with Vaseline petroleum jelly to simulate fish-egg bait.

- **Prevent car battery corrosion.** Smear Vaseline petroleum jelly on clean car battery terminals.

- **Repair stains, rings, and minor scratches in wood furniture.** Cover each scratch with a liberal coat of Vaseline petroleum jelly, let sit for 24 hours, rub into wood, wipe away excess, and polish as usual.

- **Remove chewing gum from hair.** Apply Vaseline petroleum jelly and work into hair until gum slides off.

- **Stop a faucet from screeching.** Remove the handle and stem, coat both sets of metal threads with Vaseline petroleum jelly, and replace.

- **Lubricate roller skate and skateboard wheels.** Smear Vaseline petroleum jelly around the cylinders on the wheels so they roll faster.

- **Remove a ring stuck on a finger.** Coat finger with Vaseline petroleum jelly and slide the ring off.

- **Remove candle wax from carpet or upholstery.** Place a VIVA Ultra paper towel over the wax. Gently press the paper towel with a warm iron. The iron will melt the wax and the paper towel will absorb it.

- **De-silk an ear of corn.** Shuck an ear of corn, then wipe it in a single stroke from top to bottom with a dampened VIVA Ultra paper towel.

- **Prevent cast-iron skillets from rusting.** Place a VIVA Ultra paper towel between your cast-iron pots and pans in the cupboard. VIVA absorbs the moisture that can promote rust.

- **Sprout seeds before planting.** Cut a three-inch strip from a VIVA Ultra paper towel, dampen it, and lay it on top of a strip of Saran Wrap. Place the seeds on top of the paper towel at the intervals recommended on the seed packet. Cover with another strip of damp VIVA Ultra paper towel, then roll the paper and plastic together, place in a Baggie, and store in a warm place. When the roots begin to sprout, remove the Baggie, unroll the Saran Wrap, plant the strip of VIVA Ultra paper towel in a well-tilled garden bed, cover with a fine layer of soil, and water thoroughly. The VIVA Ultra paper towel acts as a mulch to inhibit dehydration and soon dissolves, ensuring a perfectly spaced row of seedlings.

Invented
1967

The Name

VIVA, the Spanish word for *live*, apparently signifies the paper towel's longevity. Ultra alludes to the paper towel's additional strength and absorbency.

A Short History

In 1879, brothers Clarence and Irvin Scott founded the Scott Paper Company and began selling paper bags out of pushcarts on the streets of Philadelphia. Capitalizing on the growth of indoor plumbing in the late nineteenth century, Scott started making toilet paper, supplying more than 2,000 customers by the turn of the century. In 1902, the company introduced its first brand-name toilet paper, trade-marked Waldorf, followed in 1914 by ScotTissue, supported by the company's first advertising campaign. Print ads featured a small boy declaring, "They have a pretty house, Mother, but their bathroom paper hurts."

In 1907, unsanitary conditions in Philadelphia schoolrooms, where teachers used cloth towels to clean bathroom mishaps, prompted the Scott Paper Company to invent the paper towel. The company introduced the paper towel roll under the ScotTissue brand in 1931 and later invented perforated embossing to add softness and absorbency.

Scott Paper introduced VIVA paper towels in 1967. In 1995, Kimberly-Clark, the maker of Kotex tampons, Huggies disposable diapers, and Kleenex tissues, bought Scott Paper for $7.4 billion.

✳Ingredients

Processed wood pulp, wet-strength resin, paper ink, adhesive

✳Strange Facts

- Kimberly-Clark owns about 700,000 acres of timberland, and also makes disposable surgical gowns, sterile wrapping for surgical instruments, and groundwood printing papers and paper specialty products for the tobacco and electronics industries.
- From its corporate flight department, Kimberly-Clark set up Milwaukee-based regional airline Midwest Express in 1984 to transport its employees. Kimberly-Clark sold its interest in the airline in public offerings in 1995 and 1996.
- VIVA Ultra paper towels are made from both long and short wood fibers. The long fibers are obtained from softwood trees, such as pine and spruce, and are used primarily for strength. The short fibers are obtained from hardwood trees, such as oak and maple, and are used primarily for softness.

✳ *Distribution*

- Kimberly-Clark also makes Huggies baby wipes, Kleenex tissues, Huggies disposable diapers, Kotex, New Freedom, and Depend.
- Kimberly-Clark has plants in the U.S. and 25 foreign countries. Its products are sold in 150 countries.

For More Information

Kimberly-Clark Corporation, 401 North Lake Street, P.O. Box 349, Neenah, WI 54957-0349. Or telephone 1-800-272-6882.

WD-40

WD-40

• Stops Squeaks
• Protects Metal
• Loosens Rusted Parts
• Frees Sticky Mechanisms

DANGER. FLAMMABLE. CONTENTS UNDER PRESSURE. HARMFUL OR FATAL IF SWALLOWED. KEEP OUT OF REACH OF CHILDREN. SEE OTHER CAUTIONS ON BACK.

NET WEIGHT 8 OZ./226g (9.3 FL.OZ)

- **Attract fish.** When sprayed on fishing bait, WD-40 covers up the scent of human hands on the bait to better lure fish, according to *USA Today*. The WD-40 Company receives hundreds of letters from consumers confirming this use but prefers not to promote WD-40 as a fishing lure because the petroleum-based product could potentially pollute rivers and streams, damaging the ecosystem.

- **Cure mange.** While spraying a dog with WD-40 gets rid of parasitic mites, according to *USA Today*, the WD-40 Company feeling that the potential misuse of the product is too great, refuses to condone using WD-40 to cure mange on animals.

- **Prevent squirrels from climbing into a birdhouse.** Spray WD-40 on the metal pole or wires.

- **Remove a ring stuck on a finger.** Several medical journals claim that WD-40 is the perfect cure for a toe stuck in the bathtub faucet, a finger stuck in a soda bottle, or a ring stuck on a finger.

- **Clean decorative snow from windows.** Spray windows with WD-40 before spraying with artificial snow so the decorative spray will wipe off easier.

- **Prevent dead insects from sticking to your car.** Spray WD-40 on the hood and grille so you can wipe bugs off easily without damaging the finish.

- **Remove chewing gum, crayon, tar, and Silly Putty from most surfaces.** Spray on WD-40, wait, and wipe.

- **Make hangers glide over a clothes rod.** Spray WD-40 on the clothes rod so hangers can be pushed back and forth easily.

- **Clean clogged spray-paint-can nozzles.** Remove the nozzles from the spray-paint can and the WD-40 can, place the nozzle from the spray-paint can on the WD-40 can, give it a couple of quick squirts, and re-place both nozzles.

- **Remove oil spots from driveways.** Spray with WD-40, wait, then blot. The mineral spirits and other petroleum distillates in WD-40 work as a curing agent.

- **Thread electrical wire through conduits.** Spray WD-40 on electrical wire to help it glide through winding conduits.

- **Prevent grass clippings from clogging up a lawn mower.** Spray WD-40 on the underside of the lawn mower housing and blade before cutting the grass.

- **Clean sap from gardening equipment.** Spray with WD-40, wait, and wipe clean.

- **Prevent mud and clay buildup on bicycles.** Spray the bicycle with a thin coat of WD-40.

- **Remove baked-on food from a cookie pan.** Spray WD-40 on cookie pan and wipe clean. Then wash with soap and water.

- **Remove dirt and grime from barbecue grills.** Remove the grill from the barbecue, spray with WD-40, wait, and wipe clean. Then wash with soap and water.

- **Remove chewing gum from the bottom of a shoe or sneaker.** Spray on WD-40, wait, and pull the gum free.

- **Keep dogs, maggots, and flies out of trash cans.** Coat the trash cans with a thin layer of WD-40.

- **Take squeaks out of new shoes.** Spray WD-40 into the leather and shine.

- **Remove grease stains from linen.** Spray WD-40 directly to the stain, rub it in, let soak for a few minutes, then wash through a regular cycle.

- **Take squeaks out of a box-spring mattress.** Remove the fabric covering the bottom of the box-spring mattress (simply by removing the staples) and spray the springs with WD-40. Staple the fabric back in place with a staple gun.

- **Polish wood furniture.** Spray WD-40 on a cloth and wipe.

- **Clean crayon from a blackboard.** Spray WD-40 on the crayon marks, let soak for ten minutes, then blot clean with a cloth.

- **Free a tongue stuck to frozen metal.** Spray WD-40 on the metal around the tongue.

Invented
1953

The Name

Norman Larsen, president and head chemist at the Rocket Chemical Company, developed a *water displacement* formula on his 40th try, naming it WD-40.

A Short History

The aerospace industry needed a product to eliminate moisture from electrical circuitry and to prevent corrosion on airplanes and Atlas Missile nosecones. The newly developed WD-40 worked so well, engineers working at the Rocket Chemical Company began sneaking it out of the plant for home use on squeaky doors and stuck locks. WD-40 became available to the public in 1958, and in 1961, a sweet fragrance was added to overcome the smell of the petroleum distillates. In 1969, the Rocket Chemical Company was renamed the WD-40 Company, after its only product. The WD-40 Company makes the "secret sauce," then sends it to packagers who add the solvent and propellant.

Ingredients

Petroleum distillates, fragrance

Strange Facts

- In 1964, John Glenn circled the earth in *Friendship VII*, which was covered with WD-40 from top to bottom.
- The WD-40 Company went public on the NASDAQ exchange in 1973. The initial 300,000 shares, available at $16.50, closed that same day at $26.50.
- WD-40 makes more than a million gallons of the "secret sauce" every year.

Distribution

- WD-40 can be found in four out of five American homes. It is distributed to 115 countries around the world.
- Worldwide sales of WD-40 in 1994 were $112 million.

For More Information

WD-40 Company, P.O. Box 80607, San Diego, CA 92138-0607. Or telephone 1-619-275-1400.

Wesson Corn Oil

- **Moisturize skin.** Massage Wesson Corn Oil into your skin, wait fifteen minutes, remove the excess oil with paper towels, then take a hot bath.

- **Make bubble bath.** Mix two cups Wesson Corn Oil, three tablespoons of liquid shampoo, and one-quarter teaspoon your favorite perfume. Mix the solution in a blender at high speed.

- **Prevent cat hair balls.** Add a teaspoon of Wesson Corn Oil to one cat meal daily.

- **Add a shine to your dog's coat.** Add a teaspoon of Wesson Corn Oil to each food serving.

- **Condition hair.** Massage lukewarm Wesson Corn Oil into dry hair, cover hair with a shower cap for thirty minutes, then shampoo and rinse thoroughly.

- **Remove oil-based paint from skin.** Use Wesson Corn Oil instead of turpentine.

- **Season a cast-iron skillet.** Rub a drop of Wesson Corn Oil on the inside of the pan to keep it seasoned. Place a paper towel over and under the skillet when storing. To season a new cast-iron skillet, grease with unsalted Wesson Corn Oil and warm in an oven for two hours. Repeat after washing the skillet for several weeks.

- **Remove rust spots from a cast-iron skillet.** Apply Wesson Corn Oil, let stand, then wipe thoroughly. Repeat if necessary.

- **Prevent car doors from freezing in winter.** Rub the gaskets with Wesson Corn Oil to seal out water without harming the gaskets.

- **Remove white spots or watermarks from wood furniture.** Dip a cloth in Wesson Corn Oil, then into cigar or cigarette ashes. Rub with the grain, across the spot, until it disappears.

- **Prevent snow from sticking to a shovel.** Coat the shovel with Wesson Corn Oil.

- **Remove decals.** Saturate the decal with Wesson Corn Oil.

- **Oil wooden spoons, cutting boards, and butcher blocks.** Put Wesson Corn Oil on a paper towel, rub it into the wood, then wipe clean.

- **Soothe tired feet.** Rub warmed Wesson Corn Oil into your feet, wrap in a damp, hot towel, and sit for ten minutes.

- **Remove glue from furniture.** Apply a dab of Wesson Corn Oil and rub.

- **Remove a splinter.** Soak the wounded area in Wesson Corn Oil for a few minutes to soften the skin before trying to remove the splinter.

- **Break in a new baseball mitt.** Rub a few drops of Wesson Corn Oil into the palm of the glove, place a baseball in the glove, fold the mitt around it, and secure with rubber bands. Tuck the mitt under a mattress and leave overnight.

- **Remove burrs, tar, and sticky substances from a dog's hair.** Saturate the area with Wesson Corn Oil. Wash with dog shampoo, rinse immediately, and brush clean.

- **Clean the sap from a Christmas tree from your hands.** Rub your hands with Wesson Corn Oil and wipe clean with a paper towel.

- **Remove price tags from appliances or the price-tag sheet from an automobile.** Apply Wesson Corn Oil. Let sit and then scrape away.

- **Make cleaning a barbecue grill easy.** Before cooking, coat the grill with Wesson Corn Oil. Clean when the grill is cool to the touch.

- **Remove paper stuck to a wood surface.** Saturate the paper with Wesson Corn Oil, let sit for a while, and gently peel the paper off.

- **Keep your sink shining.** Wipe the sink with a few drops of Wesson Corn Oil on a soft cloth.

- **Treat ear mites in cats.** Put a few drops of Wesson Corn Oil into your cat's ear and massage. Then clean out all debris with a ball of cotton. Repeat daily for three days, and the mites should be gone. The oil soothes the cat's sensitive skin, smothers the mites, and promotes healing.

Invented
1899

The Name

Wesson Corn Oil is named after company founder Dr. David Wesson.

A Short History

In 1899, Dr. David Wesson, a plant chemist with the Southern Cotton Oil Company in Savannah, Georgia, developed the technology to deodorize cottonseed oil, creating the very first edible vegetable oil known in the industry. In 1900, Wesson started a refinery in Savannah to produce Wesson oil for the retail market. Wesson later developed the hydrogenation process used to produce a "hogless lard" called Snowdrift, laying the foundation for the highly successful Wesson Oil & Snowdrift Company.

In 1960, the company merged with Hunt Foods & Industries, founded as the Hunt Brothers Fruit Packaging Company in 1890 by Joseph and William Hancock Hunt in Santa Rosa, California, to become Hunt-Wesson, Inc. The company was acquired in 1990 by ConAgra, Inc., founded in 1919 when four flour mills joined to form Nebraska Consolidated Mills, headquartered in Omaha.

✳Ingredient

Corn oil

✳Strange Facts

- Corn oil is obtained from the germ of the kernel. The crude oil is extracted by crushing and milling the kernels. Caustic soda is mixed into the oil and heated, allowing most of the impurities and fatty acids to separate from the oil. Bleaching clay is then added under vacuum at elevated temperatures to remove the color from the oil. The oil is then placed in a vacuum, and steam is forced through it, deodorizing the refined oil. The result is a pure, delicate oil with a natural flavor and taste.
- Today all Wesson oil available to the public is packaged in plastic bottles. The last glass bottle was used in 1984.
- Florence Henderson, best known as Carol Brady on *The Brady Bunch*, was spokesperson for Wesson oil for many years on television, touting "Wessonality."

✳Distribution

- Wesson was the first vegetable oil on the market.
- Wesson makes Wesson All Natural Vegetable Oil (from soybean oil), Wesson Corn Oil, Wesson Sunflower Oil, Wesson Canola Oil, Wesson Best Blend, Wesson Stir Fry Oil, Wesson No-Stick Cooking Spray, and Wesson Shortening.

For More Information

ConAgra Foods, One ConAgra Drive, Omaha, NE 68102. Or telephone 1-877-528-0745.

Wilson Tennis Balls

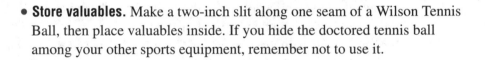

- **Store valuables.** Make a two-inch slit along one seam of a Wilson Tennis Ball, then place valuables inside. If you hide the doctored tennis ball among your other sports equipment, remember not to use it.

- **Fluff your down jacket in the dryer and reduce static cling.** Throw in a handful of Wilson Tennis Balls to fluff the down while the jacket is tumbling in the dryer.

- **Childproof the sharp corners of furniture.** Cut old Wilson Tennis Balls into halves or quarters and use Scotch Packaging Tape to affix the sections over sharp corners of coffee tables, end tables, cabinets, dining room tables, and other pieces of furniture that might be dangerous to a small child.

- **Make parking cars in your garage easier.** Hang a Wilson Tennis Ball on a string from the garage ceiling so it will hit the windshield at the spot where you should stop your car.

- **Prevent a chrome trailer hitch from getting scratched.** Slit a Wilson Tennis Ball and put it over the trailer hitch as a protective cover.

- **Make a walker glide more easily.** Cut a hole in two Wilson Tennis Balls and fit them on the back feet of the walker.

- **Give yourself a foot massage.** Roll your foot over a Wilson Tennis Ball.

- **Remove cobwebs from unreachable places.** Wrap a Wilson Tennis Ball inside a dust cloth secured with a few rubber bands, then toss at the distant cobweb.

- **Play "basket tennis."** Remove the bottom of an empty coffee can, and nail the can above the garage door. Use a Wilson Tennis Ball to play basketball.

- **Strengthen your grip.** Squeeze a Wilson Tennis Ball in each hand.

- **Prevent snoring.** Sew a Wilson Tennis Ball inside a pocket on the back of your pajama top to prevent you from sleeping on your back.

- **Prevent a deck chair from slipping through the cracks of a dock.** Slit four Wilson Tennis Balls and fit them on the feet of the deck chair.

- **Make a back massager.** Put several Wilson Tennis Balls inside a sock and tie the sock at the end. This type of massager is frequently used by a labor coach to massage the back of a woman in labor.

- **Keep your car door open without wasting the battery.** Wedge a Wilson Tennis Ball into the doorjamb to depress the interior light switch.

✳Invented
1914

✳The Name

When the Ashland Manufacturing Company was forced into receivership in 1914, a group of bankers decided to rename the company Wilson and Company to capitalize on President Woodrow Wilson's popularity at the time.

A Short History

In 1913, the Chicago-based meat-packing firm of Schwartzchild and Sulzberger created the Ashland Manufacturing Company as a subsidiary to sell violin strings, surgical sutures, and strings for tennis rackets—all by-products of animal gut. The company soon branched out into making tennis rackets, camping equipment, fishing tackle, bicycles, automobile tires, and phonographs.

In 1914, a New York banking firm took over the company and selected Thomas E. Wilson, a vice president of the meat-packing firm, to manage the company. The bankers chose Wilson because they had already decided to rename the company Wilson and Company to capitalize on President Woodrow Wilson's popularity. Thomas E. Wilson began expanding the company by purchasing other sporting goods companies that manufactured baseball masks, tennis rackets, baseballs, baseball gloves, and uniforms.

The company also went through a number of name changes until 1931, when it became known as Wilson Sporting Goods Co. In the 1940s, Wilson created an advisory staff of sports figures who field-tested equipment and offered suggestions on improving it. In 1970, PepsiCo purchased the company, and in 1989, Wilson was acquired by Amer Group Ltd., an international conglomerate based in Helsinki, Finland, and involved in marketing motor vehicles, paper, communications, and tobacco.

Ingredients

Duraweave felt, high-grade wool, copolymer fibers, rubber, adhesive, ink

Strange Facts

- In 1930, a can of three Wilson Tennis Balls sold for $1.50 in the Sears & Roebuck catalog. In 1990, that same can of balls sold for less than $2.
- Once a Wilson Tennis Ball is removed from its pressurized can, the rebound of the balls decreases over time due to pressure loss. The rebound loss, however, is only between .032 and .038 inches per day.
- Wilson is the only ball used at all United States Tennis Association national championships.

- Since 1979, Wilson has been the official ball of the U.S. Open.
- A number between one and eight is imprinted on each Wilson Tennis Ball to help players keep track of their tennis balls while playing.
- Wilson Tennis Balls are packaged in specially designed, 100 percent recyclable, pressurized containers capable of keeping the balls fresh for years when unopened.
- Duraweave is an exclusive Wilson felt developed with high-grade wool uniquely interwound with copolymer fibers to form a tight, uniform weave. The result is a long-lasting tennis ball with enhanced play and consistency.
- According to United States Tennis Association specifications, tennis balls must weigh between 2 and 2.06 ounces, measure between 2.575 and 2.7 inches in diameter, and when dropped from a height of 100 inches onto a solid, concrete base, rebound to a height of between 53 and 58 inches.

Distribution

- Wilson Tennis Balls are sold throughout the world, including France, Germany, England, Japan, Singapore, Hong Kong, and Latin American countries.
- Wilson also makes tennis rackets, tennis shoes, footballs, basketballs, baseball gloves, golf clubs, and golf balls.

For More Information

Wilson Sporting Goods Co., 8700 West Bryn Mawr Avenue, Chicago, IL 60631. Or telephone 1-800-WIN-6060.

Wonder Bread

- **Clean wallpaper.** Use two-day-old crustless slices of Wonder Bread to rub down the wallpaper.

- **Remove corns.** Make a poultice of one crumbled piece of Wonder Bread soaked in one-quarter cup Heinz Vinegar. Let poultice sit for one-half hour, then apply to the corn and tape in place overnight. If corn does not peel off by morning, reapply the poultice for several consecutive nights.

- **Deodorize a stale lunch box.** Soak a piece of Wonder Bread in Heinz Vinegar and leave it inside the closed lunch box overnight.

- **Erase pencil marks from paper.** Ball up a small piece of Wonder Bread (without the crust) and use it as you would an eraser.

Invented
1921

The Name

Elmer Cline, the Taggart Baking Company vice president appointed to merchandise a new one-and-a-half-pound loaf bread, was awed by the sight of the sky filled with hundreds of colorful hot-air balloons at the International Balloon Race at the Indianapolis Speedway. The wonder of that sight prompted Cline to name the new bread Wonder Bread, and colorful balloons have been featured on the Wonder Bread wrappers ever since.

A Short History

In 1921, Taggart Baking Company of Indianapolis, Indiana, decided to go along with a postwar trend to bring out a one-and-a-half-pound loaf of bread. To promote the new bread's debut, company trucks delivered helium-filled balloons to children in Indianapolis neighborhoods. Messages attached to the balloons urged mothers to try new Wonder Bread. Continental Baking Company bought Taggart in 1925, and Wonder Bread soon became a national brand. In 1930, Wonder Bread was introduced in sliced loaves to a first suspicious, then enthusiastic, public. In 1996, Interstate Bakeries Corporation (IBC) acquired Continental Baking Company, making IBC the largest wholesale baker of fresh delivered bread and cake in the United States.

Ingredients

Enriched wheat flour (barley malt, niacin, iron [ferrous sulfate], thiamine mononitrate, riboflavin), water, high-fructose corn syrup, yeast, contains 2 percent or less of: salt, vegetable oil (contains one or more of: canola oil, corn oil, cottonseed oil, soybean oil), soy flour, calcium sulfate, sodium stearoyl lactylate, monoglycerides, starch, yeast nutrients (ammonium sulfate), leavenings (monocalcium phosphate), vinegar, wheat gluten

Strange Facts

- Continental Baking Company was not the only producer of Wonder Bread. The Seven Baker Brothers Co. of Pittsburgh also produced a bread named Wonder, and there was some dispute as to which company had used the brand name first. When the Pittsburgh company went out of business around 1930, Continental bought the trademark rights.

- In 1941, Continental Baking Company joined in the government-supported bread-enrichment program, adding vitamins and minerals to Wonder Bread. Known as the "quiet miracle," bread enrichment nearly eliminated beriberi and pellagra and brought essential nutrients to people who previously could not afford nutritious foods.
- Wonder Bread does not contain any cholesterol or saturated fat.
- Wonder Bread has been endorsed on television by Howdy Doody and Buffalo Bob, and was praised in song by the Happy Wonder Bakers quartet.
- In the 1970s, Continental Baking Company became the first national wholesale baking company to print freshness dates and nutritional information on bread product wrappers. The move came at a time when the whole-grain bread revolution threatened to erode white bread's market share.
- In 1986, Continental Baking Company introduced Wonder Light, with only forty calories per slice, compared with approximately seventy-five calories per slice of regular bread.
- In 1993, the New York State record black bullhead catfish was caught at Wantagh Mill Pond with a piece of Wonder Bread.
- In 1996, artist Michael Gonzalez's show at the Huntington Beach Art Center featured paintings incorporating Wonder Bread wrappers.
- In his book, *The Total Package*, design critic Thomas Hine compares the Wonder Bread wrapper with the monstrance, the ornate container that holds the bread used in Roman Catholic liturgy. According to Hine, the monstrance calls attention to the invisible presence of Christ within the bread; the Wonder Bread wrapper calls attention to the invisible nutritional additives advertised to build strong bodies twelve ways.

Distribution

- Wonder Bread is the best-selling bread in the United States.
- Thousands of loaves of fresh Wonder Bread are distributed to store shelves on more than seven thousand delivery routes from Continental's forty bakeries across the country.

- Interstate attributes Wonder Bread's popularity to the company's continuing commitment to freshness, consistent product quality, and colorful merchandising and advertising campaigns.

For More Information

Interstate Brands Corporation, P.O. Box 419627, 12 East Armour Boulevard, Kansas City, MO 64111. Or telephone 1-816-502-4000.

Worcestershire Sauce

- **Remove tarnish from copper pots.**
  With a soft cloth, rub Worcestershire
  Sauce on the tarnish.

- **Polish brass.** Apply Worcestershire
  Sauce with a damp cloth.

- **Repair scratched woodwork or furniture.** Use a cotton ball to apply
  Worcestershire Sauce to the
  scratched surface.

Invented
1835

The Name
Worcestershire Sauce was named for the town of Worcester, England,
which is in the shire (county) of Worcester.

A Short History

In 1835, when Lord Marcus Sandys, governor of Bengal, retired to Ombersley, England, he longed for his favorite Indian sauce. He took the recipe to a drugstore on Broad Street in nearby Worcester, where he commissioned the shopkeepers, John Lea and William Perrins, to mix up a batch. Lea and Perrins made a large batch, hoping to sell the excess to other customers. The pungent fishy concoction wound up in the cellar, where it sat undisturbed until Lea and Perrins rediscovered it two years later when housecleaning. Upon tasting the aged sauce, Lea and Perrins bottled Worcestershire sauce as a local dip. When Lea and Perrins's salesmen convinced British passenger ships to put the sauce on their dining room tables, Worcestershire Sauce became an established steak sauce across Europe and the United States.

Ingredients

Water, vinegar, molasses, high fructose corn syrup, anchovies, hydrolyted soy and corn protein, onions, tamarinds, salt, garlic, cloves, chili peppers, natural flavorings, and échalotes

Strange Facts

- To this day, the ingredients in Worcestershire Sauce are stirred together and allowed to sit for up to two years before being bottled.
- An advertisement in 1919 falsely claimed that Worcestershire Sauce was "a wonderful liquid tonic that makes your hair grow beautiful."
- In a famous photograph taken on September 30, 1938, of Neville Chamberlain having dinner with Adolf Hitler, Benito Mussolini, and Edouard Daladier, a bottle of Lea & Perrins Worcestershire Sauce sits on the table.

Distribution

- Lea & Perrins Worcestershire Sauce is the best-selling dark Worcestershire Sauce in the world.

For More Information

Lea & Perrins, Inc., Fair Lawn, NJ 07410. Or telephone 1-201-791-1600.

Wrigley's Spearmint Gum

- **Lure crabs.** Chew a piece of Wrigley's Spearmint Gum briefly and use it as bait on a fishing line.

- **Repair a leaking gas tank temporarily.** Patch the leak with a piece of well-chewed Wrigley's Spearmint Gum.

- **Alleviate an earache caused by a cold, sinus infection, or allergy.** The muscular action of chewing Wrigley's Spearmint Gum will open the eustachian tubes (leading from the back of the throat to the middle ear).

- **Seal a punctured garden hose.** Patch the holes with chewed Wrigley's Spearmint Gum.

- **Keep mealworms and other pests away from pasta.** Place a few sticks of wrapped Wrigley's Spearmint Gum on the shelf near open packages of noodles, macaroni, or spaghetti. Spearmint repels these household pests.

- **Adhere plastic bathroom tiles.** If a tile comes loose, put a little piece of chewed Wrigley's Spearmint Gum on each corner and press back in place.

- **Fill cracks in a wall or in a clay flowerpot.** Use a well-chewed stick of Wrigley's Spearmint Gum.

- **Relieve an earache caused by the change in pressure in an airplane.** Open the eustachian tubes in your ears by chewing Wrigley's Spearmint Gum on an airplane flight.

- **Repair a loose pane of glass temporarily.** Use a wad of chewed Wrigley's Spearmint Gum as window putty.

- **Fix eyeglasses.** In an emergency, put a small piece of chewed Wrigley's Spearmint Gum in the corner of the lens to hold it in place.

- **Improvise caulking compound.** Use a piece of well-chewed Wrigley's Spearmint Gum to seal holes.

- **Fix a hem temporarily.** Reattach a drooping hem with a dab of chewed Wrigley's Spearmint Gum.

- **Retrieve a coin or piece of jewelry that has fallen down a drain.** Tie a fishing weight to a long string, chew a piece of Wrigley's Spearmint Gum briefly, stick it on the bottom of the weight, dangle it down the drain, let it take hold, then pull up.

✳Invented
1893

✳The Name

Wrigley's Spearmint Gum is named after company founder William Wrigley Jr. and the common garden mint (*Mentha spicata*), better known as spearmint because of the sharp point of its leaves.

✳A Short History

William Wrigley Jr. started his career at the age of thirteen when, following his expulsion from school, his father put him to work selling soap door-to-door. In 1891 he moved to Chicago to sell soap and baking powder. At twenty-nine, he started his own business in Chicago—with a wife and child and $32 in cash. When he began offering customers free chewing gum made of spruce gum and paraffin by Zeno Manufacturing, customers offered to buy the gum. Convinced that chicle, a naturally sweet gum base being imported from Central America for the rubber industry, would work as a main ingredient in chewing gum, Wrigley developed two gum flavors, Lotta Gum and Vassar. In 1893, Wrigley introduced Spearmint and Juicy Fruit gums, offering dealers counter scales, cash registers, and display cases for volume purchases. In 1898, he merged with Zeno Manufacturing to form Wm. Wrigley Jr. & Co, and by 1910, after pumping huge amounts of money into advertising, Wrigley's Spearmint Gum was the leading U.S. brand.

Ingredients

Sugar, gum base, corn syrup, dextrose, softeners, natural flavors and BHT (to maintain freshness)

Strange Facts

- In 1915, William Wrigley Jr. sent four free sticks of gum to every person listed in a U.S. phone book.
- The spear-bodied elf character William Wrigley began using before World War I to promote Wrigley's Spearmint Gum turned into the cheerful Wrigley gum boy of the 1960s.
- During World War II, gum, considered an emergency ration, was also given to soldiers to relieve tension and dry throats on long marches. GIs used chewed gum to patch jeep tires, gas tanks, life rafts, and parts of airplanes. Wrigley advertisements recommended five sticks of gum per day for every war worker, insisting that "Factory tests show how chewing gum helps men feel better, work better."
- William Wrigley was the first distributor to place gum next to restaurant cash registers.
- The Wrigley family bought Catalina Island in 1919 and the Arizona Biltmore Hotel in 1931, built the Wrigley building in Chicago in 1924, and owned the Chicago Cubs for fifty-seven years.
- The company did not raise the original five-cent price of Spearmint, Juicy Fruit, and Doublemint gums until 1971, when management reluctantly agreed to raise it to seven cents.

- Before World War II, the basic ingredient of all chewing gum was chicle, the sap of the sapodilla tree indigenous to Central and South America. When chicle became difficult to obtain during World War II, the gum industry developed synthetic gum bases such as polyvinyl acetate, supplied almost entirely by the Hercule Powder Company, an explosives manufacturer.
- Psychiatrists have called gum chewing oral masturbation.
- Americans chew approximately $2.5 billion worth of gum every year.
- The average American chews 168 sticks of gum each year.
- According to *The Great American Chewing Gum Book* by Robert Hendrickson, if all the sticks of gum chewed in America each year were laid end to end, it would equal a stick of gum five million miles long. That's long enough to reach the moon and back ten times.
- Since World War II, American soldiers have been issued gum with their K rations and survival kits.
- William Wrigley Jr.'s grandson, William Wrigley, owns 25 percent of the company and serves as CEO.

✳Distribution

- In 1993, the Wm. Wrigley Jr. Company sold over $1.4 billion worth of gum.
- The Wm. Wrigley Jr. Company has 49 percent of the $1.6 billion domestic gum market and is the number-one chewing gum maker in the world.
- Since the collapse of communism, Wrigley's sales to the former Soviet Union have surged about 20 percent every year since 1989. For two years in a row, sales of Juicy Fruit, Hubba Bubba, Big Boy, and other Wrigley's brands doubled in Central and Eastern Europe. Foreign sales now account for 45 percent of the company's business.
- Wrigley gums include Arrowmint, Big Boy, Big G, Big Red, Cool Crunch, Doublemint, Dulce 16, Extra, Freedent, Hubba Bubba, Juicy Fruit, Orbit, P.K., Spearmint, and Winterfresh.

For More Information

Wm. Wrigley Jr. Company, 410 North Michigan Avenue, Chicago, IL 60611. Or telephone 1-312-644-2121.

Ziploc Storage Bags

- **Keep passports waterproof.** Store your passport in a Ziploc Storage Bag.

- **Protect important papers.** Store tax forms, important records, canceled checks, receipts, warranties, and instructions in a Ziploc Storage Bag.

- **Store camping items.** Carry utensils, food, clothes, maps, medications, and first aid supplies in Ziploc Storage Bags.

- **Carry a wet sponge or cloth for sticky fingers.** Travel with your own dampened wipe in a Ziploc Storage Bag.

- **Separate lingerie, scarves, gloves, hosiery, and handkerchiefs.** Organize your smaller garments in Ziploc Storage Bags.

- **Keep jewelry together.** Organize rings, earrings, necklaces, and brooches in Ziploc Storage Bags.

- **Improvise a diaper changing mat.** In an emergency, a jumbo Ziploc Storage Bag can be used as an easy-to-tote changing mat.

- **Carry dirty diapers in a baby bag without any offending odors.** Keep extra Ziploc Storage Bags in your baby bag so you can seal dirty diapers until you can dispose of them properly. This is especially considerate when visiting friends' homes.

- **Carry snacks.** When traveling, pack snacks in Ziploc Storage Bags.

- **Carry a change of baby clothes.** Pack a change of clothes for a baby in a Ziploc Storage Bag. In separate bags, store a pacifier, cotton balls, and medication. Place all the items in a jumbo zippered Storage Bag and keep it in the baby bag.

- **Pack toiletries when you travel.** Keep all your toiletry items together in a Ziploc Storage Bag and prevent any unexpected leaks or spills.

- **Store game pieces.** Never lose dice, cards, playing pieces, or small toys again.

- **Pack seasonal items away.** Store leftover holiday greeting cards, valentines, and Halloween decorations in Ziploc Storage Bags.

- **Pack a child's suitcase with ease.** Organize your children's outfits in jumbo Ziploc Storage Bags. Put a matching top, bottom, a pair of underwear and socks in each bag so kids know exactly what they're going to wear each day of a vacation.

- **Marinate meats.** Combine your food marinade ingredients in a Ziploc Storage Bag and refrigerate.

- **Store crayons.** Keep a few crayons in a Ziploc Storage Bag for trips so kids always have something to do in restaurants or while traveling.

- **Store leftovers.** Keep leftovers for single servings in Ziploc Storage Bags for quick meals.

- **Organize store coupons.** Keep coupons in Ziploc Storage Bags for easy reference.

- **Make potpourri.** Collect dried roses, juniper sprigs, tiny pinecones, strips of orange rind, bay leaves, cinnamon sticks, whole cloves, and allspice berries. Mix a few drops of rose, cinnamon, and balsam oils with orrisroot (available at your local crafts store). Add all ingredients and seal in a Ziploc Storage Bag for a few weeks to mellow, turning the bag occasionally.

- **Store jigsaw puzzles.** Keep all the pieces in a Ziploc Storage Bag so you never lose that one pivotal piece of the puzzle again.

- **Store screws, nuts, and bolts.** Organize nuts, bolts, drill bits, nails, washers, and screws in the workshop.

- **Store crafts.** Organize paintbrushes, ribbons, beads, glues, and strings in Ziploc Storage Bags.

- **Store leftover garden seeds.** Seal seeds and put them in a cool, dry place until ready for planting.

- **Pipe icing on a cake.** Fill a pint-size Ziploc Storage Bag with icing, twist the bag to force icing to one corner, seal, and use scissors to snip a small bit off the corner. Squeeze out icing to make polka dots or squiggles or to write names. Use a separate bag for each color.

- **Clean a showerhead.** If a showerhead cannot be removed for cleaning, fill a Ziploc bag with vinegar, wrap it around the showerhead, and secure in place overnight with a rubber band.

Invented
1970

The Name

Ziploc is a clever hybrid of the words *zipper* and *lock*—a mnemonic device to remind consumers that the bags zip shut and lock tight.

A Short History

Herbert H. Dow founded the Dow Chemical Company with the discovery of salt deposits in northern Michigan, expanding into the research, development, and manufacture of industrial chemicals. Dow started manufacturing consumer products in 1953 with the introduction of Saran Wrap, followed by Handi-Wrap in 1960, Dow Oven Cleaner in 1963, and Scrubbing Bubbles in 1966. In 1970, Dow unveiled the Ziploc Storage Bag with its patented tongue-in-groove "Gripper Zipper," providing a virtually airtight, watertight seal that revolutionized plastic bags.

✳Ingredient

Polyethylene

✳Strange Facts

- Ziploc Storage Bags were the first food storage bag with the zipperlike seal available to consumers.
- Consumers rate Ziploc Storage Bags as the easiest bags to close.
- Ziploc Brand Bags are recyclable under the plastic recycling number 4, although, as of this writing, it is difficult to find a local recycling center able to recycle this type of plastic.
- Ziploc Storage Bags may be used for microwave reheating, and Ziploc Freezer Bags may be used for microwave reheating and defrosting. Vent the zipper one inch to allow steam to escape, and use the reheat or defrost setting only for a short amount of time. Do not microwave foods high in sugar or fat in a Ziploc Storage Bag; foods high in sugar or fat content respond quickly to microwave energy and may melt the bag. Ziploc Sandwich Bags should not be used in the microwave because they are too thin.
- Do not boil food in Ziploc brand bags. The bags will soften at 195°F, which is below the temperature of boiling water.

✳Distribution

- DowBrands manufactures Ziploc Storage Bags, Ziploc Freezer Bags, Ziploc Sandwich Bags, Ziploc Vegetable Bags, and Ziploc Snack Bags.

For More Information

DowBrands L.P., P.O. Box 68511, Indianapolis, IN 46268-0511. Or telephone 1-800-428-4795.

And Much, Much More

Dawn

Kill insects on plant leaves. Mix one-half cup Dawn dishwashing detergent to one pint water. Spray on both sides of plant leaves, let sit for one hour, then spray clean with water. **For More Information:** Procter & Gamble, Cincinnati, OH 45202. Or telephone 1-800-725-DAWN.

Heinz Ketchup

Clean tarnish from copper. Rub with Ketchup. **For More Information:** H. J. Heinz Co., P.O. Box 57, Pittsburgh, PA 15230. Or telephone 1-412-456-5700.

Liquid Paper

Camouflage stained grout. Simply paint the grout with Liquid Paper. **Cover up scuff marks on white shoes.** Touch up with Liquid Paper.

For More Information: The Gillette Company, Stationery Products Division, Box 61, Boston, MA 02199. Or telephone 1-800-884-4443.

Pampers

Control heavy bleeding. Use a pair of Pampers as a compress.

For More Information: Procter & Gamble, Cincinnati, OH 45202. Or telephone 1-800-285-6064.

Parsons' Ammonia

Clean jewelry. Soak in equal parts of Parsons' Ammonia and warm water for ten minutes. Rub gently with a cloth or soft brush and allow to air dry. Do not use on pearls.

For More Information: The Dial Corporation, Consumer Information Center, 15101 N. Scottsdale Road, Scottsdale, AZ 85254. Or telephone 1-800-528-0849.

Phillips' Milk of Magnesia

Minimize oily skin. Apply Phillips' Milk of Magnesia as a thin mask over your face, let dry, then rinse off with warm water.

For More Information: The Charles H. Phillips Co., Bayer Corporation, Consumer Care Division, Gulfport, MS 39501. Or telephone 1-800-331-4536.

Preparation H

Prevent shaved horsehair from growing back white. Apply Preparation H to the shaved skin of the horse every day until the hair grows back properly.

For More Information: Whitehall-Robins Healthcare, 1 Campus Drive, Parsippany, NJ 07054. Or telephone 1-201-660-5500.

Slinky

Improvise a radio or television antenna. During the Vietnam War, communications soldiers would toss a Slinky over a high tree branch as a makeshift radio antenna.

For More Information: James Industries, Inc., Beaver Road Extension, Hollidaysburg, PA 16648. Or telephone 1-814-695-5681.

Tampax Tampons

Control heavy bleeding. A tampon can be used as a compress for wounds or lacerations.

For More Information: Tambrands Inc., Palmer, MA 01069. Or telephone 1-800-523-0014.

The Fine Print

Sources

- *All-New Hints from Heloise* by Heloise (New York: Perigee, 1989)
- *Another Use For* by Vicki Lansky (Deephaven, MN: Book Peddlers, 1991)
- *Ask Anne & Nan* by Anne Adams and Nancy Walker (Brattleboro, VT: Whetstone, 1989)
- *Can You Trust a Tomato in January?* by Vince Staten (New York: Simon & Schuster, 1993)
- *Chicken Soup & Other Folk Remedies* by Joan Wilen and Lydia Wilen (New York: Fawcett Columbine, 1984)
- *Coca-Cola: An Illustrated History* by Pat Watters (New York: Doubleday, 1978)
- *A Dash of Mustard* by Katy Holder and Jane Newdick (London: Chartwell Books, 1995)
- *Dictionary of Trade Name Origins* by Adrian Room (London: Routledge & Kegan Paul, 1982)
- *The Doctors Book of Home Remedies* by the Editors of *Prevention* Magazine (Emmaus, PA: Rodale Press, 1990)
- *The Doctors Book of Home Remedies II* by Sid Kirchheimer and the Editors of *Prevention* Magazine (Emmaus, PA: Rodale Press, 1993)
- *Encyclopedia of Pop Culture* by Jane and Michael Stern (New York: HarperCollins, 1992)
- *Famous American Trademarks* by Arnold B. Barach (Washington, D.C.: Public Affairs Press, 1971)
- *From Beer to Eternity* by Will Anderson (Lexington, MA: The Stephen Greene Press, 1987)
- "Have a Problem? Chances Are Vinegar Can Help Solve It" by Caleb Solomon (*Wall Street Journal*, September 30, 1992)
- *Hints from Heloise* by Heloise (New York: Arbor House, 1980)
- *Hoover's Company Profile Database* (Austin, TX: The Reference Press, 1996)
- *Hoover's Handbook of American Business 1994* (Austin: Reference Press, 1994)

- *Hoover's Handbook of World Business 1993* (Austin: Reference Press, 1993)
- *Household Hints & Formulas* by Erik Bruun (New York: Black Dog and Leventhal, 1994)
- *Household Hints and Handy Tips* by *Reader's Digest* (Pleasantville, NY: Reader's Digest Association, 1988)
- *Household Hints for Upstairs, Downstairs, and All Around the House* by Carol Reese (New York: Henry Holt and Company, 1982)
- *How the Cadillac Got Its Fins* by Jack Mingo (New York: HarperCollins, 1994)
- *How to Work Wonders with the Wonder Jelly* (Trumbull, CT: Chesebrough-Pond's USA)
- *I'll Buy That!* by the Editors of *Consumer Reports* (Mount Vernon, NY: Consumers Union, 1986)
- "Is There Anything Vinegar Is Not Good For?" by Lora Rader (*Country Stock & Small Stock Journal*, March-April 1993)
- *Kitchen Medicines* by Ben Charles Harris (Barre, MA: Barre, 1968)
- *Make It Yourself* by Dolores Riccio and Joan Bingham (Radnor, PA: Chilton, 1978)
- *Mary Ellen's Best of Helpful Hints* by Mary Ellen Pinkham (New York: Warner/B. Lansky, 1979)
- *Mary Ellen's Greatest Hints* by Mary Ellen Pinkham (New York: Fawcett Crest, 1990)
- "More Than You Want to Know About SPAM" by Judith Stone (*New York Times Magazine*, July 3, 1994)
- "A Most Favored Food" by Alice M. Geffen and Carole Berglie (*Americana*, May-June 1989)
- *The New Our Bodies, Ourselves* by The Boston Women's Health Book Collective (New York: Touchstone, 1992)
- *Our Story So Far* (St. Paul, MN: 3M, 1977)
- *Panati's Extraordinary Origins of Everyday Things* by Charles Panati (New York: HarperCollins, 1987)
- *Practical Problem Solver* by *Reader's Digest* (Pleasantville, NY: Reader's Digest, 1991)
- *Rodale's Book of Hints, Tips & Everyday Wisdom* by Carol Hupping, Cheryl Winters Tetreau, and Roger B. Yepsen Jr. (Emmaus, PA: Rodale Press, 1985)
- *Symbols of America* by Hal Morgan (New York: Viking, 1986)

- *The Tabasco Cookbook* by Paul McIlhenny with Barbara Hunter (New York: Clarkson Potter, 1993)
- "WD-40," (*USA Today*, 1993)
- *A Whole Houseful of Uses for Heinz Vinegar* (Pittsburgh, PA: H. J. Heinz, 1993)
- *Why Did They Name It . . . ?* by Hannah Campbell (New York: Fleet, 1964)
- *The Woman's Day Help Book* by Geraldine Rhoads and Edna Paradis (New York: Viking, 1988)

Trademark Information

"Alberto VO5" is a registered trademark of Alberto-Culver USA, Inc.

"Alka-Seltzer" is a registered trademark of Miles, Inc.

"Arm & Hammer" is a registered trademark of Church & Dwight Co., Inc.

"Aunt Jemima" is a registered trademark of the Quaker Oats Company.

"Avery" is a registered trademark of Avery Dennison Corporation.

"Barbasol" and "Beard Buster" are registered trademarks of Pfizer Inc.

"Bounce" is a registered trademark of Procter & Gamble.

"Canada Dry" and the shield are registered trademarks of Cadbury Beverages Inc.

"Carnation" is a registered trademark of Nestlé Food Company.

"Cascade" is a registered trademark of Procter & Gamble. Photograph used by permission.

"ChapStick" is a registered trademark of American Home Products Corporation.

"Clairol" and "Herbal Essences" are registered trademarks of Clairol.

"Clorox" is a registered trademark of The Clorox Company.

"Coca-Cola" and "Coke" are registered trademarks of the Coca-Cola Company.

"Colgate" is a registered trademark of Colgate-Palmolive.

"Conair" and "Pro Style" are registered trademarks of Conair Corporation.

"Coppertone" is a registered trademark of Schering-Plough HealthCare Products, Inc. Photograph reproduced with permission of Schering-Plough HealthCare Products, Inc., the copyright owner.

"Cover Girl" and "NailSlicks" are registered trademarks of Noxell Corp.

"Crayola" is a registered trademark of Binney & Smith Inc.

"Crisco" is a registered trademark of Procter & Gamble. Photograph used by permission.

"Dannon" is a registered trademark of the Dannon Company.

"Dawn" is a registered trademark of Procter & Gamble.

"Dixie" is a registered trademark of James River Corporation.

"Efferdent" is a registered trademark of Warner-Lambert.

"Elmer's Glue-All" and Elmer the Bull are registered trademarks of Borden.

"Endust" is a registered trademark of Sara Lee Corporation.

"Forster" is a registered trademark of Forster Manufacturing Company, Inc.

"Frisbee" is a brand name and a registered trademark of Mattel, Inc., used with permission. Mattel, Inc. makes no endorsement of the uses of Frisbee discs other than as sports toys.

"Geritol" is a registered trademark of Beecham, Inc.

"GLAD" is a registered trademark of First Brands Corporation.

"Gold Medal" is a registered trademark of General Mills, Inc.

"Hartz" is a registered trademark of Hartz Mountain Corporation.

"Heinz" is a registered trademark of H. J. Heinz Company.

"Huggies," "Kleenex," and "Cleans Like a Washcloth" are registered trademarks of Kimberly-Clark Corporation.

"Ivory" is a registered trademark of Procter & Gamble.

"Jell-O" is a registered trademark of Kraft Foods, Inc. Photograph used with permission.

"Jif" is a registered trademark of Procter & Gamble.

"Kingsford" is a registered trademark of Kingsford Products Company.

"Kingsford's" and the Kingsford logo are registered trademarks of CPC International Inc.

"Kiwi" is a registered trademark of Sara Lee Corporation.

"Krazy" is a registered trademark of Borden, Inc.

"L'eggs" and "Sheer Energy" are registered trademarks of Hanes.

"Lipton," "The 'Brisk' Tea," and "Flo-Thru" are registered trademarks of Thomas J. Lipton Company.

"Liquid Paper" is a registered trademark of Liquid Paper Corporation.

"Listerine" is a registered trademark of Warner-Lambert.

"Lubriderm" is a registered trademark of Warner-Lambert Co.

"MasterCard" is a registered trademark of MasterCard International.

"Maxwell House" and "Good to the Last Drop" are registered trademarks of Kraft Foods, Inc. Photograph used with permission.

"Maybelline" is a registered trademark of Maybelline.

"McCormick" and "Schilling" are registered trademarks of McCormick & Company, Inc.

"Tidy Cats" and "Kitty Litter" are registered trademarks of Purina Pet Products.

"Turtle Wax" and "Super Hard Shell" are registered trademarks of Turtle Wax, Inc.

"20 Mule Team" and "Borax" are registered trademarks of United States Borax & Chemical Corporation.

"Uncle Ben's" and "Converted" are registered trademarks of Uncle Ben's, Inc.

"Vaseline" is a registered trademark of Chesebrough-Pond's.

"VIVA" is a registered trademark of Kimberly-Clark Corporation. "Works Like Cloth" is a trademark of Kimberly-Clark Corporation.

"WD-40" is a registered trademark of the WD-40 Company.

"Wesson" is a registered trademark of ConAgra Foods.

"Wilson" is a registered trademark of Wilson Sporting Goods Co. Used with permission.

"Wonder" is a registered trademark of Interstate Brands Corporation.

"Worcestershire Sauce" is a registered trademark of Lea & Perrins.

"Wrigley" is a registered trademark of Wm. Wrigley Jr. Company.

"Ziploc" is a registered trademark of DowBrands L.P.

Index

Backpacks
    GLAD Trash Bags, 125
    Oral-B Mint Waxed Floss, 213
    Scotchgard, 249
Baked-on food. *See* Pots and pans
Baking ingredients
    Miller High Life, 196
    Tang Drink Mix, 287
Baking pans, lining
    Reynolds Cut-Rite Wax Paper, 239
Bandages
    Alberto VO5 Conditioning Hairdressing,
        2
    Conair Pro Style 1600, 66
    Scotch Packaging Tape, 252
Barbasol, 30–33
Barbecue grills
    Arm & Hammer Baking Soda, 19
    GLAD Trash Bags, 124
    Kingsford Charcoal Briquets, 184
    Maxwell House Coffee, 184, 186
    Reynolds Wrap, 243
    Scotch Packaging Tape, 253
    Tidy Cats, 291
    WD-40, 317
    Wesson Corn Oil, 322
Barking, discouraging
    ReaLemon, 232
Baseball gloves, softening
    Alberto VO5 Conditioning Hairdressing, 5
    Barbasol, 31
    Wesson Corn Oil, 321
Basket tennis
    Wilson Tennis Balls, 325
Bathing
    Arm & Hammer Baking Soda, 17
    Carnation Nonfat Dry Milk, 42
    Clairol Herbal Essences, 50
    Coppertone, 69
    L'eggs Sheer Energy, 167
    Wesson Corn Oil, 320
Bathrooms, cleaning
    Clorox Bleach, 55
    Heinz Vinegar, 135
    Spray 'n Wash, 271
Bathtub faucets, labeling
    Cover Girl NailSlicks Classic Red, 73
Bathtubs, cleaning
    Arm & Hammer Baking Soda, 15
    Cascade, 45
    Clorox Bleach, 54, 55
    Cream of Tartar, 84
    Heinz Vinegar, 135
    L'eggs Sheer Energy, 168
    Turtle Wax, 294
    20 Mule Team Borax, 298
Batteries, loose
    Reynolds Wrap, 242
Bed sheets, warming
    Conair Pro Style 1600, 67
Bedtime, preparing children for
    SueBee Honey, 278

Bed wetting
    SueBee Honey, 278
Bicycles
    Alberto VO5 Conditioning Hairdressing, 5
    Pam No Stick Cooking Spray, 220
    WD-40, 317
Birdbaths
    Frisbee, 115
Bird feeders
    Clorox Bleach, 55
    Hartz Parakeet Seed, 131
Birdhouses
    WD-40, 316
Bleach, strengthening
    Arm & Hammer Baking Soda, 19
Bleach spots, covering
    Crayola Crayons, 80
    Food Coloring, 109
Bleeding, controlling
    ChapStick Lip Balm, 47
    Lipton Tea Bags, 172
    Pampers, 343
    ReaLemon, 231
    Tampax Tampons, 346
Bloodstains, removing
    Kingsford's Corn Starch, 156
Bloody Mary
    Tabasco Pepper Sauce, 283–84
Boats
    Alberto VO5 Conditioning Hairdressing, 5
    Clorox Bleach, 53, 54, 55
    Vaseline Petroleum Jelly, 309
Bolts. *See* Nuts and bolts
Books
    Avery Laser Labels, 26
    Forster Toothpicks, 112
    Kingsford's Corn Starch, 157
    Saran Wrap, 246
    Scotch Packaging Tape, 253
    VIVA Ultra Paper Towels, 312
Boots
    Alberto VO5 Conditioning Hairdressing, 3
    Conair Pro Style 1600, 65
    Crisco All-Vegetable Shortening, 88
Bottle caps
    Cover Girl NailSlicks Classic Red, 74
    Vaseline Petroleum Jelly, 309
Bottles
    baby. (*see* Baby bottles)
    corking
        Scotch Packaging Tape, 252
    removing glue from
        Alberto VO5 Hair Spray, 9
    washing
        L'eggs Sheer Energy, 168
Bounce, 34–36
Bra pads
    Krazy Glue, 164
Brass, cleaning or polishing
    Alberto VO5 Hair Spray, 9
    Endust, 106
    Gold Medal Flour, 129

Brass, cleaning or polishing *(cont.)*
  ReaLemon, 231
  Worcestershire Sauce, 332
Bread, baking
  Miller High Life, 196
Brick, cleaning
  Clorox Bleach, 53
Bubble bath
  Clairol Herbal Essences, 50
  Ivory Soap, 144
  Wesson Corn Oil, 320
Bubbles, blowing
  GLAD Flexible Straws, 121
Bucket, improvising
  Clorox Bleach, 55
Bumpers, cleaning or polishing
  Alberto VO5 Conditioning Hairdressing, 5
  Arm & Hammer Baking Soda, 19
  Coca-Cola, 58
  Reynolds Wrap, 242
  S.O.S Steel Wool Soap Pads, 264
Bumper stickers, removing
  Conair Pro Style 1600, 66
  Heinz Vinegar, 137
  Turtle Wax, 293
Burglars
  Scotch Packaging Tape, 253
Burns, treating
  Lipton Tea Bags, 172
  Miracle Whip Salad Dressing, 200
  Reddi-wip, 234
  Star Olive Oil, 274
  SueBee Honey, 277
Bursitis, relieving
  Star Olive Oil, 275
Buttermilk substitute
  Cream of Tartar, 84
Buttons, securing
  Maybelline Crystal Clear Nail Polish, 189
  Oral-B Mint Waxed Floss, 213

C

Cables, organizing
  Scotch Packaging Tape, 253
Cakes
  Conair Pro Style 1600, 66
  Forster Toothpicks, 112, 113
  Oral-B Mint Waxed Floss, 213
  Pam No Stick Cooking Spray, 221
  Ziploc Storage Bags, 340
Calculators, labeling
  Cover Girl NailSlicks Classic Red, 74
Cameras, labeling
  Avery Laser Labels, 26
  Cover Girl NailSlicks Classic Red, 74
Camping supplies
  GLAD Trash Bags, 124, 125
  Maxwell House Coffee, 185
  Oral-B Mint Waxed Floss, 213

  Scotchgard, 249
  Ziploc Storage Bags, 338
Canada Dry Club Soda, 37–40, 87
Candles. *See* Wax candles
Candlestick holders, cleaning
  Alberto VO5 Conditioning Hairdressing, 5
Candy
  Avery Laser Labels, 26
  Maxwell House Coffee, 186
Canker sores, relieving
  Dannon Yogurt, 92
Can openers
  Oral-B Toothbrush, 217
Carnation Nonfat Dry Milk, 41–43
Carpets
  adhering to floor
    Pink Pearl Eraser, 224
  cleaning or deodorizing
    Arm & Hammer Baking Soda, 17
    Barbasol, 30
    Canada Dry Club Soda, 37
    Heinz Vinegar, 138
    Kingsford's Corn Starch, 156
    Spray 'n Wash, 271
    VIVA Ultra Paper Towels, 313
Carpet stains. *See* Stain removers
Cascade, 44–46
Cat litter
  Arm & Hammer Baking Soda, 17
  Maxwell House Coffee, 186
  20 Mule Team Borax, 296
Catnip ball
  L'eggs Sheer Energy, 168
Cats
  Alberto VO5 Conditioning Hairdressing, 3
  Alberto VO5 Hair Spray, 9
  Bounce, 35
  Reynolds Wrap, 242
  Scotch Packaging Tape, 252
  Silly Putty, 261
  Tabasco Pepper Sauce, 283
  Wesson Corn Oil, 320, 322
CAT scanners
  Silly Putty, 261
Caulk
  Clorox Bleach, 54
  Wrigley's Spearmint Gum, 335
Ceilings, painting
  GLAD Trash Bags, 124
Chairs, deck
  Wilson Tennis Balls, 325
ChapStick Lip Balm, 47–49
Cheese, slicing
  Oral-B Mint Waxed Floss, 214
Chewing gum. *See* Gum, removing
Chicken bones, turning to rubber
  Heinz Vinegar, 136
Chicken pox, soothing
  Quaker Oats, 227
China
  Arm & Hammer Baking Soda, 18
  Clorox Bleach, 53

G

Game boxes and pieces
  Huggies Baby Wipes, 141
  Scotch Packaging Tape, 253
  Ziploc Storage Bags, 339
Garages
  Wilson Tennis Balls, 324
Garbage
  Arm & Hammer Baking Soda, 17
  Clorox Bleach, 53
  L'eggs Sheer Energy, 168
  Tidy Cats, 290
  WD-40, 318
Garbage disposals
  Arm & Hammer Baking Soda, 16
  Clorox Bleach, 56
  Heinz Vinegar, 136
  20 Mule Team Borax, 297–98
Garden hoses, repairing
  Forster Toothpicks, 113
  Wrigley's Spearmint Gum, 334
Gardens. *See also* Flowers; Plants
  Maxwell House Coffee, 184
  McCormick/Schilling Black Pepper, 192
Garlic
  Forster Toothpicks, 113
  L'eggs Sheer Energy, 168
Gas tank leaks, fixing
  Wrigley's Spearmint Gum, 334
Gelatin mold, improvising
  Maxwell House Coffee, 186
Geritol, 118–20
GLAD Flexible Straws, 121–23
GLAD Trash Bags, 124–27
Glass, cleaning or repairing
  Cascade, 44–45
  Clorox Bleach, 56
  Colgate, 62
  Heinz Vinegar, 138
  20 Mule Team Borax, 297
Glass windshields. *See* Windshields
Gloves
  Conair Pro Style 1600, 66
  Gold Medal Flour, 129
  Kingsford's Corn Starch, 157
  Lubriderm, 178
  Scotchgard, 249
Glue
  applying
    Forster Toothpicks, 112
  dispensing
    SueBee Honey, 278
  homemade
    Elmer's Glue-All, 109
    Food Coloring, 109
    Gold Medal Flour, 128
  removing
    Alberto VO5 Hair Spray, 9
    Coppertone, 70
    Jif Peanut Butter, 150
    Wesson Corn Oil, 321

Gold, cleaning or polishing
  Colgate, 62
  Pink Pearl Eraser, 225
Gold Medal Flour, 128–30
Golf balls
  Cover Girl NailSlicks Classic Red, 73
  Pink Pearl Eraser, 225
Golf clubs
  Alberto VO5 Conditioning Hairdressing, 5
  S.O.S Steel Wool Soap Pads, 264
Grass
  fertilizing
    Listerine, 175, 195
    Miller High Life, 195
  killing
    Heinz Vinegar, 135
    Morton Salt, 207
Grass seed
  Lipton Tea Bags, 171–72
  Maxwell House Coffee, 185
Gravy, thickening
  Kingsford's Corn Starch, 158
Grease, removing from
  appliances, furniture, or walls
    Cascade, 44–45
    Coppertone, 70
    Endust, 105
  fabrics
    Canada Dry Club Soda, 37
    Coca-Cola, 59
    Crayola Chalk, 78
    Kingsford's Corn Starch, 157
    WD-40, 318
  glass, porcelain, or pots
    Alka-Seltzer, 11
    Canada Dry Club Soda, 38
    Cascade, 44–45
  skin
    Alberto VO5 Conditioning Hairdressing, 1
    Barbasol, 30
    Clairol Herbal Essences, 50
    Coppertone, 70
    Crisco All-Vegetable Shortening, 87
Grease, spilled
  Morton Salt, 207
Grease fires
  Tidy Cats, 291
Greenhouse
  Saran Wrap, 246
Grills. *See* Barbecue grills
Grout, cleaning
  Clorox Bleach, 56
  Liquid Paper, 343
  Oral-B Toothbrush, 216
Guitar pick
  MasterCard, 181
Gum, removing
  Jif Peanut Butter, 150
  Miracle Whip Salad Dressing, 201
  Spray 'n Wash, 271
  Vaseline Petroleum Jelly, 308
  WD-40, 317, 318

H

Hair
  conditioning
    Alberto VO5 Conditioning Hairdressing, 2
    Arm & Hammer Baking Soda, 18
    Aunt Jemima Original Syrup, 23
    Canada Dry Club Soda, 38
    Heinz Vinegar, 137
    Miracle Whip Salad Dressing, 200
    Reddi-wip, 234
    Star Olive Oil, 275, 277
    SueBee Honey, 277
    Wesson Corn Oil, 320
  cutting
    Scotch Transparent Tape, 256
  dandruff
    Listerine, 176
    Morton Salt, 207
    ReaLemon, 230
  detangling
    Alberto VO5 Conditioning Hairdressing, 3
  highlighting
    Lipton Tea Bags, 171
    Maxwell House Coffee, 185
    ReaLemon, 230
  removing sticky substances from
    Alberto VO5 Conditioning Hairdressing, 2
    Jif Peanut Butter, 150
    Miracle Whip Salad Dressing, 201
    Spray 'n Wash, 271
    Vaseline Petroleum Jelly, 308
  shampooing
    Kingsford's Corn Starch, 157
    Miller High Life, 195
    Quaker Oats, 227
    Tang Drink Mix, 287
  static electricity in
    Alberto VO5 Conditioning Hairdressing, 2
  styling
    Alberto VO5 Conditioning Hairdressing, 2
    Jell-O Gelatin, 147
    Miller High Life, 196
Hair balls, preventing
  Alberto VO5 Conditioning Hairdressing, 3
  Wesson Corn Oil, 320
Hairbrushes, washing
  Clairol Herbal Essences, 50
  20 Mule Team Borax, 296
Hair dye stains
  Alberto VO5 Conditioning Hairdressing, 2
  Vaseline Petroleum Jelly, 310
Halloween candy, labeling
  Avery Laser Labels, 26
Ham, baked
  Coca-Cola, 59
Hands. See also Fingernails
  freshening
    Colgate, 62
  moisturizing
    Coppertone, 69

ReaLemon, 231
    Star Olive Oil, 231
  strengthening
    Silly Putty, 261
    Wilson Tennis Balls, 325
Hands, cleaning off
  berry stains
    ReaLemon, 231
  grease and grime
    Alberto VO5 Conditioning Hairdressing, 1
    Arm & Hammer Baking Soda, 18
    Barbasol, 30
    Clairol Herbal Essences, 50
    Crisco All-Vegetable Shortening, 87
    Huggies Baby Wipes, 141
  ink
    Coppertone, 70
    Crisco All-Vegetable Shortening, 88
  paint, varnish, or sap
    Alberto VO5 Conditioning Hairdressing, 1
    Coppertone, 70
    Spray 'n Wash, 271
    Wesson Corn Oil, 322
Hangnails, preventing
  Lubriderm, 178
Hangover, relieving
  Maxwell House Coffee, 185
  SueBee Honey, 277
Hartz Parakeet Seed, 131–33
Hawaiian grass skirt
  GLAD Trash Bags, 125
Heinz Ketchup, 342
Heinz Vinegar, 134–41, 328
Hem, fixing
  Wrigley's Spearmint Gum, 335
Hemorrhoids, relieving
  Huggies Baby Wipes, 141
  Kingsford's Corn Starch, 158
Hiccups, curing
  Heinz Vinegar, 136
High chairs, cleaning
  Arm & Hammer Baking Soda, 19
Honey, measuring
  Pam No Stick Cooking Spray, 278
Horsehair
  Preparation H, 345
Horse hooves, shining
  Alberto VO5 Conditioning Hairdressing, 3
Household cleanser
  20 Mule Team Borax, 297
Huggies Baby Wipes, 141–43
Humidifiers, deodorizing
  ReaLemon, 231
  20 Mule Team Borax, 299

I

Ice cream, flavoring
  McCormick/Schilling Black Pepper, 192–93
Ice makers, defrosting
  Conair Pro Style 1600, 66

Immune system, enhancing
    Dannon Yogurt, 91
Indigestion, relieving
    Canada Dry Club Soda, 38
    Heinz Vinegar, 135
Ingredients, measuring
    Pam No Stick Cooking Spray, 278
    Reynolds Cut-Rite Wax Paper, 239
Ink stains, removing
    Alberto VO5 Hair Spray, 8
    Colgate, 62
    Coppertone, 70
    Crisco All-Vegetable Shortening, 88
    ReaLemon, 230
Inner tubes, sealing
    Krazy Glue, 164
Insect bites, soothing
    Alka-Seltzer, 12
    Arm & Hammer Baking Soda, 17
    Carnation Nonfat Dry Milk, 42
    Coppertone, 70
    Heinz Vinegar, 135
    Ivory Soap, 145
Insects
    killing
        Alberto VO5 Hair Spray, 8
        Dawn, 342
    repelling
        Aunt Jemima Original Syrup, 24
        Bounce, 34
        Coppertone, 69
        Miller High Life, 195
Invisible ink
    ReaLemon, 230
Ironing
    Reynolds Wrap, 242
Irons, cleaning
    Heinz Vinegar, 137
    Reynolds Wrap, 244
Itching, relieving
    Heinz Vinegar, 135
    Ivory Soap, 145
    Quaker Oats, 227
Ivory Soap, 144–46

J

Jeans, softening
    Morton Salt, 206
Jell-O Gelatin, 147–49
Jellyfish stings, relieving
    Star Olive Oil, 275
Jewelry
    cleaning or polishing
        Alka-Seltzer, 11
        Canada Dry Club Soda, 37
        Colgate, 62
        Efferdent, 99
        Parsons' Ammonia, 344
        Pink Pearl Eraser, 225
        Star Olive Oil, 274

retrieving from pipes
        Wrigley's Spearmint Gum, 335
storing
        Crayola Chalk, 78
        GLAD Flexible Straws, 121
        Ziploc Storage Bags, 338
Jif Peanut Butter, 150–52
Joint compound, drying
    Conair Pro Style 1600, 67

K

Ketchup bottles, unclogging
    GLAD Flexible Straws, 121
Keys, lubricating
    Pam No Stick Cooking Spray, 221
Kingsford Charcoal Briquets, 153–55, 184
Kingsford's Corn Starch, 85, 87, 109, 156–60
Kiwi Shoe Polish, 161–63
Knitting needles
    GLAD Flexible Straws, 122
Knots, detangling
    Kingsford's Corn Starch, 157
Kool-Aid mustaches
    Colgate, 62
Krazy Glue, 164–66

L

Labeling instruments
    Avery Laser Labels, 26–27
    Cover Girl NailSlicks Classic Red, 73–74
Labels, removing
    Coppertone, 70
Laryngitis, soothing
    Lipton Tea Bags, 172
    ReaLemon, 172
    SueBee Honey, 172
Laundry. *See also* Stain removers
    Arm & Hammer Baking Soda, 18, 19
    Bounce, 35
    Cascade, 44, 45
    Heinz Vinegar, 136
    Lipton Tea Bags, 171
    McCormick/Schilling Black Pepper, 192
    Morton Salt, 207
    20 Mule Team Borax, 298
Laundry bags
    GLAD Trash Bags, 124
Laundry detergent
    Arm & Hammer Baking Soda, 15
    20 Mule Team Borax, 298
Lava lamp, homemade
    Canada Dry Club Soda, 37
Lawn mowers
    Pam No Stick Cooking Spray, 220
    WD-40, 317
Leather, conditioning
    Alberto VO5 Conditioning Hairdressing, 3
    ChapStick Lip Balm, 47

Leather, conditioning (cont.)
  Endust, 105
  Turtle Wax, 293
  Vaseline Petroleum Jelly, 309, 310
Leaves, preserving
  Reynolds Cut-Rite Wax Paper, 238
L'eggs Sheer Energy, 167–70
Lightbulbs, greasing
  Vaseline Petroleum Jelly, 309
Lingerie ribbons
  Maybelline Crystal Clear Nail Polish, 190
Lint
  Heinz Vinegar, 137
  L'eggs Sheer Energy, 168
  Oral-B Toothbrush, 217
  Scotch Packaging Tape, 252
  Silly Putty, 261
Lips, moisturizing
  Alberto VO5 Conditioning Hairdressing, 2
  Coppertone, 69
  Vaseline Petroleum Jelly, 309
Lipstick stains
  Canada Dry Club Soda, 87
  Crisco All-Vegetable Shortening, 87
  Vaseline Petroleum Jelly, 310
Lipton Tea Bags, 171–74
Liquid Paper, 343
Listerine, 175–77, 195
Lubriderm, 178–80
Lunch boxes, deodorizing
  Heinz Vinegar, 138, 328
  Wonder Bread, 328

M

Machine parts, rattling
  Silly Putty, 261
Makeup
  Alberto VO5 Conditioning Hairdressing, 2
  Carnation Nonfat Dry Milk, 41
  Reddi-wip, 235
  Vaseline Petroleum Jelly, 309
Makeup, clown. See Clown makeup
Mange, curing
  WD-40, 316
Maple frosting
  Aunt Jemima Original Syrup, 23
Maple Yogurt Smoothie
  Aunt Jemima Original Syrup, 23
Maraca, improvising
  Uncle Ben's Converted Brand Rice, 302
Marble, polishing
  Crayola Chalk, 78
Marital relations, improving
  Reddi-wip, 235
Masking tape, marking
  Forster Toothpicks, 113
Massages
  Coppertone, 70
  Wilson Tennis Balls, 325
MasterCard, 181–83

Mattresses
  Arm & Hammer Baking Soda, 19
  Krazy Glue, 164
  Scotchgard, 249
  20 Mule Team Borax, 298
  WD-40, 318
Matzah balls, fluffy
  Canada Dry Club Soda, 37
Maxwell House Coffee, 184–88
Maybelline Crystal Clear Nail Polish, 172, 189–91
McCormick/Schilling Black Pepper, 192–94
Measuring cups
  Cover Girl NailSlicks Classic Red, 73
  Pam No Stick Cooking Spray, 278
Meat
  marinating
    Heinz Vinegar, 134
    Miller High Life, 195
    Ziploc Storage Bags, 339
  tenderizing·
    Lipton Tea Bags, 172
    Nestea, 210
Medicine, labeling
  Cover Girl NailSlicks Classic Red, 74
  Maybelline Crystal Clear Nail Polish, 189
  Scotch Transparent Tape, 257
Medicine cabinets
  Alberto VO5 Conditioning Hairdressing, 4
Megaphone, improvising
  Clorox Bleach, 56
Melons, growing
  Maxwell House Coffee, 185
Metal, polishing
  Crayola Chalk, 78
Metal file, cleaning
  Scotch Packaging Tape, 252
Metal sliding board, resurfacing
  Reynolds Cut-Rite Wax Paper, 239
Mice, trapping
  Jif Peanut Butter, 150
Microwaves
  Arm & Hammer Baking Soda, 15
  Mr. Coffee Filters, 203
  ReaLemon, 231
  Reynolds Cut-Rite Wax Paper, 239
Mildew. See Mold and mildew
Milk baths
  Carnation Nonfat Dry Milk, 42
Milk paint
  Carnation Nonfat Dry Milk, 41
Milk substitute
  Reddi-wip, 234
Miller High Life, 195–99
Miracle Whip Salad Dressing, 200–202
Mirrors
  Barbasol, 30
  Conair Pro Style 1600, 65
  Mr. Coffee Filters, 203
  SPAM Luncheon Meat, 267
Mold and mildew
  Clorox Bleach, 53, 55, 56
  Heinz Vinegar, 135

Rust *(cont.)*
  removing
    Coca-Cola, 58, 59
    Cream of Tartar, 84
    Heinz Vinegar, 136
    Morton Salt, 206
    ReaLemon, 206, 231
    Reynolds Wrap, 242
    S.O.S Steel Wool Soap Pads, 264
    20 Mule Team Borax, 298
    Wesson Corn Oil, 321

S

Saddles, lubricating
  Alberto VO5 Conditioning Hairdressing, 3
Salad bowls
  Crisco All-Vegetable Shortening, 88
  Reynolds Cut-Rite Wax Paper, 240
Salad greens, drying
  Conair Pro Style 1600, 65
Salt, declumping
  Uncle Ben's Converted Brand Rice, 302
Sap, removing
  WD-40, 317
  Wesson Corn Oil, 322
Saran Wrap, 246–48
Sausages, cooking
  Forster Toothpicks, 113
Sawdust, removing
  Bounce, 35
Scarecrows, creating
  Dixie Cups, 126
  GLAD Trash Bags, 126
School supplies
  Avery Laser Labels, 26
  Scotchgard, 249
Scoopers
  Clorox Bleach, 54
Scorch marks, removing
  Heinz Vinegar, 137
Scotchgard, 249–51
Scotch Packaging Tape, 252–55, 324
Scotch Transparent Tape, 256–60
Screwdriver (drink)
  Tang Drink Mix, 287
Screwdriver (tool)
  Crayola Chalk, 77
Screw holes, tightening
  Elmer's Glue-All, 103
Screws
  screwing in
    ChapStick Lip Balm, 47
    Forster Toothpicks, 113
    Ivory Soap, 145
    Saran Wrap, 246
    S.O.S Steel Wool Soap Pads,
     265
  storing
    Huggies Baby Wipes, 142
    Maxwell House Coffee, 186
    Ziploc Storage Bags, 340

Scuff marks
  Arm & Hammer Baking Soda, 18
  Colgate, 63
  Coppertone, 70
  Liquid Paper, 343
  Pink Pearl Eraser, 224
Seeds, grass. *See* Grass seed
Seeds, plant. *See* Plants
Septic tanks, maintaining
  Arm & Hammer Baking Soda, 16
Sewing machines
  Crayola Crayons, 80
  Forster Toothpicks, 113
  VIVA Ultra Paper Towels, 312
Sewing patterns
  Scotchgard, 249
  Scotch Transparent Tape, 257
Shampoo
  Kingsford's Corn Starch, 157, 158
  Miller High Life, 195
  Quaker Oats, 227
  Tang Drink Mix, 287
  Vaseline Petroleum Jelly, 310
Shaving
  Alberto VO5 Conditioning Hairdressing, 2
  ChapStick Lip Balm, 47
Shaving cream
  Clairol Herbal Essences, 50
  Jif Peanut Butter, 150
  Lubriderm, 178
  Maybelline Crystal Clear Nail Polish, 189
  Reddi-wip, 234
  Star Olive Oil, 274
Shoelaces, frayed
  Elmer's Glue-All, 102
  Scotch Packaging Tape, 254
  Scotch Transparent Tape, 257
Shoe polish, applying
  Mr. Coffee Filters, 203
  Reynolds Cut-Rite Wax Paper, 238
Shoes
  cleaning or polishing
    Alberto VO5 Conditioning Hairdressing, 3
    ChapStick Lip Balm, 47
    Colgate, 63
    Coppertone, 70
    Endust, 105
    Geritol, 118
    Huggies Baby Wipes, 142
    Lubriderm, 178
    Turtle Wax, 293
    Vaseline Petroleum Jelly, 310
    WD-40, 318
  deodorizing
    Arm & Hammer Baking Soda, 18
    Bounce, 35
  drying
    Conair Pro Style 1600, 65
  repairing
    Alberto VO5 Conditioning Hairdressing,
     3
    Krazy Glue, 164

About the Author

Joey Green, author of *Polish Your Furniture with Panty Hose* and *Paint Your House with Powdered Milk*, got Jay Leno to shave with Jif peanut butter on the *Tonight Show*, had Katie Couric drop her diamond engagement ring into a glass of Efferdent on the *Today* Show, and has been seen polishing furniture with SPAM on *CNN Headline News* and cleaning a toilet with Coca-Cola in the *New York Times*. A former contributing editor to *National Lampoon* and a former advertising copywriter at J. Walter Thompson, Green is the author of ten books, including *Selling Out: If Famous Authors Wrote Advertising, Hi Bob! (A Self-Help Guide to the Bob Newhart Show)*, and *The Partridge Family Album*. A native of Miami, Florida, and a graduate of Cornell University, he wrote television commercials for Burger King and Walt Disney World, and won a Clio Award for a print ad he created for Eastman Kodak. He backpacked around the world for two years on his honeymoon, and lives in Los Angeles with his wife, Debbie, and their two daughters, Ashley and Julia.